RETROSPACE

Collected Essays on Chicano Literature
Theory and History

Bruce-Novoa

Arte Publico Press
Houston
Texas
1990

This volume is made possible through a grant from the National Endowment for the Arts, a federal agency.

Arte Público Press
University of Houston
Houston, Texas 77204-2090

Bruce-Novoa
    RetroSpace / Juan Bruce-Novoa.
      p.   cm.
    Includes bibliographical references.
    ISBN 1-55885-013-9
    1. American literature—Mexican American authors—
History and criticism—Theory, etc. 2. American literature
—Mexican American authors—History and criticism.
3. Mexican Americans—Intellectual life. 4. Mexican Americans in literature. I. Title.
PS153.M4B74 1990
810.9'86872073—dc20   89-18371
                                                            CIP

The paper used in this publication meets the minimum requirements of the American National Standard for Permanence of Paper for Printed Library Materials Z39.48-1984. ∞

To Mary Ann and Juan Carlos
For Horst

In memory of my Mother,
whose death,
like a door,
closed a period of creativity.

Table of Contents

Preface

These essays represent a decade and a half of writing on Chicano literature. My intention was to select, from over seventy published articles, those that treated theory and/or the historical aspects of the literature. Two rather personal essays frame the collection. The first, though I didn't realize it at the time, declared my position on the Chicano Movement's cultural production. To a great extent, I remain faithful to that original statement, both in its perspective and the implied goal of opening our cultural production to the representation of segments of the Chicano community that, for whatever reasons, are excluded or ignored. The last essay was written in response to an invitation to speak about Chicano criticism from the perspective of a participant in the creation of the field. It forced me to reconsider my years of activity in Chicano studies, as well as how and why I became involved. In a way, the two essays mark a cycle that moves from spontaneous intervention in an almost non-existent field, to highly self-conscious participation in a now established amd flourishing one. In between fall essays of a more academic tone.

The essays' main purpose is the exposition of my way of conceptualizing Chicano literature, which differentiates them from those that address specific works or genres, which I reserve for a future volume. Most of the essays appear with only minor editorial changes: "Freedom of Expression and the Chicano Movement," "Chicanos in Mexican Literature," "Hispanic Literature in the United States," "Pluralism Versus Nationalism: U.S. Literature," "Chicano Literary Production: 1960-1980," "Chicanos in Mexican Literature," "Canonical and Noncanonical Texts," and "The Topological Space of Chicano Literature." For "The Space of Chicano Literature," perhaps the most influential article in the collection, I have included a previously unpublished, expanded version. Three essays appear for the first time here: "Chicano Literary Space: Cultural Criticism/Cultural Production," "Spanish-Language Loyalty and Literature," and "Surviving Our Decade." Two essays, "A Case of Identity, What's in Name: Chicanos and Riqueños," and "Charting the Space of Chicano Literature" are translated for the first time. Many of these texts are difficult to find in the original publications, having been published in ephemeral or foreign journals. This volume makes them available again.

Grouping the articles together, moreover, creates a new context, arising from their intertextual relationship. As unified, instead of loose texts dispersed among other authors' work, the reading assumes a different meaning and value. The book becomes the image of the theory by making material and concrete the implied space in which these essays have always moved. Readers can now follow the development of this space and overhear the intertextual dialogue which, in the end, writes the text of a persona to whom my name has been appended. I cannot claim to control that persona or its text in the reader's mind. I simply want this volume to be helpful, one more aperture in the space of Chicano literature.

Bruce-Novoa
Irvine, California

RetroSpace

I

1 Freedom of Expression and the Chicano Movement; An Open Letter to Dr. Philip Ortego

Dear Philip:

At the recent joint conference held in Denver of the Colorado Council of Hispanic Educators and the American Association of Publishers, I listened to you deliver the keynote address. You had arrived that morning feeling quite ill with an upset stomach, but thanks to a suggestion drawn from the curanderismo of my past—warm coca-cola—you seemed to be in your usual top form. You proceeded to reprimand the publishers for the lack of minority authors in their catalogues, and briefly recounted the various paths that minorities, especially Mexican Americans, had taken in the past and the new developments in the present scene. During the speech, you called for a new aesthetic, one not biased in favor of the Anglo writer, one that would allow the Chicano contributions to American culture to take their rightful place alongside those of other groups: a new literary aesthetic, a Chicano aesthetic, by which to judge the works of Chicano authors.

Later, I rose to address the two groups myself. I also called for a new aesthetic, artistic as well as critical. I deplored, as I always have, the existence of any pre-established definition of the characteristics of art and its sub-types. Those that have been proffered by segments of the Chicano Movement are no less oppressive than those so long held by the Anglo critics. I called for complete freedom to write about anything, in any way and in any language, without cultural, regional or political prerequisites. No restrictions from outside nor inside the Movement. To compliment this freedom, a new critical approach: post analysis instead of prejudgment.

At the luncheon, six of us sat around a small table discussing the talks we had heard. You expressed agreement with my views, whereupon

13

the head editor of Ginn and Company, in a friendly but argumentative manner, posed the question of the possible contradiction between the new cultural aesthetic you called for and the apparently acultural one I had proposed. At the moment both of us answered, denying any such conflict between the two, and moved on to other subjects. However, now that the memory of that question returns to me, the answer merits further amplification, not for you, but for the public. Therefore, I have chosen this hybrid of open letter-essay, hoping it might be published where it will reach the most people. I sincerely believe some of the comments herein are overdue.

The educational process, not only in the United States but almost everywhere, is the imposition of pre-formulated norms on students. No substantial effort is made to teach people how to become their own source of standards—how to read. Instead, they are taught what to read and what to find in the books. This especially has been true of the field of literature. The practice is so pervasive that when one group rebels against the standards imposed upon them by the majority, they counter with another set of norms just as rigid, which they in turn begin to teach as "the" way. We have seen this happen in the Chicano Movement. It is sad to see a supposedly revolutionary program resort to the same oppressive tactics it condemns. Let me explain.

In the field of the visual arts, as in everything, the Mexican influence upon the Chicano is undeniable. Dr. Jacinto Quirarte's recent book, *Mexican American Artists*, justifiably begins with the Spanish-Mexican presence. Chicano artists of today have a tradition they can call upon whenever they so choose. I in no way deny them this right. However, I do deny the right of anyone, Chicano or Other, to define what is Chicano art in a manner which would exclude any artist of Mexican American descent. The variety of different types of artists included in his book lead me to believe that Dr. Quirarte would agree, and I am sure that you [Dr. Ortego] also do. There seems to be no problem. Wrong. The problem is that many people, some in positions of influence, disagree quite strongly.

The Chicano Movement, or better said, sections of it, have had the tendency to establish norms young artists must follow to qualify as Chicanos. The possible choices for artists are: (1) to work within certain norms and be recognized as Chicano, though often only regionally, since the norms will vary from area to area; (2) to work according to their own norms and try to somehow resist exclusion; (3) to dedicate themselves to art and forget the external classifications. As you may have already guessed, my preference is definitely number three, though number two is not totally unacceptable, and may well be an intermediate step towards three.

In the visual arts the general norm for Chicanos has been the imitation of Mexican muralism. The heavy presence of Rivera, Orozco and, especially, Siqueiros is obvious in the works of Raul Solache, recently featured in *Siempre*, Ernesto Palomino, or in the multitude of murals on the walls of barrio buildings throughout the Southwest. The technical execution of the works varies all the way up and down the scale; and do not misunderstand, the content and its social significance are not the point in question.

What I object to is making this one style of painting synonymous with "the Chicano style" and canonizing it as the standard from which to judge others. I object to the imposition of it on the young artist.

The glorification of this type of muralism probably is an outgrowth of a misconception of Mexican art. People tend to think that the Mexican artist is a muralist in the line of Siqueiros, etc. They reject other very fine painters because they are not readily identifiable as Mexican. In the past I have tried to combat this false impression by assigning José Luis Cuevas' "Cactus Curtain" essay to my classes; but it is the minority that understands that what Cuevas negates is the imposition of any norms upon the artists, nationalistic or aesthetic, be they under the rubric of Mexican, American, Chicano, whatever. More exposure to the varied, different contemporary Mexican artists—Vicente Rojo, Soriano, Cuevas, Fernando García Ponce, Manuel Felguérez, Gironella, Lilia Carrillo, Toledo, Arnaldo Cohen, Corzas, Von Gunten... —might serve to expand the imaginative reach of Chicanos. More important, it would destroy the basis of the argument that muralism is the Mexican form of visual art.

The literary scene is different, but at once, basically the same. Different in that the molds are not Mexican; the same because those imposed can be just as rigid and oppressive. The Chicano author is expected to meet certain criteria to be Chicano. Anglo publishers seek material readily identifiable so they can display their tokens. Chicano publishers insist on Movement so they can, among other things, relate to the heavy side of the revolution. (Exceptions are known.) This is a harmful and dangerous situation. The cases of Chicano students, aspiring to be writers, being told by some super-movement teacher that their work is not "Chicano enough" and therefore unacceptable are much too common. The stories, plays, poems, published by Chicano publishing houses have become the models one must fit into or risk rejection, and the majority of what they publish is "Movement." What is Chicano to these people?

Chicano literature is in danger of being handcuffed to superficial characteristics. Not that Chicanos do not use words such as *carnal, bato, ese* in everyday speech. Many do. Still others find it necessary to adopt them into their vocabulary to move in certain circles. Writers may face the rejection of their material by those they consider their own people if they do not include them. The standard formula for a successful Chicano piece calls for five or six *carnales*, a dozen *eses* and *batos*, a sprinkle of Spanish and a well placed "*Chinga tu madre*." Again, I do not deny the right of the author to use this or any language. What I attack is the need to utilize it to sell the work as Chicano.

Language is not the only so-called "Chicano trait." The barrio experience is considered a key one. But not all Chicanos have seen a barrio. Nor have they ever worked in the fields as others would like us to think. None of these experiences are invalid, but none can be called exclusively the Chicano experience. And the whole question of the selling of machismo as a virtue and the chaining of the woman to a false image are too lengthy to develop here. Suffice it to say, these self imposed stereotypes are as harmful, if not more so, than the rest.

Those closely affiliated with the more visibly militant segments of the Chicano movement insist on a political posture in literature. Much of what has been published by Chicano publishers falls into the category of "Movement" material, that is, its subject matter is the political struggle and it is usually highly propagandistic. However, more and more young people are being turned off by the rhetoric, especially of those groups professing hatred and racism. These young Chicanos pose a problem for those older movement members who claim to know what Chicano art is. Young Chicano artists more and more are willing to ignore the militant organizations that would predefine their art. It is encouraging to note that Luis Valdez, in his talks at the national teatro conference last year, and in his troupe's latest Denver performance, supported such a posture. It is the healthy answer to a dangerous problem.

After this lengthy explanation of the situation as I perceive it, the question still stands: How do Dr. Ortego's cultural aesthetic and my apparently acultural aesthetic agree? Simply thus: Dr. Ortego asks for the evaluation of Chicano writing according to different norms than the Anglo experience. He calls for the acceptance of bilingualism, biculturalism, diverse heritages and traditions, etc. In short, that such work be judged according to the culture that produced it and not by one extraneous and hostile. However, Dr. Ortego has never to my knowledge insisted on any set of characteristics to qualify authors or their work as Chicano. He has studied the field and works produced by persons of Mexican American descent, and commented on the general scope as well as individual examples. The material he has chosen for publication in his role as editor and critic in no way shows a preformulated bias. He emphasizes divergence and takes pride in the great variety found among us.

I ask for an even more basic commitment to literature that I believe necessary before Dr. Ortego's can be truly possible. We agree, I believe, because he recognizes that what I seek may produce what he seeks, and cannot hinder it. I ask for a very difficult change in our way of approaching anything. I have often said to my classes that how a person reads a book is usually the same way he treats people. What I want is post-analysis, that is, for the critic, publisher, reader, anyone, to read first, without any pre-established norms, without fixed absolutes. Enter a book not to see something in particular, but open to whatever it contains. The book will reveal itself. If the writer is Mexican American, the experience is also. If he or she has falsified it, the material itself has ways of exposing the liar. It is extremely difficult to lie in fiction, because fiction creates its own logic excluding what does not fit. The writer who tries to pervert the inner relationships of a story will find it denouncing the heavy handedness to every reader.

Books are. Read them for themselves and not for what they represent. For in truth, they represent only themselves. Each is unique. Years from now, critics will come to study what were the characteristics of Chicano literature of our time. Hopefully, they will find such an enormous wealth of divergent material that simple classification will be impossible. Not that they will be stopped, for literary historians make the impossible possible, usually through the process of falsification by amputation. (Or should that read mutilation?) *Ni modo* (sic). But it will be tragic if they find their job already done, the censuring and excluding having been carried out by over zealous, narrow minded, misguided Chicanos them(our)selves.

I believe very strongly in the strength of our culture, call it Mexicano, Mexican American, Hispano, Chicano. If left alone to its own paths, the products will be a source of pride to all, a shining multitoned gem whose beauty lies in its ever changing facets. Dr. Ortego has demanded that the American experience be opened to include the sum total of all its parts as well.

Estamos de acuerdo, Doctor. Y ahora, si me permite, sugiero también que somos compadres, porque hace unos días, juntos, bautizamos esta nueva estética. Y tal vez tengamos que defenderla coma a una hija querida. Sin más por el momento, quedo su afmo., atno., y ss.

Bruce-Novoa

La Luz (Sept. 1973): 28-29.

2 Pluralism vs. Nationalism: U.S. Literature

What we much too casually refer to as national literatures are actually rather special phenomena. If we accept Walter J. Ong's distinction between literature and oral tradition—the former being written and printed texts, while the latter is a code of orally transmitted knowledge—then relatively few groups have literature. Munro E. Edmonson found that of the three thousand languages in existence in the 1960s only seventy eight had a literature (323, 332). Ong states that only one hundred and six of the tens of thousands of languages that have possibly existed have been committed to writing to a degree sufficient to have produced literature (7). National literatures are, then, relatively rare, while oral tradition is comparatively ubiquitous.

Rarity aside, nationhood and literature have found themselves closely allied, particularly in the Occident since the advent of print. Ong points out that certain regional dialects invested heavily in writing, eventually developing chirographically beyond those around them until they assumed the status of national languages. The utilization of writing in the building of national states has long been acknowledged. While George Steiner rightfully credits the German Romantics with setting the precedent for European and U.S. academics with respect to creating national identity through the teaching of one's literary heritage, he fails to note that nationalistic *políticos* in Spain had waged literary warfare against Franks and Moors centuries before romanticism. And Tlacaelel, the mastermind behind Aztec ascendency in pre-Columbian Mexico, certainly realized the significance of written texts when he ordered Indian codices burned and rewritten in terms more favorable to the Aztecs almost a century before the Spaniards would repeat the burning to impose a European rewriting of history. National literatures and national histories go hand in hand, as chauvinistic, rhetorical weapons, selective representations designed to produce a coherent, flattering self-portrait. These textual *axis mundi* inform succeeding generations of citizens and can expand to colonize foreigners. In the process, enemies are defined, territories drawn, suffrage granted, and the fundamental national definition of good and evil established.

The United States, born into the print age, did not manage to avoid the nationalistic pattern. Despite efforts to jettison old-world prejudices, the founders of American literature displayed an intolerance equal to that of European nationalistic critics who scorned the upstart U.S. writers. While we must acknowledge the great variety of opinions within the U.S. heritage as usually studied, from an outsider's point of view Timothy Dwight characterized the U.S. literary canon's chauvinism rather well in his 1776 valedictorian address at Yale University: it would reflect a "people, who have the same religion, the same manners, the same interests, the same language, and the same essential forms and principles of civil government ... A people, in all respects one ... indeed a novelty on earth" (Spencer, 3). Chauvinistic and arrogant and political. Needless to say, there are still too many who would like to see Dwight's ideal realized, even if it would have to be imposed by law.

From the start, then, whether looking into the past to salvage texts, or creating new ones, the guardians of the U.S. literary canon have excluded other major language groups within or bordering on its national territory. That canon has been the handmaiden, or mother, to U.S. historiography's paradigms of British stock, the melting pot, and westward expansion. Students are not taught to conceive of the U.S.A. as a product of multiple and simultaneous national colonization efforts, all of which ruthlessly displaced Native American nations. Nor did students, until recently, find literary anthologies that, juxtaposed to Cotton Mather, include samples of Native American oral tradition, and most of the anthologies that have now taken in such materials are usually snubbed by English Departments as "those American Studies anthologies." Although one can often find reference to French influence in the founding fathers, one will never encounter the early writings of French explorers or missionaries, nor their Spanish counterparts in anthologies of U.S. literature. Nor, for that matter, African oral tradition or Amish songs. Is Cotton Mather's "American pen" vision more basic to our present situation than the journal of Cabeza de Vaca's wanderings from Florida to Mexico, or Villagrá's epic poem on the settlement of New Mexico, both from the sixteenth century. Their mere existence debunks U.S. paradigms of cultural exclusivity and English priority. Would the study of *Moby Dick* from the perspective of the U.S. expropriation of the Spanish Empire—proposed first by José de Onís, and later by Carlos Fuentes—be less enlightening than a strictly New England perspective? At least it should be understood that the U.S. literary/historical canon has been realized at the expense of a pluralistic perspective more genuinely reflective of the U.S. experience.

In 1883, after a century of anti-British rhetoric that established an independent U.S. canon, Whitman, the apotheosis of that process, recognized the danger of its incestuousness: "Impress'd by New England writers and schoolmasters, we Americans tacitly abandon ourselves to the notion that our United States have been fashion'd from the British Islands only ... which is a very great mistake" (Moquin, 224). Whitman went on to decry the materialism of British and German stock, predicting that balance would come from the Spanish and Native American characters. Unfortunately, Whitman, as was often the case, was far ahead of his time and of his fellow Anglo Americans.

However, it is doubtful that even Whitman envisioned a polyglot canon. His was still the melting-pot ideal, and the new ingots were to speak a common language. Since his time, the U.S. canon has been forced to expand, but in a manner we could characterize as the fulfillment of the literary founding fathers' dream of Americanization. That is, the New England predominance has been eroded by a series of minority writers: Southern, Jewish, Black, and women, with a few midwesterners thrown in. As U.S. letters seemed to founder in midtwentieth century, it has been from these minority groups that new breath has come. As the Mexican critic García Ponce noted in 1968, "American intellectuals have been forced to face the fact that their most significant literary works have been written by authors belonging to two minority groups: Jews and Blacks" (*Entry*, 48). Yet the all-embracing code—the Americanizing agent—remains American English, with its inherent biases.

Recently, a different pressure has been exerted on the U.S. canon, in the form of media, print and electronics, which bespeaks an American experience, but does so in Spanish. These media service the growing Spanish-speaking and reading population of the U.S. citizens or residents. This phenomenon must be distinguished from the Spanish-language literature written in the U.S. by visitors who are not, and do not intend to be, permanent residents of the U.S. This new literary expression presents itself as a legitimate product of the U.S., and, as such, demands a radical change in the ideal of one common language and culture. While still relatively small in the number of texts produced, this new U.S. literature represents the most significant challenge to Anglo-American chauvinism. The repressed pluralism lamented by Whitman has begun to surface as threat to the very material of the canon, language. However, language is not ahistorical, and this U.S. Hispanic challenge affects thematic content as well as form.

Succinctly, what U.S. Hispanic literature and history infuse into the U.S. canon is radical dialectics. It could be argued that Black, Jewish, Feminist and even mainstream American writers challenge the U.S. paradigms of identity, but it is the language difference—a difference present even in Hispanic texts written in English—that makes U.S. Hispanic literature a radical expression of a more general threat to the predominant canon. Nationalism has been associated with monolingualism; now the question arises of the polyglot state. And this inherently means pluralism as an alternative to the monism of Timothy Dwight's one common people. This new presence demonstrates the truth of a radical statement made by Frederic Jameson: "American literature has therefore become problematic, not to say impossible, because if it limits itself to the traditional language and form of a national literature it misses the basic truths about itself, while if it attempts to tell those truths it abolishes itself as literature" (*Marxism*, 339-400). Ironically, U.S. Hispanic literature infuses a negative dialectic even into Jameson's declaration—he came to the above conclusion after myopically repeating a U.S. ideologeme, that capitalism has eliminated the economic lower class from U.S. territory itself.[1] A cursory reading of Chicano literature reveals the nationalistic trap into which even our foremost Marxist critic can fall when he reads only canonically.

Minor myopias aside, Jameson's *The Political Unconscious* provides a practical formulation for studying the dialectic dilemma of the U.S. canon confronted with U.S. Hispanic expression. Jameson posits the following:

> Semantic enrichment and enlargement of the inert givens and materials of a particular text must take place within three concentric frameworks, which make a widening out of the sense of the social ground of a text through the notions, first, of political history, in the narrow sense of punctual event and a chroniclelike sequence of happenings in time; then of society, in the now already less diachronic and time-bound sense of a constitutive tension and struggle between social classes; and, ultimately, of history now conceived in its vastest sense of the sequence of models of production and the succession and destiny of the various human social formations, from prehistoric life to whatever far future history has in store for us. (75)

It is obvious that his proposal, taken seriously and applied, would radically alter the concept of American literature.

However, I would venture the following emendation. While Jameson privileges the critical act with the power to enrich and enlarge the text, I propose that it is minority literature in general, and U.S. Hispanic in particular, that practices the critical dialectic on the inert text of the U.S. canon. What falls to critics is not the Promethean role of savior—a nostalgia for individual heroism latent in Jameson's unconscious —but the less glorious one of witness and interpreter. It is the literature, as material product of a people, that dialogues with the logocentric U.S. canon, and the critic participates as one more producer among many.

Allow me to suggest how Chicano literature fulfills Jameson's tripartite dialectic. In the first stage, that of political history, specific events in time, Chicano literature and history have infused into the traditional U.S. canon the simple fact of a prior Spanish presence. This seems so trite as to be discounted, yet the fact that the majority of educated U.S. citizens do not factor this presence into their national equation demonstrates that what is trite for us—U.S. Hispanics —is radically new within the context of the canon we are asked to accept. Other events or data within the first stage would include the figures on Hispanic average wage, represive labor conditions, discriminatory education policies, political disfranchisement, over representation on society's casualty lists such as prison populations and deaths during combat, etc.

In the second stage, Jameson states, society's ideologemes come under scrutiny; that is, "the smallest intelligible unit of the essentially antagonistic collective discourses of social classes" (76). They manifest themselves as either pseudoideas or protonarratives (87), which in the U.S. would include the melting pot, westward expansion of civilization, stereotypes of the evil outsider, and even Jameson's assumption that there are no lower class workers within the territorial U.S. The facts from stage one engage the ideologemes and deconstruct them. How can the melting pot be a reality if Spanish speakers were present from the beginning and still have not been melted down? It is enough for Sergio Elizondo to write, "They reached our ranches" (*Perros*, 7) to evoke an image of Spanish-Mexican priority in the form of a highly developed social system of land ownership and to proffer a new paradigm for U.S. history. At a time when a major campaign has taken place to remind Americans that many of their ancestors passed through Ellis Island, Chicano history reminds us that immigration across the Mexican border has been equally significant, and perhaps more so for the future. The humanity, in its most universal sense, of Chicano characters debunks the ideologeme of the evil, dark-skinned Mexican. The early *actos* by the Teatro Campesino do the same to Jameson's extraterritorial lower class.

In the third stage, Jameson sees the work as a "field of force in which the dynamics of sign systems of several distinct modes of production can be registered and apprehended" (98). Systems in conflict share codes, but reveal contradictions within them. Thus, the Bill of Rights as a signifier in American tradition is evoked by Chicano literature to attack the status quo of American discriminatory justice. The basic values of simplicity, respect, family, love of nature, equal opportunity— all of them are utilized to simultaneously evoke the ideal and the betrayal of it by society. Finally, both English and Spanish are forced into confrontation to form a new interlingual product, the reflection of the cultural synthesis being realized in America.

In this third state, in addition, conflicts of the present day are studied in the context of permanent cultural evolution. Considered in this perspective, Chicano and other ethnic literatures of our time are understood to be, not fads as some claim, but the current surface sign of a deep structural dialectic present from the very beginning in the United States' search for a literary and cultural identity. This forces us to reconsider that search as a process of selection, exclusion and repression carried out by elite groups, closely identified with the central national project, that intend to focus attention on themselves and distract it from those groups they wish to relegate to the margins of the national psyche. In a much wider scope, national literatures everywhere should be studied as the product of such a dialectic, including cases such as England, France, Spain, Germany and certainly the Soviet Union. In this context, U.S. literature will then be seen within a historical struggle between centralizing and decentralizing forces, between majority and minority groups, and between mainstream imposition and peripheral resistance.

The pressure to revise the concept of American literature and culture is clearly evident. Recent studies and new anthologies attempt to open the canon, while denouncing the elitist manipulations of it. In the 1970s The Feminist Press initiated a project titled *Reconstructing American Literature* designed to study, criticize, and reformulate the history of U.S. literature and its canonizing process. One goal of the project was to organize the findings into several publications, including a university level anthology. The anthology, now being carried out by D.C. Heath and Co., will incorporate many of the traditionally excluded groups. Meanwhile, other major publishers, including Norton, have been rushing to cash in on what is perceived as the new trend—or necessity—by cutting and pasting into their standard anthologies a limited number of ethnic and women writers. Critics also have begun to reconsider the U.S. canon. Marcus Klein's book *Foreigners, The Making of American Literature, 1900-1940* makes a strong case for considering contemporary U.S. literature as a product, not of the New England/Puritan tradition, but of the displacement of that tradition by the mass immigrations to the U.S.A. of the early twentieth century. Literature and culture in the U.S. became, he claims, essentially polyglot—by which Klein means that American English was forced to accept new foreign influences. U.S. Hispanic literatures of today demand a fuller polyglot expression. They would take what Klein sees as the revolution in American literature to its logical extreme.

The dilemma of U.S. literature is also extreme. It is no longer a matter of if it should or will expand to absorb new words or new expressions within a national literature, but that of an insistent, multivoiced call for a restructuring of U.S. literature—and culture—into the polyglot expression of many nations within a common frontier. A dilemma between nationalism and pluralism.

Council of National Literature Quarterly Report 6. 1-2 (Jan.-April 1983): 13-18.

3 Hispanic Literatures in the United States

The literature of Hispanic peoples in the United States is certainly not a recent development. It was the first literature in a European language to be written on the continent. Before any permanent English settlement appeared on the American shores, Cabeza de Vaca had wandered from Florida to Mexico and published his famous account of the journey. In the mid-1500s Coronado and De Soto led expeditions into the territory now occupied by the U.S.A., producing more chronicles. By that time, the eastern seaboard, later the site of the English colonies, had already been explored and named in Spanish—and naming your environment is perhaps the most elementary form of poetry. That English names came to replace the Spanish is an accurate sign of the conflictive relationship that has persisted between the two groups of settlers and their respective written expressions.

In other parts of the continent, the Spanish presence was more permanent. In the second half of the sixteenth century, the Oñate expedition to settle New Mexico produced not only another of the many epic poems composed by the Spanish conquistadors everywhere from North America to Tierra del Fuego, but also the first performances of European drama within what is now the U.S.A. Through the years, in spite of isolation and the rather primitive conditions of the northern provinces of Nueva España (later Mexico), the Spanish-speaking population maintained a rich oral tradition of stories, poetry and drama. Specialists, such as Aurelio Espinosa and Arturo Campa, began gathering this material during the first half of our century. Their studies, documenting the fact of the existence of a Hispanic literary tradition, proved that this material was the direct heir to Spanish peninsular literature, such as the medieval ballads and religious dramas. This is not unusual. Similar phenomena can be found—or could be until recently—in most

Latin American countries where technology or non-Spanish migrations have not wiped out the traditional culture. In the U.S. Southwest, the Hispanic inhabitants of New Mexico were anxious to maintain their language as an essential foundation of culture; thus the first book printed in the area, shortly before the take-over by the United States, was a grammar and spelling manual.

Since 1848, when the territory now comprising the states of Arizona, California, Nevada, Utah, New Mexico, Texas and half of Colorado passed from Mexican to U.S. ownership, a continuous Spanish journalistic tradition has existed in the Mexican communities that survived in the area. Some strictly literary pieces appeared from time to time, and now it is becoming clear that the Hispanic writers living in the U.S.A. were not totally unaware of the literary trends in Latin America, as many people, including specialists, thought only a few years ago. However, official literary history—both U.S. and Mexican versions— ignored this activity and still does for the most part. In Puerto Rico, which has been occupied since 1898 by the U.S.A., literature has continued within the traditions of a Latin American country. The U.S. presence has affected Puerto Rican literary expression, certainly, but the literature that is culturally comparable to Chicano literature is that written by Puerto Ricans living on the mainland, mostly in the northeastern coastal region. Wherever Hispanic immigrants or migrants have settled for any length of time, there usually has appeared some form of journalistic media, and literature has been produced.

In addition, there exists a steady and highly significant outpouring of writing by Latin American visitors to the United States. Authors like Sarmiento, José Martí, Mariano Azuela, Martín Luis Guzmán, Carlos Fuentes, Octavio Paz, Angel Rama, José Agustín, Jorge Luis Borges, and many others have spent time in this country; and it, in turn, has entered into their writing. Yet they were visitors; their writings, though pertinent to the comprehension of the U.S. American experience, belong more legitimately to Latin American letters and should not be mistaken for that which this essay treats. Space does not allow me to differentiate thoroughly between these two bodies of writing. Suffice it to say that there is a centuries-old tradition of Hispanic writing done in and about the United States, written by Latin Americans deeply concerned with the implications of the U.S.A. and who viewed the country and its people from the perspective of sojourners. Moreover, they usually wrote for readers in their home countries. The literature which concerns us here was written by permanent residents of this country, insiders in spite of being an ethnic and linguistic minority often excluded from the mainstream; and their literature is, for the most part, directed at and read by other permanent residents of the United States.

Racial and ethnic awareness surged to prominence during the 1950s and 60s with the rise of the Black civil rights movement. Following closely behind, and greatly influenced by the Black example, came the efforts by Hispanics, Asian Americans and Native Americans (Indians) to win the same civil rights. These easily recognizable minorities overshadowed other ethnic groups, such as the Poles, Italians, Irish and others, who, though apparently assimilated into the general society, still maintain traditions and, in some cases, their own language, and feel themselves to be distinct and separate entities from those people of English (and Protestant) extraction.

The decade of the 60s shattered the ideal of a national cultural homogeneity that some had believed realized during W.W.II, the legendary end product of the melting pot. The citizenry of the U.S.A. is still, it was discovered, a *de facto* conglomerate of many national groups that immigrated to this country in the recent past (the last 100 years) and some—few—who were here prior to that. It really should not shock anyone that in 200 years, a relatively brief period on the historical scale of human existence, a country, which has steadily embraced such huge numbers of immigrants of widely divergent origins, has not managed to meld them into a single cultural character. Much older countries with less influx have not done so either; one need only travel through Great Britain, France, Spain, India, China, or the Soviet Union to realize the lie of their offical monological culture voice. Within this setting of unrest, division and shattered ideals, there arose the literary activity of Hispanic groups living in the United States, predominantly Chicanos and Puerto Ricans, with an as yet ambiguous Cuban presence.

We can eliminate from our discussion the Cuban literary production in the U.S.A. up to this point. Their main literary activity comes, so far, from writers who consider themselves exiles more than U.S. citizens or permanent residents, although this will probably change in the near future. The journal *Escandalar* (New York) is an example. The editorial board includes major Latin American writers; its content is entirely in line with the latest trends in Latin America; the literature published neither treats nor engages the U.S. experience. This is not to say that it is less valid or undesirable, but only that as literary production it is still essentially Latin American. The journal could be published in Mexico City without any significant change in orientation. Perhaps this derives from the fact that the exiled Cuban literati continue to think of themselves as part of that distinguished group of sojourners mentioned above, with every intention of returning someday to their mother country as soon as they get the opportunity. The younger generations will probably change this tendency, having grown up for the most part in the U.S.A. and experiencing Cuba only through the nostalgic memories ᴏг their elders. But that literature lies in the future and, thus, outside the concerns of this essay.

Although it is convenient for government agencies—as well as some leftist organizations—to lump Chicanos and Puerto Ricans (and any other Hispanics) together under any of several rubrics, this is as much an illusion as that of a monolithic U.S. national character. The groups are diverse and their literature cannot be reduced to simple generalizations without doing each violence. It is more instructive to compare and contrast them to understand the reasons why they differ and how the differences affect the literature. Ironically, one can take the supposed common denominators, which outsiders utilize to unite Chicanos and Puerto Ricans, and identify points of divergence: Spanish heritage, Latin American historical roots, miscegenation, minority status in the United States as immigrants and a common language.

Both groups acknowledge antecedents in Hispanic culture, but its significance for each certainly differs. This is closely tied to their history as Latin Americans. Mexican culture underwent a strongly anti-Spanish period after independence in 1821 and again during the Revolution of 1910. The Mexican nation developed a non-Spanish identity. Puerto Rico remained a Spanish colony until the end of the 19th century and then passed directly into the U.S. sphere of influence, never developing the same independent identity as Mexico. One could say that, to date, Puerto Rico has not achieved independence and remains a colony. Some Chicanos claim that the U.S. Southwest is also colonized territory; but even so, it was independent for almost thirty years. Immigrants who have come from Mexico since 1848 bring with them a sense of independent nationality.

More significant is the fact that Chicano culture derives from inland North-central Mexico, while Puerto Rican culture is Caribbean and coastal. If Chicanos were influenced to any great extent by the eastern coastal cultural patterns of Veracruz or Yucatán, they might be more like Puerto Ricans and Cubans, but the fact is that Mexico itself is not Caribbean in its national ethos. Thus, Chicanos may well feel closer to a Columbian from Bogotá or an Argentine from Mendoza than to a native of San Juan. In addition, the Chicano movement has inherited—or chosen to appropriate—much of the agrarian ideology from the Mexican Revolution. This produces a much stronger preoccupation with property ownership—from small farms to homes, as well as the question of "owning" a national territory—than in Puerto Rican mainland literature.

This difference was reinforced through the immigration patterns that, until recently, led Puerto Ricans to the northeast coast and Mexicans mostly to the southwestern states. Although both groups are concentrated in cities and urban areas, in general terms the Puerto Ricans are urban oriented, while Chicanos tend to retain a rural quality. Chicano literature is full of campesinos and migrant farm workers. One of the prime proponents/protagonists of the literature, the Teatro Campesino of Luis Valdez, began as the propaganda arm of the United Farm Workers Union. Mainland Puerto Rican literature is more concerned with the urban ghetto and the New York style of life. Moreover, the western U.S.A. traditionally has signified the dream of land acquisition, while the eastern cities have come to represent the renters' ghetto. Add to this the ideology propagated by much Chicano literature that the Southwest belongs to the Chicanos because it was taken from Mexico through an illegal invasion, and one can understand how Chicano literature would contain a proprietary vein absent in Puerto Rican writing.

Both groups are considered minorities of mixed racial backgrounds. However, the predominant non-Spanish element differs in each case. Chicanos see themselves as Indian and Spanish; Puerto Ricans emphasize their Black and Spanish heritage. Thus Miguel Méndez, a Chicano from Arizona, calls for a close association with Native Americans, and Alurista utilizes pre-Columbian mythology as the basis for the projection of a Chicano identity. Piri Thomas, on the other hand, struggles with being black but not *a Black* in *Down These Mean Street*. This difference is compounded by the fact—suppressed in public—that there is anti-black prejudice in the Chicano (and Mexican) community, as well as a lingering resentment over what is perceived as pro-black favoritism in governmental circles. This mistrust and envy is projected onto Puerto Ricans when they emphasize their blackness. In literature the black influence is most obvious in Puerto Rican poetry written in English, with its black rhythm and penchant for repetitive words and facile rhyme. Some Chicano poets, like Alurista, have deliberately cultivated a black voice which they sprinkle into their usual style, but these usages are recognized and classified as an extraneous element. Chicano *pinto* (prison) writers sometimes show more similarity to black styles because of a predominant black presence within the prison system; but cultural and ethnic divisions seem to be spreading behind prison walls as well, and recent pinto poetry shows much more influence from Chicano writers outside the walls than from Blacks within.

In terms of miscegenation, what is shared is a status of less than full-fledged racial identification with the non-Spanish group to which each relates. Neither Blacks nor Native Americans consider Puerto Ricans or Chicanos, respectively, completely theirs.

The government often unites the groups under the rubric of Spanish-speaking people, yet the Spanish spoken is quite different, both phonetically and lexically. Once again, the difference between Caribbean and non-coastal origins is a significant factor. Moreover, the literary usage of Spanish differs. One is more likely to find Spanish and English used in the same text in Chicano writing than in Puerto Rican. Code switching, as linguists unfortunately call this mixture, was legitimized by the best Chicano poets in the 1960s—José Montoya, Alurista and Ricardo Sánchez used it extensively. "Hoy enterraron al Louie / and San Pedro o san pinche / are in for it," reads the opening of Montoya's classic poem "El Louie;" "la canería y el sol / la mata seca, red fruits / the sweat / the death / el quince la raya / juanito will get shoes," are typical verses from Alurista's collection *Floricanto en Aztlán*. Certainly not all Chicano literature is written in this interlingual form—much is only in Spanish or English, sometimes published in bilingual editions with translations from the original language.

Puerto Rican writers are much more liable to remain in one language, although recent poets—Victor Hernández Cruz, Pedro Pietri, Tato Laviera and Miguel Algarín—are utilizing code switching more and more in their writing. Both groups use anglicisms, but not the same ones, just as the Spanish slang they employ is not the same. At times the same word has entirely different meanings for the two groups. Thus, ironically, it is exactly the usages which characterize the speech of Puerto Ricans and Chicanos within the family of Latin American speech patterns that also distinguish them from each other.

It could be added that in literature both groups preoccupy themselves with the injustices suffered by Hispanic people within the U.S. sphere of influence. However, the self-appraisals of their status as a people differ considerably. Chicano literature has produced several epic-like books which attempt to create historical and mythological overviews of a Chicano nation. Works like Rodolfo Gonzales' *I Am Joaquín*, Sergio Elizondo's *Perros y antiperros*, Alurista's *Floricanto en Aztlán*, and Miguel Méndez' *Los criaderos humanos* provide an ideological base for cultural cohesion and purpose. Nothing similar has appeared to date in mainland Puerto Rican literature.

Chicano literature, in addition, has created archetypes of cultural survival despite assimilatory pressures—the *Pachuco* and the *campesino*. The former came to prominence in the 1940s when U.S. military men attacked them on the streets of Los Angeles.[2] Writers like José Montoya and Luis Valdez have transformed the Pachucos into precursors of the comtemporary Chicano consciousness. As a literary image they represent militant resistance to both U.S. and Mexican society, and thus symbolize the intercultural synthesis of Chicanismo. Campesinos, or migrant farm workers, have come to represent the exploited labor force utilized by the dominant society to maintain a high standard of living for the middle class at the expense of underpaid workers; yet they also rep-

resent Mexicans willing to leave Mexico and change their way of life
for a better standard of living in the U.S.A. Puerto Rican literature has
produced no comparable archetypes.

Immigration and deculturation are favorite subjects of both groups.
René Márquez' *La carreta* compares well with Richard Vásquez' *Chicano* or even Ernesto Galarza's *Barrio Boy*. Families leave their rural
home in the mother country to move to the urban U.S.A., where the
younger members start to adopt new ways. The family unit suffers and
the older generation longs for the lost past. Both literatures have explored the *Bildungsroman* within the milieu of immigration, though Chicanos give it more emphasis. Piri Thomas' *Down These Mean Streets*
relates a young Puerto Rican's struggles with blackness and then with
prison; Pedro Juan Soto's *Hot Land, Cold Season* explores a mainland
youth's return to Puerto Rico, where he confronts alienation. In Chicano literature José Antonio Villarreal's *Pocho*; Rudy Anaya's *Bless Me,
Ultima*; John Rechy's *City of Night* and *The Fourth Angel*; Tomás Rivera's
. . . *y no se lo tragó la tierra*; and Oscar Zeta Acosta's *The Autobiography
of a Brown Buffalo* all fall within the genre to some extent, exploring Chicano rites of passage in a variety of social settings. What distinguishes
the Chicano *Bildungsroman* is the inclusion of writing itself as an essential factor in the process of maturation. Several of the most important
Chicano novels can be read as portraits of the artists as young men.
Writing becomes the means of preserving culture and, at once, a way of
redefining it within the new situation of the United States. This concern
is not yet present in Puerto Rican literature to any great extent.

In spite of the great variety of thematic concerns and stylistic tendencies, Chicano literature manifests a unifying paradigm: to a perceived
threat to the existence of the culture, the work itself responds, becoming
a proof of survival. Within this paradigm there functions what Ramón
Saldívar calls the dialectics of difference. Chicanos in literature choose
to be other than U.S. American or Mexican. They reject the chaos of
deculturation, but in the act of defining themselves they discover a non-
Mexican identity as well. The literature is the production of a space
of difference, an intercultural synthesis between dialectical forces, be
they United States vs. Mexico, urban vs. rural, English vs. Spanish, or
even rock 'n' roll vs. polkas. To attempt to eliminate completely one or
the other is to cease to be Chicano, although certainly individuals can
prefer more U.S. or more Mexican content in their lives. Chicanismo
is the product/producer of ongoing synthesis, continually drawing from
what seem to outsiders to be opposing cultural elements. Therefore,
the literature proposes an alternative, an "inter" space for a new ethnic
identity to exist.

Mainland Puerto Rican literature, while doing the same thing, still

tends to advocate unity with the island and to disparage the creation
of a new cultural synthesis not centered in the homeland. Militant in-
dependistas discourage the idea of a separate identity for Puerto Ricans residing on the mainland, just as a small minority of Mexicanists
do among Chicanos. Yet there already exists a different cultural manifestation, sometimes pejoratively called Nuyorican. Writers like Miguel
Algarín (*Nuyorican Poetry*) and Jaime Carrero (*The FM Safe*) utilize the
term with a new pride in a similar fashion to what Chicano writers did
with the previously disparaging word Chicano in the late 1960s. This
redefinition of one's hybrid state is the first step towards an ideology of
difference.

The next logical step would be to synthesize the Nuyorican and Chicano identities into a Latino or Hispano ethnicity. In the Chicago area,
where Puerto Ricans and Chicanos live side by side, the effort has begun. The *Revista Chicano-Riqueña* was started as just such a forum for
the two groups. However, to date, very little synthesis has occurred.
Ethnicity is not a matter of rational planning, or else the melting pot
might have worked much better than it has. The two groups share a
similar situation, and perhaps they will come to share the paradigm of
resistance to chaotic destruction through the creation of a different, alternate identity. But at present the cultural differences between them
are still stronger than the will to unify. Their writing reflects those differences as much as it constitutes a literature different from the mainstream writing of the United States.

American Writing Today, v. 2 (Washington D.C.: Forum Series 1982): 250-261.

4 A Case of Identity: What's in a Name? Chicanos and Riqueños

Nations hardly ever have the luxury to develop their identity in strict introspection; extraneous factors intervene. The process usually includes some degree of contrasting with neighbors or ideal models. Nations develop in the context of other nations. Mexico and Puerto Rico are no exceptions. Their modern history has never ceased to be played out on a field of which the U.S.A. has occupied a significant, often monopolizing, percentage of space. And since the U.S.A. has long since abandoned any pretense of being a peer in the American fraternity of nations, preferring to manifestly fulfill its arrogated role of overseer of forced hegemony, Mexico and Puerto Rico naturally adopted a defensive stance of radical binary opposition: we against they.

While binary oppositions suit the needs of scientific and pseudoscientific thinking, they have the deleterious effect of characterizing the space between the two terms as a sliding scale of plus and minus values. As a result any point between the poles assumes the value of less than completely whole, of no longer one but not yet the other. From the perspective of the poles, the in between stage is no longer, or not yet, fully acceptable. Linguistic science and structuralism have influenced our cultural thought, and both are examples of the inherent negativity of binary constructs. Terms are defined by what they are not. Languages are opposed in pairs, and to be bilingual is to switch codes from one to another, not to mix them. Anything less than a complete jump from one pole to the other is termed "interference" in this way of thinking, with the negative connotations the word carries. The space between the languages is a forbidden zone of neither this nor that. Those who practice a type of speech located in the zone of mixture are linguistic outlaws for the purists at either pole.

The implications with regard to the immigrant's situation are clear.

Immigrants are judged from the extremes in opposition, and upon them are projected the demands of the binary structure. They become less than authentic natives of either side—*half-breed*; their mere existence is considered an interference into both poles, a threat to either national identity. Attempts to develop customs or languages in an *ad hoc* manner, truly reflective of the material and ideal experiential base of the immigrants, are rejected by the purists at the extremes. Mexican and Puerto Rican immigrants to mainland U.S.A., and their descendents, exemplify well this dilemma, and always have. We are all too familiar with U.S. society's negative attitude towards Mexican and Puerto Rican immigrants, but less attention has been dedicated to the attitudes of the source societies. Here I will concentrate on the latter.

Earlier in this century, during the Mexican Revolution, Mexican intellectuals were forced to spend time in the U.S.A. in communites of their compatriots who had settled in this country. Their attitude towards their hosts was sympathetic, though often patronizing, and usually less than accepting. And as we might expect, they almost always offered examples of language usage, both to illustrate their point, as well as to justify their negative reaction with regard to people who supposedly were their compatriots, and who often were extending the most gracious welcome they could muster.

Martín Luis Guzmán, considered among the best prose writers in Mexican literature, while in San Antonio, Texas in 1913, was hosted by the lawyer Samuel Belden. A linguistic purist trained in the classic tradition of correct usage, Guzmán was struck by Belden's rather curious manner of speaking Spanish. Guzmán identifies Belden as a "Medio mexicano y medio norteamericano," who spoke to him "en su español raro y difícil —ininteligible a veces—, español sin tercera persona ficticia y con sintaxis anglicizante" (227). Belden, according to Guzmán, had slid to the center of the binary scale, his speech being of a hybrid character, no longer proper Spanish, although still some recognizable form of it. The absence of the *usted* form on which Guzmán focuses signified a cultural evolution away from the formalities of Hispanic customs and propriety. Belden no longer respected the subtleties of intimacy and familiarity implicit in the use of the *usted*. Perhaps his more egalitarian environment made them irrelevant, or it could have been that he never mastered the tone of respect, just as many Chicanos today confuse the formal and informal in Spanish. This must have shocked Guzmán and his Mexican comrades with whom he traveled, almost all of whom normally addressed one another in the formal *usted*, despite years of close relationship. Belden's manner strikes Guzmán as "directa y ruda," but he goes on to add, one suspects with heavy irony, that his manner made him "simpático a primera vista y nos indujo a tratarlo desde el principio con cierta amable familiaridad" (227). Guzmán was not partial to quick familiarity, so we can read this as a commentary on how Mexican customs had degenerated in Texas, just as the language had reached a point between Spanish and English at which it teetered dangerously at the brink of incomprehension, both in the realm of language and culture.

José Vasconcelos was less generous. He too knew Belden during the same period and branded him "inculto como todos los que se crían en aquellos territorios" (785). With one sentence he condemns everyone raised in Texas, or perhaps in the U.S.A. itself. Belden is termed a "mexicano-yankee," with the disparaging connotations of the latter word. In Los Angeles, California, Vasconcelos praises the perfect Castilian of some Spanish dancers, contrasting the women's speech with "la lengua corrompida a que uno se habitúa por estos lugares" (105). The context is significant: these women are not educated, nor even particularly respectable if we take into consideration the opinion held of musical performers in the early part of the century. Yet, to Vasconcelos—like Guzmán a linguistic purist, but even more of an Anglophobe—these women are culturally preferable to the Hispanos of California, who Vasconcelos was willing to utilize for his political needs, but not cultivate for enjoyment. San Antonio, however, epitomizes for Vasconcelos — as for other Mexicans then and now—the despicable Mexican-Yankee synthesis: "No sólo lo norteamericano, también lo mexicano se volvía absurdo, bajaba de categoría en la híbrida ciudad" (786). This is the arrogance of a supposedly bilingual man, who thinks he can assume a place at one or the other pole of the binary oppositions, leaping over the middle ground without undergoing any process of transition. From this purist perspective, with utter self-assurance, he can scorn those who find themselves somewhere between the poles. His was a flagrantly elitist position, which will come as no surprise to careful readers of Vasconcelos.

Vasconcelos also receives the dubious credit for having popularized the despective name for these hybrid Mexican U.S. beings: Pochos, "palabra que se usa en California para designar al descastado que reniega de lo mexicano aunque lo tiene en la sangre y procura ajustar todos sus actos al mimetismo de los amos actuales de la región." For Vasconcelos this synthesis represented "la destrucción de la cultura latinoespañola de nuestros padres, para sustituirla con el primitivismo norteamericano que desde la niñez se infiltra en los pochos" (782). While Vasconcelos tolerated nothing less than the purity of the binary poles— either correct Spanish or correct English—he never hid his preference for the former, viewing it as a good in itself, inherently superior, and which likewise contained a scale of values rising from the lowly Mexican form to the preferred Castilian. Within his linguistic view there lay the ideologeme (see note 1) of good versus evil, and any mixing of the two contaminated the good without improving the bad. Vasconcelos judged that process to be degrading for both countries. He would have favored a strict linguistic border to maintain well defined national spaces of pure speech—no hybrids.

Among Puerto Rican writers we find similar texts, with the difference that the authors did not have to travel outside their borders to observe the same phenomena. The U.S. invasion and the subsequent juxtapositioning of the two languages and cultures, which both sides called "bilingualism" and "biculturalism," provided targets for their pens at home. In his book *El idioma de Puerto Rico*, Epifanio Fernández Vanga, a contemporary of Vasconcelos and Guzmán, included an essay titled "Hablando en gringo" (Fernández Méndez, 1056-60). The author lamented the incorrect translations from English into Spanish in local newspapers, the English syntax used by university students when they spoke Spanish, and the abuse of English words sprinkled into Spanish. As an example, Fernández Vanga takes aim at a sports report about baseball, a trivial subject, perhaps, but in truth he laments not only the degeneration of language in Puerto Rico, but also the refocusing of popular culture onto a foreign ritual. If baseball becomes the new youth ritual, where is the cultural *axis mundi*? No longer does it reside in Puerto Rico. It was no mere coincidence that the author wrote about a game between Washington and the New York Giants. The U.S.A. looms as a bicephalous monster, whose business head controls its governmental counterpart. Fernández Vanga ended his essay by recommending to his readers that they turn for relief from this U.S. influence to another article, this one taken from the Madrid paper *El Imparcial*. Like Vasconcelos, Fernández Vanga preferred peninsular Spanish to the corrupted speech of his fellow islanders.

More significant for us, however, is the fact that Fernández Vanga could not appreciate the living, vital language process that appears in his essay. The author proves unable to conceive of, and therefore unable to comment on, the possibility that the juxtaposition of Spanish and English texts, which he shuffles within his essay and which forms the textual environment of his readers, can bring into existence in some natural manner the very synthesis he so deprecates. His world vision and mental structuring capacity are strictly binary, blinding him to those possibilities. His only response is to condemn what already existed all around him—his country's new culture in evolution—and to take refuge in a foreign culture, the Spanish, the same one that had colonized and repressed his island for centuries.

Ten years later, in 1941, José M. Toro Nazario attacked bilingualism as the cause of what he interpreted as the Puerto Rican intellectual's inferiority. He asserts that "el bilingüismo nos hace conscientes del castellano al hablar inglés; conscientes del inglés al hablar castellano,' which according to the author results in the fact that Puerto Ricans now spoke slowly and that the island had become "un país de intelectuales tartamudos" (Fernández Méndez, 1065-66). Once again we find an example of the critic's blindness. Toro Nazario did not consider the possibility that this situation of having to maintain languages strictly separate in a bilingual manner, was not natural for these intellectuals; that having to speak just one language was the cause of the stammering he condemned. If they could have spoken interlingually, in their natural and by then native fashion, the problem might have disappeared along with the inferiority.

However, Toro Nazario betrays his own position when he relates an anecdote witnessed in New York's Central Park. He heard children speak both languages in "cataratas," an image connoting velocity, volume and beauty. The natural question, unvoiced by the author because its mere enunciation would put in danger his elitism, is why—if children use the two languages equally well and together—do intellectuals stammer and falter? Could it not stem from the repression inherent in Toro Nazario's binary prejudice? So blinding is this prejudice that although Toro Nazario perceives clearly the falsity of "bilingualism," he cannot bring himself to welcome the truth of interlingualism; instead, for him it is a tragedy: "La tragedia del bilingüismo está en que su proyección ... provoca un nuevo idoma. Llamadlo dialecto si os parece, pero los países bilingües sólo existen en la imaginación de los políticos malos y los pedagogos buenos" (1070). I agree, certainly, because the people of whom he spoke, like others in the same situation, are not bilingual. We are interlingual.

Yet another decade later, Jaime Benítez coined a Puerto Rican equivalent for *pocho*: "homo portorricensis imprecisus" (Fernández Méndez, 1089). Admittedly it is not as convenient as *pocho*, but it summarizes the Puerto Rican preoccupation with faltering speech, as well as the elitist stance of those who condemned the new hybrid culture. Once again the stress falls on the ill effects of bilingualism, the interference of English in Spanish: "De ahí esa frecuente tartamudez o balbuceo ... Así ha podido decirse que se es analfabeto en dos idiomas al mismo tiempo" (1193). Neither one nor the other, the Puerto Rican is stigmatized by Benítez as an imprecise being.

Underlying both the Mexican and the island Puerto Rican texts is the assumption of the correctness of the binary system. None of the writers questioned the system nor his right to use it to name and judge those supposed unfortunates caught between the poles. They were of-

fended, horrified by what they saw and heard. Yet one can imagine their
reaction had they lived to see the new phenomena apparent in at least a
segment—perhaps small but highly visible—of the immigrants and their
descendents from those two nations who challenge and reject the binary
system, preferring to live out their intercultural essence openly. These
groups claim legitimate residence in the space between the poles, and
from there they demand and excercise the right to self-determination.
They have pondered their situation, decided that it is their real state of
existence upon which they can base an identity, and chosen a name for
themselves appropriate to that identity, a sign of their own making.

Chicanos and Nuyoricans or Riqueños clearly assert a new hybrid
identity, which in turn redefines the nationalistic binary opposition into
a preliminary dialectic from which has begun to spring the logical, ir-
repressible international synthesis. The two competing logocenters—
Mexico and Puerto Rico, respectively, versus the United States—have
become opposite extremes in a new circle of cultural production, the
center of which is a new, continually dynamic *nosotros*. And whereas
before the apologists of the Latin American source societies could dis-
paragingly characterize these hybrid peoples—simply because they con-
trolled the means of cultural production, the printed word—now the
hybrids express themselves as the producers/products of their identity
in process.

When viewed from the point of synthesis, the dialectical poles assume the character of marginal others, of not-we-though-related, of
less-than-fully-us, perhaps not inauthentic in themselves, but clearly not
authentically us. They are Other, not to be envied nor emulated nor
consulted as models of behavior or speech. This is difficult to accept for
those still situated at the poles—or those who pretend to be there despite the reality of their residence within the borders of the U.S. mainland. There are those, like Chicanos of South Texas, who insist they
are Mexicans. To accept that they are not, and cannot be, threatens
their world image, displaces their illusory centrality—ironically based
on a pejorative peripheral status—and supercedes their survival strategy. They do what they can to deny the dialectical process and infuse
doubt onto the synthesis, but they are living proof that they cannot be
what they delude themselves into believing they are, Mexicans. True
Mexicans have satirized and attacked Chicanos in ways closely resem-
bling the Guzmán and Vasconcelos texts. Octavio Paz's Pachuco essay,
while couched in benevolent comprehension, is actually a reactionary
condemnation of Chicano hybridness (*Laberinto*, 9-25). More recently,
the Marxist David Ojeda rejected the Chicano concept of Aztlán as a
false dream and exhorted Chicanos to return to Mexico to help in the
class struggle (41). Others are less aggressively scornful, but they too

insist on trying to appropriate Chicanos for Mexican purposes and to lock us into a Mexican scale of values and priorities. Chicano literature and forms of speech are inevitably compared to the writing and Spanish of Mexicans, with the expected conclusion—logical from their binary perspective—that Chicano cultural production is inferior. At best the reaction has been patronizing.

Similar results can be found among Puerto Ricans. Pedro Juan Soto, whose *Spiks* could be said to prefigure Nuyorican literature, has come to disclaim the hybrid language of his own text written in New York: "Detesto ... la influencia del inglés: desde vocablos anglizados que aún no se han convertido en préstamos lingüísticos, hasta el repetido abuso del gerundio. He preferido dejar en paz tales errores y emplear lo aprendido para la redacción de otras obras" (10). Those errors are facets of Riqueño and Chicano native speech. Soto has gone on to ally himself with, to embrace, the Spanish purist pole of the binary prejudice. María Teresa Babín, while including a section on Nuyorican writers in her anthology *Borinquen*, insisted on subsuming them to the Island tradition. The forced union elicited a comparison in which the island's literature was said to be superior in richness, antiquity, complexity and refinement. Nuyorican writing was granted, however, the virtue of being recent (xxv). Even Ricardo Campos and Juan Flores, after taking Babín to task for failing to realize how different the Nuyorican writers are from the Muñocista ideals Babín exults, go on to criticize the same writers for being ignorant of what Campos and Flores posit as their true tradition: that of the Puerto Rican working class (136). Once again the new synthesis is subsumed into one of the binary poles, disguised here behind the mask of correct political ideology.

Yet to name oneself is an act of conscious self-creation, a right some cultures still grant their offspring, while other groups retain only vestiges of adult renaming rituals, like the sacrament of Confirmation among Catholics. Chicanos and Riqueños have chosen names to fit a reality— or an ideology. Their literatures are different from that of the national literature from their respective Latin American relatives. There exist ties, similarities, concordances with the once mother country and language, of course, but there are just as many with the U.S.A. In truth, the latter is more mother for many than the Latin American past of their parents, or grandparents, or ... That is exactly the point of the names, to emphasize difference in sameness, to affirm a faith in our power to synthesize a language and a culture of our own, here and now.

The names are signs of new identity, perhaps still in the making— and thus more free and liberating—but nonetheless real. The literature is both a product and producer of the sign. One can welcome, decry, denounce, belittle, or embrace and revel in it, but one cannot make it go away. Perhaps it will disappear on its own, evolving into something else, proving itself one more fleeting expression of migration writing, but it could also turn out to be the manifestation, much clearer through its extreme character, of a new cultural synthesis in full process both in Latin America and the United States. Trying to place the opposition of nations and cultures outside or above history, or to think that we can avoid the evolution of languages just because they are now in print, are illusions and delusions probably shared by the Roman elite in Spain, the creole Spanish in Latin America, the French in Viet Nam, or the Afrikaner in South Africa, just to recall a few examples. It is difficult for parents to let go of their children. Sometimes the latter must insist on their rights for the good of all concerned. Names change, new identities are forged. And it is an old literary motif that bastard children are the most loyal offspring, even though they may seem the least desirable heirs.

Imágenes e identidad: el puertorriqueño en la literatura (Río Piedras: Ediciones Huracán, 1985): 283-288.

5 Spanish-language Loyalty and Literature

The title of this essay was not of my creation. It was imposed on me by the organizers of a symposium, who, as is often the case, did not consult me when making up the program. As will become apparent, I reject its implicit division of writers into those who use Spanish and those who do not, with the further attribution of loyalty to the former and disloyalty to the latter. The title focuses attention on language usage as if language where something extraneous to the writer instead of personal and interior. I believe that the real question of the literary use of language by Chicanos lies elsewhere. Yet, I also realize that, ironically, this title accurately captures the misconceptions held by many people, including some who look favorably upon our literature. So in the end, I accepted the title as a flawed proposition which allowed me to work through it to my own position and conclusions.

From the first encounter between Spanish-speaking inhabitants and the invading foreigners who spoke, among other languages, English, the history of Texas, like that of the country itself, has been marked by efforts to eliminate Spanish from the conquered territories and impose English as the official language. Needless to say, these efforts—which periodically reappear during periods of reactionary paranoia—have not been entirely successful, for if they had we would not still be discussing the phenomena of a literature written in Spanish by U.S. citizens, and I would not be writing an essay to ponder the ideal of loyalty to the Spanish language by people who, it is implied by the title of the essay, should be writing in English. But since the history of efforts to mold a monolingual state have failed, those closely associated with that failed ideal now want us to consider if, when we write, we are loyal. Perhaps it is a polite way to ask us if we consider ourselves loyal when we speak in Spanish, and I have been asked to include in my pondering the virtues

41

or vices of bilingualism. Whatever the motivation, I will twist the topic to my own purpose, for one must, above all, be loyal to oneself.

Before we can address the question of loyalty to Spanish among recent writers—or if loyalty should even be the question —we must put the discussion into a historical context for better understanding. This is not as easy as it seems, the tradition of fictionalizing history being one of the primary genres of U.S. literature.

Misconceptions and Disinformation

Non-Hispanics conceive of Chicanos and other Latinos who maintain our language both in speaking and writing as recent immigrants. They have been trained to think of U.S. residents according to the pattern of European peoples arriving to Eastern ports of entry and blending into the English speaking mainstream in a process of assimilation over a couple of generations. The end product of this transformation is the monolingual "American." Logically, according to this formula, anyone who speaks the language of another country must be either an excellent student or a recent arrival, and those who write it by choice must have been educated somewhere other than in U.S. schools. This concept of assimilation remains so ingrained in the U.S. psyche that any deviation suffices to brand a person as exactly that, a deviant, with rather negative connotations.

This manner of reducing all immigration to, and assimilation into, the U.S. to a rigid generational scheme rests on a master fiction called American history. In this propaganda of an idealized English cultural dominance, the U.S. was settled by a slow expansion east to west into the open space always just beyond the last settlement, an area sparsely populated for the most part by savages, nomads with no crops to root them in the ground nor urban centers to keep them in place. In other words, to the west awaited uncivilized space for the taking by the English-speaking bearer of civilization. The story goes on to recount how almost a century after the founding of the country by the heirs of the first English immigrants, the flood of well-intentioned and god-fearing migrants, following a pattern of expansion into the wilderness just waiting to be claimed, encountered some small settlements of Spanish/Mexicans, isolated far from their country to the south and living in moral decadence and economic stagnation. These people were quickly outnumbered by the more progressive English speakers, who generously accepted those who wanted to stay among them. Much later, so it goes, Mexicans began immigrating into the region, repeating a standard pattern of foreigners coming to a host country. However, these Spanish

speakers supposedly have refused to follow the generational assimilation plan as defined by the more cooperative European groups, preferring to remain loyal to their native tongue. This recalcitrance is, then,
by definition at the heart of the problem. With history organized in this
way, the conclusion is unquestionably logical. The problem is that this
version of history does not accomodate all the facts, and much less the
alternative fictions of the case.

Competing Colonial Systems

From the earliest period of exploration and settlement of what is
now the territory of the U.S.A., European languages were at war—first
Spanish and French, and later others, among them English. Despite
decades of the above mentioned attempts to teach U.S. history as the
slow but inexorable expansion of the English-based colonies into the
wilderness until the newly formed country embraced what was relatively
empty space, the truth is that we would be better served—and better
educated—if we had always studied it as the close interworking of at
least three, if not more, colonial systems which competed for every inch
of territory. Moreover, while the space may have been scarcely populated by European standards, there were no unclaimed areas—all of
it pertained to some Native American tribe. Yet even if we discount
the Native Americans as somehow outside the system of civilized European competition—a position into which all European powers seemed
intent on placing them—the territories in question were claimed also by
Europeans; that is to say, there were no unclaimed spaces even in the
European sense. Every appropriation of new territory by the United
States was at the expense of some other country which then had to adjust its boundaries and redraw its maps. More often than not, a gain
by the U.S.A. represented a loss by the Spanish, and later the Mexcian
nation. And where national interests collided, languages became a defensive fortress, a besieging weapon, the matériel of war.

The eastern seaboard was first named in Spanish by exploratory expeditions charting the territory claimed and awarded to the Spanish
crown, only to be renamed by later English intruders. Of course the
Native Americans already had names for the land but, not being Europeans, they were seldom granted equal human status in the dealy serious
game of territorial pursuit. That the map of this country still preserves
Native American names may attest to the persistence of the original
inhabitants, but also to the romantic nostalgia for an idealized native
population that possessed the European immigrants once they had rid
themselves of the unbearably real Indian presence.

Establishing one official language, empowering that of the controllers, is one way of trying to insure cultural and political dominance. Yet, people have a way of speaking their native tongue despite laws and repression. Case in point, neither the Spanish nor the Mexican government succeeded in making the legal and illegal aliens who poured into their northern territories speak Spanish, even when those aliens had promised to do so in exchange for privileges and rights. These recalcitrant foreigners who flooded into the northern Mexican provinces, looking for work and the opportunity to own land, claiming only the intention of participating in the established society of the area, could not see why they also had to learn another language, even when that language was the government's official means of communication and the socially acceptable one of their hosts. The implicit logic of their steady invasion was that if enough of them came, then the country should and would naturally change its language—a worthy logic to consider, even today. But once this plague of undocumented immigrants—to avoid calling them illegal aliens—often unsavory itinerants, took over, they decided that perhaps language should not be a matter of choice and logic but of power and force. Needless to say, in spite of a history of incredible abuse in schools and the legal system, the imposition of English in the state of Texas has not produced all the desired results. While it has served to keep the Chicano population concentrated in the lowest echelons of labor and politically disenfranchised, Spanish is still spoken, in some form or another, as it is in other border areas and many inland states as well.

Unfortunately, the drawing of the linguistic battle line turned language into an ideological concern producing the situation in which the language someone speaks or writes becomes a question of loyalty or disloyalty, as if we were still speaking of war, treason, betrayal—or tormented love. And within the framework of simplistic binary opposition—this not being that—to be loyal to one language often translates as disloyalty to the other, and disloyalty to the official language, even the unofficial official one, equals betrayal.

When Father Martínez—the patriarch of the New Mexican Catholic Church from 1821 until the take over by the United States in 1849—finally managed to bring a printing press to what was then the most important cultural center of the northern Mexican provinces, the first book published was a manual to teach children how to read and write Spanish: *Cuaderno de ortografía* (Santa Fe, 1834). Martínez realized the importance of knowing one's language. He also knew, as early as the 1830s, that it was only a matter of time before the invasion by non-Spanish speakers would be unleashed—so he taught his students English as well. So the first book published in the Southwest was an attempt to strengthen the Spanish language under the impending menace of an English-language take-over.

As I have pointed out elsewhere, the *Cuaderno* has the qualities of a paradigm for Chicano literature ("Chicano Poetry"). First, while its goals were diadactic, the author realized that learning is easier through literature, so he used poetry to exemplify the lessons. When, with the 1960s Chicano civil right struggle, a resurgence of literary production occurred, much of it was diadactic, and at least part of it aimed at preserving, if not strictly the Spanish languages in opposition to English, at least a Chicano culture as opposed to an Anglo American one. Father Martínez' manual is also exemplary in that to print it he had to aquire his own press, as many Chicanos would have to do over a century later. Yet it is highly significant that most probably the press and the supplies were brought from the U.S.A. and not from Mexico. Chicano literature, together with its precursors in the Southwest, while sometimes drawing from Mexican culture for content and even form —as well as authors— is essentially a U.S. literature. Its existence has not been made possible by Mexican publishers, but by Chicanos who have either acquired the means of producing it themselves or, in fewer instances, have been accepted by U.S. mainstream publishers. Just as Fr. Martínez was scorned by the central authorities of the church in Mexico, Chicanos have been more often than not ignored by both Mexican publishers and readers. The question of language maintance in the face of English-language threat was and is itself a concern almost exclusively of those who inhabit the space of encounter, the northern provinces of Mexico in the process of becoming the Southwestern territory of the United States, a process still going on, culturally and linguistically unresolved.

U.S. Conquest

After the take over by the United States, the battle was fully engaged. Yet it was not a simple matter of selecting what language one cared to speak. From 1848 to the present century —some would say still today—to speak Spanish could suddenly become a political act, a declaration of loyalties, that could cost a person much, even their life. It is no accident that in *The Corrido of Gregorio Cortez* (Paredes) the fatal shooting of two men and the story's central action hinge on an incorrect translation of one language to another. There was a state of war, and the language, too, oral as well as written, was not only used to fight it, it was itself the battleground.

During the last half of the nineteenth century, the Southwest became a favorite topic of the new-dime novel industry centered in New

Jersey (Pettit). Mexicans were stereotyped cruelly and continually ridi-
culed for their broken speech. At the same time, Southwest Spanish-
language newspapers published satirical pieces about those *Mexicanos*
who tried to speak the language of the invaders. These satires produced
the stereotype similar to its counterpart created by Anglo American
writers. Since both sides saw the other as a menacing presence, attempts
by Mexicans to speak English were perceived and depicted as threatening and/or degrading. Hybrid speech became a sign of cultural betrayal
and moral degeneration when the speaker was Mexican. Anglo Americans could be seen as clever, smart, generous, and even kind when they
could speak a little of "those people's lingo," but Mexicans were simply
pathetic. The "half-breed" was suspect.

Twentieth Century

When the Mexican Revolution produced an influx of Mexican immigration to the U.S.A., among the newcomers were literate men and
women who deplored the state into which the Spanish language had
fallen in the supposedly Mexican centers of population. It was at this
time that *Pocho* became the term of derision used by Mexicans to characterize their brethern living in the U.S.A. Jorge Ulica's cruel satires of
Pochos in the first decades of the present century clearly demonstrates
this Mexican bias, both against intercultural speech and those who were
in the process of adopting English. Ulica was no kinder than Hollywood
script writers who invented their version of Pocho speech calculated to
get a knowing laugh from English speakers, or even from immigrants
who could look down on these half-breeds, who might themselves speak
broken English like them, but who were obviously un-American in their
loyalty to Spanish. Real immigrants were trying to learn English, not
preserve their old languages.

Some of these exiles from the Mexican Revolution, like the Lozanos
and the Munguías in San Antonio, Texas, went into publishing. One of
their goals was to serve their fellow refugees who were used to a more
refined press in their native Mexico. Another goal seems to have been to
upgrade, if not the Pochos' ability to read and speak Spanish, at least the
quality of the materials in Spanish available to them. For the educated
Mexicans, the cultural and political battle was being rapidly lost, and
the proof was the hybrid, pocho nature of such cultural production as
food and language (see my essay, "A Case of Identity"). The presses
established by the new immigrants published mostly Mexican materials.
As we could expect from the world-class authors who colaborated in *La
Prensa*, the Lozano's San Antonio newspaper, the language was often

stylistically impeccable and the ideological perspective was more in tune with the concerns of central Mexico than with those of central Texas. There was a clear hierarchy of values: authentic Mexicans were those who identified with the texts of *La Prensa*. And most authentic were those who could write them.

It should come as no surprise, however, that *La Prensa*'s reading public could not have written on the same level as its publishers and contributors. Not many English-speaking Texans could equal the quality of prose in New York based journals, nor even of *The San Antonio Light*, not then or now, especially considering Texas' scandalously high percentage of illiteracy. What concerns us here, however, is that between 1910 and 1920 a group of Mexican immigrants arrived in Texas, and other areas of the country, and revitalized publishing in Spanish, which in turn boosted the presence of Spanish-language literature on this side of the border.

While the focus of these newspapers was originally what we could term refugee or even exile—that is, they gave almost all their space to news and literature from the mother country—over the years they became steadily more U.S. oriented. Actually, they became what their originators abhorred in the beginning: cultural hybrids. It was only natural that local matters became more central to the readers as those readers came to accept the permanence of their residency in the U.S. Tremendous changes in every-day culture could not be ignored. Technological advances, the common comforts of the American style of life, such popular culture innovations as film and cars, all were transforming society and turning the children of Mexicans into non-Mexicans— call themselves whatever they might. The Spanish-language presses reflected these changes and, even more significantly, were the vehicles that both Mexicanized the changes by putting them into Spanish and Anglicized the Mexicans by promoting the new cultural fads. While apparently loyal to the Spanish language, these newspaper were promoters of a hybridism that denied harsh division along the lines of language. If Hollywood was the home of the new social idols—*La Prensa*'s prize for its community Queen contest was a new car and a night out in Hollywood with Douglas Fairbanks—why not watch the films in the original language; why not read the books in English; why not speak it?

Ironically, film, which did so much to transform society, from the start repeated the same stereotypes about Mexicans as the earlier dime novels. Even before sound, the Mexican was a villain, and the worst Mexican was the hybrid or half-breed: the greaser (Lamb), prototype of Hollywood's version of a Chicano. With sound, language became central to the characterization: broken English with a Latin accent became the sign of treachery or buffoonery, as mentioned above. Not that other non-English groups fared much better—U.S. society of the early twentieth century was openly antiforeigner (they call it nativistic, but to repeat that is to fall into a rhetorical trap as well as to falsify history) and expressed its sentiments crudely and blatantly. What is striking is that while most of these groups slowly faded from the screen, the Latino (usually Mexican) has remained consistently present and unchanging into the present (Bruce-Novoa, "The Hollywood Americano"). The double messages from the media reinforced the attitude that hybridization was dangerous.

The logical conclusion was that one must remain loyal to one's culture or attempt to pass entirely into the other—and once again, we must remember that this was the Mexican's alternative, because becoming latinized was once a rather fashionable trend for the Anglo American. In Hollywood, Betty Grable, Don Ameche or even Maureen O'Hara could go Latin; Roy Rogers appropriated Mexican ballads and big bands played tangos and mambos with translated lyrics, or even synthesized transculturated forms like "Mambo Italiano." So why complain when an inoffensive and sincere Frank Dobey did the same with the Mexican Tale? Yet literature written by Chicanos was limited to a few writers, most of whom published in small presses, whether in Spanish or English. True, most Spanish-language newspapers did give a different perspective on society, often pointing out the racism and injustices overlooked or even practiced by the English-speaking press, but in general the literature of the period was a mere translation of dominant English-language texts.

Chicano Literature

It was not until the end of the 1950s and start of the '60s that Chicanos began to publish in larger, although still not great, numbers, most notably after the rise of Chicano civil rights movements across the Southwest. Also, the appearance of contemporary Chicano literature roughly coincides with the demise of many Spanish-language publications, so there was a need to create new publishing houses to print the new literature. These small publishers, while having the advantage of targeting a specific readership, could not afford to misread their audience's abilities. They knew, or soon found out, that the Chicano reading public had shifted their preference towards English, a natural shift considering that most Chicanos are trained in school systems where only English is spoken and live in this country where English is the language of privilege and power. Within the Chicano community, those most likely to buy a book are those most assimilated into the general society, that is, those who speak and read English. True, there are some writers—Tomás Rivera, Sergio Elizondo, Rolando Hinojosa and Miguel Méndez—who wrote in Spanish with the conscious purpose of preserving the language. With the exception of Méndez, the choice to write in Spanish was just that, for they could have just as easily written in English, as all three have demonstrated in one text of another. Not all Chicano writers have this facility with both languages.

To anyone working in Chicano literature in the late 1960s it was obvious that the linguistic relationships among Chicano texts, authors and readers were complex. While many, if not most, Chicano audiences responded with a surge of recognition to the Spanish used by the Teatro Campesino in their early Actos, at times the reaction was more to the mere fact of usage of the language in a public forum than to complete comprehension of the meaning. The Campesino's plays, as they move from those designed for the predominantly Spanish-speaking farm workers to those aimed at an urban audience, featured progressively less Spanish (Valdez, *Actos*). While the use of some Spanish, often the very basic familial type, was accepted and even encouraged, there was a general recognition that Spanish was no longer the preferred language of Chicano readers. This was clearly demonstrated when the first major Chicano publishing house, Quinto Sol (Berkeley, California), decided that any text in Spanish would have to be printed bilingually— accompanied by an English translation—but those written in English could be published without a Spanish version. The economic facts behind the decision were convincing: English, not Spanish, sold books. (This logic has been repeated recently by Chicano and Latino publishers who prefer English texts because books in Spanish, they say, do not sell.)

On the other hand, another possibility arose in the '60s that proved quite marketable then: the interlingual text. These are pieces written in a blend of Spanish and English. They are not bilingual in that, in the best examples, they do not attempt to maintain the two language codes separate, but exploit and create the potential junctures of interconnection. This results in a different code, one in which neither monolingual codes can stand alone and relate the same meaning. Translation becomes impossible, and purists from either language deny its viability. Monolinguals, from either side of the border, often react to it as if they were being personally insulted. Although lexical interlingualism (the use of words in both languages in the same text) received a great deal of attention as an innovation during the Movement phase of the literature, it was not the predominant mode of Chicano writing, even in the late sixties, and never has been.

What we now call Chicano literature—that is, writing by anyone of

Mexican heritage residing permanently in the U.S.A.—should not be taken as an attempt to preserve the Spanish language. Nor should it be judged in terms of loyalty or disloyalty to that language. As I indicated at the start, the question is incorrectly stated, if what we seek is to understand the literary production of the Chicano community. We should not ask if Chicano writers are loyal or not to Spanish, but rather, what is their language of preference? Chicano writers, like any writers, tend to use the language they control best. If that happens to be English, as in the majority of cases, then that is the writer's native language. After all, Chicanos are citizens or permanent residents of this country and have a perfect right to claim its national heritage as their own. That many Chicano writers nostalgically wish they could write in Spanish is a separate problem; that they write in English, out of choice or necessity, is significant.

A writer's loyalty lies with writing itself before any consideration of the preservation of one or another language. I speak of creative writers. Politicians, polemists or even academics, for whom language is simply a means to an end, not an end in itself, are a different matter, but then they seldom produce writing of literary merit worth mentioning. The writer who attempts to use a language that she or he does not control well will be denounced by the text itself. Unfortunately we have many instances of this, not only with Spanish, but with language period. Too many texts proclaim that the author knows or cares little about language. In those cases, it matters nothing if the text is in Spanish or not, for bad writing is not worth preserving, nor does it convincingly express the need to maintain the language as it has been used.

This instinctual use of one's personal native idiom is, however, much more complex than a simple preference for English over Spanish. It is interlingualism—not bilingualism. Chicanos blend Spanish and English, at times in obvious ways, such as juxtaposing words from both languages, but more often in such sublte fusions of grammar, syntax or cross-cultural allusions that monolingual readers will hardly notice. Interlingualism is a linguistic practice highly sensitive to the context of speech acts, able to shift add-mixtures of languages according to situational needs or the effects desired. This practice rejects the supposed need to maintain English and Spanish separate in exclusive codes, but rather sees them as reservoirs of primary material to be molded together as needed, naturally, in the manner of common speech.

This interlingual form of expression is the true native language of Chicano communities, even though some members speak only English or only Spanish—as a whole, the language spectrum covers these and every potential blend. It is to whatever form of interlingualism she or he has experienced and internalized that the Chicano writer is loyal, because in so being s/he is loyal to her/himself, and thus, loyal to the nurturing culture and, more importantly, loyal to writing. In addition, a writer has no obligation to accept cultural, social, or class determination tied to language. Writers can just as well be loyal to an ideal self, a potential identity, an existence to be created and explored through language so different from the one imposed by the happenstance of birth and environment that perhaps no one from that context could recognize it. This is just as valid. To ask writers to consider external political questions, such as loyalty to one or another national language defined by power centers foreign to them and their art, is to ask them to betray themselves, their native language and their art for the sake of an abstract, ideal culture not of their choosing. Real culture is what resides in the works of art when they are faithfully realized by artists who seek nothing more than to produce the work.

The true language of the artist is that which comes naturally, without any considerations outside of the personal act of creating literature. (And please do not misunderstand: natural speech and training in writing skills are not at odds; technique, as in any art, liberates the artist to express what is most natural. Without technique, inability to attain desired effects prevents the utilization of the full range of natural expression.) Pervert this relationship of the artist with the chosen media, and what culture is worth preserving? For that matter, without them, what real culture would there be?

Previously unpublished.

6 Mexico In Chicano Literature

> *To become aware of our history is to become aware of our singularity. It is a moment of reflective repose before we dedicate ourselves to action ... It does not matter, then, if the answers we give to our questions must be corrected by time.*
>
> Octavio Paz, *The Labyrinth of Solitude*

Upon awakening and finding himself surrounded by Anglo American reality, menacing even in its indifference, always oppressive even when opening its doors to this stranger—since they can't call us foreigners—Chicanos, like the adolescent described by Octavio Paz on the first pages of *The Labyrinth of Solitude*, are surprised by our existence, by the singularity of our being, and we become a question mark: What are we? Where are we from? How did we arrive at how and where we find ourselves now? Our origin has been and, though with diminishing intensity, continues to be a central topic of Chicano problematics; and as creation and creator of Chicano reality, Chicano literature has treated the theme extensively.

Certainly not every Chicano author looks towards Mexico. Such in the case of some of the New Mexican writers like Rudy Anaya, author of the best seller *Bless Me, Ultima*, and the members of the Academia de la Nueva Raza, who can sink their hands in a rich Hispanic tradition, almost as old as the discovery of Mexico; and others, perhaps the healthiest, who go about the vital task of creating a tradition through writing itself, without seeking any type of support outside the texture of language. Here, however, my concern is to see how, in the search for origins, Chicano literature has represented, interpreted and recreated the image of Mexico.

Our response to the Anglo American tradition surrounding us is clear: Mexican tradition, offering a multiplicity of faces, which Chicano literature, in turn, selectively reflects. For the sake of brevity, I have divided the treatment of Mexico's image in Chicano literature into the five categories: 1) the pre-Columbian Indian; 2) Mestizaje; 3) the Revolution and Immigration; 4) Paradise lost; 5) the Disillusionment of Reencounter.

1. *The Pre-Columbian Indian*

Hispanophobia is nothing new in Mexico and its presence in Chicano literature is, on the one hand, inherited, and, on the other, a reaction against any element of European culture, synonymous with capitalism, imperialism and oppression. Today's Yankiee is the contemporary version of the Spaniard of the conquest and colonial periods, and the Frenchmen and Englishmen of the seventeenth and eighteenth centuries. All of them represent foreign power which has violated the indigenous people's original purity. The poet Ricardo Sánchez writes that "the Chicano—whose names comes from Meshicano, the original name of the Aztecs (the Spaniard heard about these Indians coming from Aztlán, so he called them Aztecs)—has traditionally been on the receiving end of the exploitative, racist and imperialistic debauchers of the world. First the gachupín and, later, the gringo [sic]" (*Canto*, 32-33). Although Sánchez credits the Spaniards for having intermarried with the Indians, he does not absolve them of the sin of being white men. This ambivalent attitude is typical.

A kind of romantic noble savage arises from the literature. The pre-Columbian Indians appear as creators of a culture more advanced than the conquerors' European one. Supposedly they were free, honest and healthy, with a firm sense of their value and dignity as human beings. This romantic vision traces Chicano geneology back to Indian nobility, overlooking the oppression which the majority of indigenous peoples of the lower classes suffered and the harsh realities of their way of life.

Following this line, a protagonist of *Pocho*, José Antonio Villarreal's novel, reminds a Mexican General—who has praised well-educated women from Mexico and the U.S.A. who have sex with Mexican officials —that "our ancestors were princes in a civilization possibly more advanced than this one" (8). When Alurista writes that Moctecuhzoma Ilhuicamina sent an expedition north in search of Aztlán, he centers the concept of Aztlán in Aztec thought, simultaneously fixing its location in the U.S. Southwest (Valdez, 1972, 332-33). The same poet tones his poetry with words such as *Ehecatl, Tonatiu, Quezalcoatl, Teo-*

catl, *Moctezuma*, and *Ometeotl*. When he protests the Anglo American's arrogation of the figure of the "vaquero" in order to turn him into
a racist, Indian-slaying cowboy, Alurista affirms that the precursors of
the Mexican Charros, "indios fueron / de la meseta central / and of the
humid jungles of Yucatán / nuestros MAYAS" (Shular, 31). He fails to
mention, however, that the cattle system, with its typical vaquero cos-
tume and equipment, were brought from Spain—as was the cattle itself.

The best known work of this type is Luis Omar Salinas' "Aztec Angel." "I am an Aztec angel" Salinas sings in each of five stanzas, but the
angel wanders lost in the oppression of Anglo American society. The
poem ends with the following verses: "my Mexican ancestors / chew my
fingernails / I am an Aztec angel / offspring / of a woman / who was beautiful (*Crazy Gypsy*, 51). The woman is, of course, the indigenous side of
the couple which engenders the mestizo, and not only is she noble but
beautiful to the point of stereotype, repeated constantly, as in Leonardo
Elias' "Aztec Mother": "Thank you beautiful bronze mother, for being
/ yourself all this time. From the conquest of Mexico, / to the present
day, you are still the beautiful bronze / afterglow in my heart (177).

Chicano mestizaje is undeniable, but, as in Salinas and other authors, while the Indian mother is highlighted, the Spanish father is usually relegated to silence. However, Alurista, poet laureate of Chicano
nationalism, has taken Hispanophobia to impossible lengths by negat-
ing the European father. In "Bronce rape" he creates a Chicano version
of the Leda and the Swan myth, in which an Indian woman is raped
by the god Ehecatl, with the mestizo born of the union. Alurista extends Chicano lineage back to the very Aztec gods and creates a type
of virgin birth: "el mestizo / ante el altar / nació sin padre / pero sí con
mucha madre (Alurista, *Ombligo*, 52). Thus, the glorification of the pre-
Columbian Indian reaches its logical extreme with the elimination of the
Spaniard from the primordial couple and the mythological deification
of Chicano origins.

2. *Mestizaje*

Other Chicanos emphasize the mestizaje process itself, turning it
into the virtue that distinguishes us from the Europeanized North American and making Mexico the cradle of a new race. For the majority
of Chicanos the mestizo is our racial symbol, iconographically represented in the Chicano head made up of the profiles of the engendering
couple; but—as in the first category—the male Spanish side is consistently depicted as negative, although exceptions can be found among
the New Mexicans and a few Californios who, rightfully, give promi-

nence to their Spanish ancestry without tinging it pejoratively. The epic poem *I Am Joaquín*, which displays the characteristics of the previous category, does not exclude the Spaniard, but limits his participation in the total image.

> I am Cuauhtémoc
>
> proud and noble,
>> leader of men,
> king of an empire
> civilized beyond the dreams
>> of the gachupín Cortés,
> who also is the blood
>> the image of myself.
> I am the Mayan prince.
> I am Nezahualcoyotl,
> great leader of the Chichimecas.
> I am the sword and flame of Cortés,
>> the despot.
>> And
> I am the eagle and the serpent of
>> the Aztec civilization. (16)

Here, as in countless other works, the Spaniard is depicted as the callous violator, the tyrant master, the "Patrón." This Hispanophobia falls to a bitter level in Villarreal's second novel, *The Fifth Horseman*, set in the Mexican Revolution. The hateful Gachupín, the educated son of a noble, but destitute, family, comes to Mexico to marry the patrón's daughter, strictly out of economic need. Horror of horrors, he doesn't care if his future wife is a virgin, which she is not, thanks to the seductive prowess of the mestizo protagonist Heraclio Inés, a true son of the people, although his deeds mark him as a hero selected by the gods who obviously have read Campbell's *The Hero with a Thousand Faces*. The Gachupín tries to control the young Heraclio, but the latter, endowed with natural intelligence and honesty, wins every intellectual or moral skirmish that the former sets up. In addition to being a cowardly and decadent pervert, the Gachupín has the characterisitic perhaps least acceptable in Mexico: naiveté. He accepts the word of revolutionaries who, of course, kill him when he surrenders—clearly, not all mestizos are as honorable as Heraclio. The revolutionaries are not to be blamed, however, for as Villarreal explained in *Pocho*, to play a Gachupín dirty doesn't count. Moreover, the Gachupín's failure to distinguish between the noble mestizo, Heraclio, who saves his life, and the lower form of the species who take it, reveals yet another facet in the Spaniard's lack of new-world skills. Mexico belongs to the mestizo, and by extension so does the rest of America.

However, *I Am Joaquín*, in which the poem's persona assumes all
the names of the Indians, Spaniards and mestizos of Mexican history
until it flows into the Chicano, is the most representative work in this
category. Despite the negativity attributed to the Spaniards, they justify
themselves by bringing the Christian religion, which allowed indigenous
people entré into the colonial social structure, instead of excluding them
as occurred in the United States.

> As Christian church took its place
> in God's good name,
> to take and use my virgin strength and
>   trusting faith,
> the priest,
>   both good and bad,
>   took—
> but
>   gave a lasting truth that
>   Spaniard
>   Indian
>   Mestizo
> were all God's children.
> And
>   from these words grew men
>   who prayed and fought
>   for
> their own worth as human beings,
>   for
>
>   that
>   GOLDEN MOMENT
>   of
>   FREEDOM.   (20)

We should note, however, that with few exceptions, for Chicano authors mestizaje is not an on-going process, open towards the future, but
rather a historical phenomena that took place before their time, fixed
and finished in the past. That is to say, Chicano authors disallow the
possibility of a further Chicano-Anglo American mestizaje. Mestizaje
is a condition predating the encounter with the Anglo Americans, one
which strengthens us and makes it possible to go on resisting oppression
and racial genocide—used in many instances as synonyms for interra-
cial marriage—attributed to "Whites" (Chicanos are not supposed to
consider themselves white, but brown). Mestizaje, then, is considered
a Mexican process, now finished, no longer to be actively carried out in
the U.S.A.

In a unique category with respect to the above discussion is Miguel
Méndez' short story "Tata Casehua." The title also names the protagonist, a fantasmal figure who guards the oral history of the Yaqui of

Sonora and Arizona, a tribe whose members enjoy dual citizenship. Tata Casehua laments all mestizaje. The "Yori," Yaqui for enemy, is the hated White who produced mestizaje by spilling his poisonous blood into Indian veins. Mestizos, who cruelly and pitilessly pursue and exterminate the Yaqui, however, are not Anglo Americans here, but Mexicans. For Tata Casehua, mestizaje equals death, so becoming Mexican equals to die. It is no coincidence that Méndez was excluded from the second edition of *El espejo/The Mirror*, the first anthology of Chicano literature, and that he is not always listed among the most representative Chicano authors, in spite of his undeniable talent. His view on this key element in Chicano thought is hardly orthodox.

3. *The Mexican Revolution and Immigration*

Migration is the failure of roots. Displaced men are ecological victims. Between them and the sustaining earth a wedge has been driven. Eviction by droughts or dispossession by landlords, the impoverishment of the soil or conquest by arms—nature and man, separately or together, lay down the choice: move or die. Those who are able to break away do so, leaving a hostile world behind to seek an uncertain one ahead.

> The Mexicans who left their homeland in the six decades beginning in 1880 represented one of the major mass movements of people in the western hemisphere. During three-and-half centuries they had lived within a caste-bound, immobile society molded on Spanish colonial traditions ... in 1910 the revolution was one of people wanting in, not out; they fought to regain possession of the ground they lived on. Migration came only after defeat. (Valdez, 1972, 127-132)

In this way Ernesto Galarza, a Mexican-born Californian, explained the migration that brought and continues to bring the great majority of Chicanos to the U.S., and he gives us some keys to comprehending the image that has been created of that phenomena. In this category, for one reason or another, Mexico goes from Aztec Angel to an exterminating angel expelling the faithful children who would have preferred to remain in their country. This migration, however, is given a positive twist by Galarza by describing it as one of those great movements of people that have produced Western culture.

Chicano authors usually associate this migration theme with the Mexican Revolution. Both Villarreal's *Pocho* and Richard Vázquez' novel *Chicano* begin with an exodus from Mexico during the Revolution. In the latter, the Sandoval family flees to keep their son from being drafted into the Federal army. In *Pocho*, Juan Rubio, a coronel in Villa's Northern Division and a relative of Zapata, crosses the border for good only when Villa's assassination signals the last in a series of betrayals against the people and the complete abandonment of the revolutionary ideals. Why stay in Mexico when Obregón's triumph assures oppression, injustice and a general dehumanizing condition? Coronel Rubio, a pure Mexican macho, patriot and hero, is also a realist. Octavio Romano sums up this realistic pessimism about post-revolutionary Mexico when he states "The day came when everyone in Mexico feared everyone else. On that day, Mexico was born" (78). The story which forms the context for his statement is significantly titled "Goodbye Revolution—Hello Slum," another explanation of migration. Mexico becomes unlivable during the Revolution. After the war ends, it continues the same, leaving no alternative but to flee.

Migration is thus justified by the impossibility of living humanely and humanly in Mexico. If with this strategy Chicanos emphasize the negative side of Mexican reality, while at the same time carefully and perhaps exaggeratedly underscoring the positive logic of our unavoidable decision, it is partially a defensive reaction. We know only too well that many Mexicans consider Chicanos renegades, sellouts or simply foreigners.

There are no prodigal sons in this relationship, perhaps because when someone returns, the changes are already too radical, and because the return is hardly ever permanent. Chicano writers affirm their Mexicanness, but they simultaneously justify their migration.

The extreme case of this strategy is *The Fifth Horseman*. While Villarreal insists that the protagonist is fictitious, he takes pains to establish his representative role. "There was no Heraclio Inés, as there were tens of thousands of Heraclio Ineses who died for a right they believed was theirs" (v). The protagonist is everything a mythological hero should be, as stated above, but after proving himself equal to the required tasks, surviving the voyage through the kingdom of death and returning with the message of salvation as is befitting a hero, he must take that message to Aztlán, the U.S.A., because in Mexico there no longer can be found the proper land in which to plant the seed of regenerated life. Heraclio must escape to the U.S.A., although he thinks it will only be for a few years.

Heraclio Inés, chosen hero of destiny, undeniable patriot, proven supermacho, will see those few years turn into fifty, as did José Rubio in *Pocho*, Neftalí Sandoval in *Chicano* and countless other characters. They became the fathers of Pochos and Mexican Americans, or Pachucos like José Montoya's Louie or the Lowriders like J.L. Navarro's Tito, or the grandfathers of the Aztec Angels: the Chicanos. And if Villarreal and others have exaggerated the case in justifying migration, it has not exceeded the level of disinterest, ignorance and rejection with respect to Chicanos practiced by Mexicans.

4. *Paradise Lost*

Juan Rubio didn't plan to remain in the U.S.A., but each passing year found him still in California, dreaming of returning to Mexico. And there were many more like Rubio. In the realm of dreams and nostalgia, Mexico becomes the longed-for past of the characters.

Neftalí Sandoval (*Chicano*) remembers his village where he ran freely, and he wants to return. Richard Rubio, Juan's U.S. born son, realizes that his mother's memories of Mexico are beautiful, but that his, all imaginary since he has never been there, are even more so. Lupe (*The Plum Plum Pickers*) talks continually about Mexico and Guadalajara, but knows that for her those places no longer really exist. The poetry—both that which celebrates indigenous virtues, as well as that which emphasizes mestizaje—tends to foster nostalgia. Mexico assumes the image of a country where more positive traditional values continue to be the cultural basis of communal life. In contrast to the oppression, racism, poverty and supposed inmorality of the U.S., Chicano literature opposes the justice, tolerance, happiness and morality of the Mexican people. The negative judgments about the impossiblity of living in Mexico, expressed to justify migration, are now forgotten. Viewed from the U.S. through the perspective of years, or from the total lack of knowledge on the part of those who have never directly experienced the country, Mexico is the antithesis of the U.S.A. So paradise calls us, drawing us back.

5. *The Disillusion of the Re-encounter*

The idealization of the paradise lost prepares the way for the return to Mexico. In Oscar Zeta Acosta's *The Autobiography of a Brown Buffalo*, the cycle of revolution, exodus and idealization reaches its logical end. The protagonist, after a geographic and spiritual voyage through the most readily identifiable traits of Anglo American culture, from W.W.II to the 1960s, rejects the American Dream. The schizophrenic conflict between the Mexican and U.S. sides, which in Nick C. Vaca's excellent story "The Week in the Life of Manuel Hernández" leads to suicide, in *Brown Buffalo* results in the return to paradise.

In Mexico—although just across the border in Juárez—Brown Buffalo feels at home. He finds two prostitutes, beds down with them both, gets drunk in the "Cantina de la Revolución" and spends a week drinking Tequila, eating tacos and making love. A Mexican paradise! Then he is arrested for insulting the manager of a sleezy hotel. In jail he is stripped, mistreated, robbed and the judge, which to the Buffalo's exasperation turns out to be a woman, tells him, in perfect English—since he doesn't speak Spanish— "Why don't you go home and learn to speak your father's language?" (Acosta, 1972, 194) But, where is his home if not in Mexico, his father's country? Later, when he crosses back over the border, the U.S. guard tells him that he doesn't look "American." Both countries reject him, revealing his true condition: he is not bicultural, but intercultural, and there follows shortly after a key declaration in Chicano literature, especially because it has been produced by the re-encounter with Mexico:

> My single mistake has been to seek an identity with any one person or nation or with any part of history ... What I see now, on this rainy day in January, 1968, what is clear to me after this sojourn is that I am neither a Mexican nor an American. I am neither a Catholic nor a Protestant. I am Chicano by ancestry and a Brown Buffalo by choice. Is this so hard for you to understand? Or is it that you choose not to understand for fear that I'll get even with you? Do you fear the herds who were slaughtered, butchered and cut up to make life a bit more pleasant for you? Even though you would have survived without eating of our flesh, using our skins to keep you warm and racking our heads on your living room walls as trophies, still we mean you no harm. We are not a vengeful people. Like my old man used to say, an Indian forgives, but he never forgets ... that, ladies and gentlemen, is all I meant to say. That unless we band together, we Brown Buffalos will become extinct. And I do not want to live in a world without Brown Buffalos. (199)

Acosta seems to open the door, previously forbidden, to a mestizaje between Chicanos and Anglo Americans, or, at least, he asks for a more humane coexistence based on ecological need.

Tep Falcon, a Chicana poet and product already of this new mestizaje, also takes us on a voyage through the American way of life. She confronts it directly in a questioning monologue that culminates with the image of mestizaje concretely expressed in a linguistic symbol.

> amerika, amerika, ¿donde estás?
> i've been trying to find you
> but i always miss you
> yesterday you took a plane to peking
> the day before you were on a coffee break
> and today you must see the pyschiatrist
> aye amerika ... slow down [sic]
> necesito hablar contigo
> amerika, amerika, dime ¿donde estás?
> you say this afternoon you must bomb hanoi
> cocktails at eight

and tomorrow you are making another trip
to the moon
amerika, amerika tengo un regalo para ti
let me give you peace, love and time
let me teach you to spell your name with a c
america, america, qué bonita that sounds to me [sic]
aye amerika, ¿donde vas ahorita?
i have been chasing you for 120 some years
but you can not wait [sic]
the only time you saw me
was when you took my land and cuerpo
yet somehow you overlooked my soul
pero ahora tengo un regalo and you have no time
the gift, amerika, is la lengua mexicana
be it spanish, pocho or spanglish
let me teach you to spell your name with a c
america, america—que bonita

The turn towards this new mestizaje brings my essay to a well-rounded end, but literature's perversity is that it escapes the structures that would cage it—and the Brown Buffalo returns once again to Mexico.

In Acosta's second novel, *The Revolt of the Cockroach People*, Brown Buffalo, who has become a leader in the Los Angeles Chicano movement, takes a short vacation in Acapulco. Tired of the constant struggle for civil rights, he leaves satisfied with his revolutionary efforts. For Brown Buffalo, Mexico is no longer paradise lost, but a refuge and haven. Mexican reality, however, once again destroys his illusions. His brother, who lives in Mexico, makes him see that the Chicano movement is a rhetorical farse compared to the land reform struggle in Acapulco lead by one Lopitos, a field worker who, after inciting the poor to rebel and take possession of the unused lands of U.S. citizens, was assassinated by the government. Mexico represents here a model of real revolution and its risks, a point of contrast, an accusing angel. Of course, Brown Buffalo sees only a small part of Mexico, because once again he spends most of his time in a bar, listening to rock music or making love to prostitutes. The Mexico that dominates his time is an extension of the U.S.A, the same one that killed Lopitos. In other words, the struggle against oppression is not national, probably not even ethnic, but one of international class struggle. Mexico teaches him this lesson.

The image of Mexico changes radically in Acosta's work, and perhaps it marks a new stage in Chicano literature, a new consciousness that after the reflective pause, the ponderings about origins, and the creation of corresponding images, we have to start to pursue our future within a social and geographic situation that, like mestizaje, is undeniable. Undeniable, surely, but as Tep Falcon would like, perhaps we can change the K to a C.

Initiation rites are playful. While they teach historical lessons that assure the survival of tradition and culture, they also require a break with the mother and an encounter with the threat of death. The only past which really becomes the future is that which leads people within themselves to what they have when they no longer are thinking about themselves, to that which they retain after they forget what they had to learn during the days of exhaustive readings. Who knows how many images of our origins will still be remembered when—and if—we finally begin to move forward? Perhaps someday we will be able to see this literature, which I have analyzed so briefly here, as the product of a first period of self-consciousness like the one Paz writes about, and, if that is true, then we should also remember that, "it does not matter, then, if the answers we give to our questions must be corrected by time." For they are, now, finally, *our* questions—not anyone else's, especially not the Anglo American's nor the Mexican's—but ours, to be worked out in our time and in our literature—and only by us.

Revista de la Universidad de México 29.5 (January 1975): 13-18.

7   Chicanos In Mexican Literature

> Let me not to the marriage of true minds
> Admit impediments. Love is not love
> Which alters when it alteration finds ...
>
> Shakespeare, *Sonnet CXVI.*

In *Triga*, the Mexican poet Francisco Segovia included a poem in-
spired by his enounter with Chicano culture as he experienced it during
a sojourn in Texas and, in particular, in his readings of Chicano literature. While the poem's title, "La lengua y el gusto (103), announces a
play on language and food, it also promises, through reference to taste
or *gusto*, a judgment as to value in the form of good taste. Two epigraphs
contextualize the brief poem and, perhaps, tell us more than Segovia's
verses. The first, taken from the Chicano poet Ricardo Sánchez, can
be read as Segovia's perception of the Chicano situation: "it becomes
imperative to pick up estoque and filero / crying out the anguish of mi
alma / when you, bastard of the jive lenguaje ... [sic]" Segovia fore-
grounds as his synecdoche for Chicanismo the militant, even violent,
protest typical of Sánchez' work. The epigraph also underscores the act
of crying out in response to someone who can *jive*, that is, misrepresent
and fool others through the distortion and manipulation of language.
Sánchez' speech is, at the same time, interlingual, not only in its use of
Spanish and English, but also in his characteristic leaps of diction from
imperative to *bastard of jive*, or *estoque* to *filero*. One might argue with
Segovia's choice of Sánchez to represent Chicanismo, but this is not yet
the place to correct his vision—my purpose is to interpret that choice
first.

The second epigraph dialogues with the first. From Dante's *Inferno*
Segovia quotes the transcription of Nimrod's unintelligible words—
"Raphel maí amech zabí aalmos"—cried out to Virgil and Dante when

the voyagers come across this infamous builder of the Tower of Babel in hell, chained among other evil giants. Virgil first admonishes Nimrod to cease trying to voice his complaint, because God's punishment has turned his speech into a language comprehended by its speaker alone. Virgil suggests that, rather than try to speak, he should limit his efforts to blowing the horn hung at his neck. Then the epic guide explains to Dante that Nimrod's cries accuse only himself, for his evil idea of the Tower—of trying to transcend human limitations and reach a godly level, perhaps god himself, through a man-made structure—provoked God's wrath, bringing down upon humankind the curse of misunderstanding: the multiplicity of languages in the world today, a metaphor of social chaos. Virgil closes ominously: "Let us leave him alone, and not speak in vain; for such is every language to him, as his to others which is known to no one" (Dante, 46). Segovia's own poem will reach much the same conclusion, as we will see below. But it is more pressing to decipher first the intertextuality Segovia has created.

The verse from Dante establishes a context of the entire Western tradition of high-culture literature, from ancient to modern, passing through the great *summa* of Dante's opus. Virgil can be read here to signify good taste—*el buen gusto*—and Dante as the reader who has been brought face to face with the hellish creature in the form of Sánchez. Segovia can be seen as Virgil, in his relationship with the reader and Sánchez, but also as Dante, inasmuch as Segovia himself wandered through the nether regions of Texas where he encountered Sánchez. Thus, hell equals the U.S. Southwest, especially Texas, and Segovia's sojourn assumes the significance of a passage through the inferno on his way to higher and more glorious levels of existence. Segovia's sustaining companion during his foray into darkness was the literary tradition of countless hero/narrator/ survivors of epic wanderings. From that tradition Segovia gleans the wisdom of those defenders of the pure and noble canon of high culture, that is: forget Sánchez and his ilk, for to speak to them is to speak in vain, to waste time.

This reference to Babel and the biblical explanation of humankind's fall from the cosmic grace of social unity—symbolized in one language— into the chaos of multiple and mutually exclusive languages focuses our attention on the problem of cross-cultural conflict and the age-old search for a means of conflict-resolving communication. Yet Sánchez' verses express the same conflict and need for resolution.

Segovia adds one more twist to this intertextual frame by quoting Dante from Angel Crespo's translation into Spanish. Of course, in one sense it makes no difference, because Nimrod's words, expressed in no real language, remain the same in any translation. Yet Segovia achieves several things. He implies that translation from one language to another is the viable response to our post-Babel condition. At the same time, Nimrod's unintelligibility remains constant, implying that it, as well as its Chicano equivalent, defy translation because they are not a language. Thus, in the context of mutual understanding through translation, Nimrod's speech act—though it may attract our attention, perhaps even our admiration for its sonority and sensual beauty—remains pathetic, ultimately a lonely, isolated cry in the darkness. Translation signifies unity and a successful passage from one region to another, just as the text and the classical tradition have passed from Dante to Virgil to Segovia, writers of three different languages in three different epochs. Interlingualism, on the other hand, seems to signify suspension—detention—between the earthly and heavenly lives, that is, the death and hell of unintelligible speech.

Segovia is not the first Mexican writer to pen a reaction to Chicano culture. Since the turn of the century there have appeared numerous references to Chicanos in Mexican letters. What makes Segovia's significant is that it follows what we can see as a tradition formed by those texts, a coherent body of texts that allows us to extrapolate a Mexican high-culture, or literary, view of Chicanos—and I emphasize high culture because what follows does not necessarily apply to popular culture expressions in Mexico. That view holds, in general terms, the following points. Chicano culture is a social aberration, revealed or signified through the synecdoches of languages and food. Chicano culture is synthetic, hybrid, no longer Mexican, yet not U.S., and therefore negative; a degenerative, as opposed to generative, creative process. It is a threat to purity (Mexican) and good taste (Occidental). Chicanos are victims lost in and condemned by their geographical happenstance.

In their fictionalized autobiographies, Martín Luis Guzmán and José Vasconcelos recalled their travels in the U.S. Southwest during the Mexican Revolution (see Chapter 4). Like Segovia, both authors resided for time in San Antonio, Texas, and they seem to have suffered the same trama of feeling as though they had descended into the lower depths of a Dantesque inferno. Both were hosted by Samuel Belden, who appears in their texts as a personification of the Mexican/U.S. synthesis. Guzmán's observation on Belden's curious speech is highly relevant: "español raro y difícil—ininteligible a veces" (227). Belden is transformed here into Sánchez' prefiguration, a Nimrodian reincarnation, speaking a language at once familiar and uninteligible, a monstrous perversion. Guzmán goes on to characterize this speech by focusing specifically on its lack of "tercera persona ficticia." Like Nimrod, Belden attempts to leap across the strict limit of grammatical decorum, a rhetorical equivalent of Nimrod's attempt to transcend the natural limits of gravity and the spheres of existence. Guzmán here assumes the position of the surprised divinity, or its surrogate—perhaps Virgil or Dante—challenged by the over ambitious Belden/Nimrod who refuses to respect the "natural" limits of his lowly existence. His punishment is to be reduced to a friendly brute, chained through Guzmán's ironic prose to his less than admirable image in a chapter of Guzmán's wanderings dedicated to his passage through hell. Vasconcelos summarized that image when he called Belden "inculto," an ultimate insult in the context of the highly cultured group to which both Guzmán and Vasconcelos belonged. When Vasconcelos extends his characterization to "todos los que se crían en aquellos territorios" (785), he condemns the entire population of San Antonio, Texas, and perhaps the Southwest itself. As for Segovia, for Guzmán and Vasconcelos San Antonio represented a hinterland of cultural degeneration, an inferno populated by half-caste monsters, into which they had been cast by ill fortune, the Mexican Revolution.

Both revolutionary writers also symbolized Chicano society in images of food. Belden took both of them to San Antonio restaurants. Guzmán recalls "restaurantes mexicanos—restaurantes patrióticos de cocina nacionalista sintética ... culto de los colores patrios y una misma efigie del cura Hidalgo ... y en todos, por supuesto, comíamos unos mismos manjares sabrosísimos, tan sabrosos que por momentos resultaban de un mexicanismo excesivo o desvirtuado por interpretaciones demasiado coloristas de nuestro color local (228). Guzmán ironically exalts the San Antonio Mexican cuisine to a level of inauthenticity attributed to hybridism and lack of sublety—behind *sabrosísimos* hides "too spicy and unrefined." In the process Guzmán's relegated Chicano food to the synthetic, superficially nationalistic. Mexican Americans' food, the result of their need to establish a clear identity with Mexico—a cry for recognition from within the nether region of U.S. control—is too rich in its extreme synthesis of Mexicanism, proving ultimately foreign to the authentic Mexican Guzmán claims to be. In other words, Guzmán found Chicano food to be a Nimrodian feast, the setting in which it was served, an absurd, infernal parody of Mexico.

Vasconcelos is more direct. When Belden takes him to the best restaurant to eat, not ersatz Mexican food, but real Texan fare, steak, Vasconcelos is appalled at the huge slice of meat, served with no sauce—no subtleties here, just a brutal slice of life. When one recalls the thinly sliced, well-cooked Mexican steaks, or the delicately flavored French cuisine preferred by the Mexican upper classes, Vasconcelos' reaction to Texas style steak can be understood. Thus Belden almost assumes the image of a cannibal proudly offering the civilized explorer a hunk of human thigh. And we must remember that the Mexican writers considered Belden a Mexican American, so even though Belden was treating Vas-

concelos to Texan food, Vasconcelos' comments can be read as a criticism of a Chicano's taste. Later Vasconcelos, the man usually associated
with the Raza Cósmica synthesis, issues an even harsher condemnation
of hybrid Chicanismo when he makes reference to Chicano food he was
subjected to in San Antonio: "No sólo lo norteamericano, también lo
mexicano se volvía absurdo, bajaba de categoría en la híbrida ciudad
[de San Antonio] que ha hecho negocio de revolver tamales con enchi-
ladas, frijoles con carne, todo en un mismo plato" (786). Like Nimrod,
Chicano cuisine refuses to respect the natural Mexican boundaries, the
hierarchical divisions that distinguish good from average or bad taste.
This over ambitious mixture of the building blocks of a meal produces
a monstrous conglomerate no longer truly expressive of the native code
which it claims to spring from—a cultural production rendered incom-
prehensible to the monolingual consumer and too exotic for the bilingual, a chaotic amalgam fit only for its creator, the Chicano Nimrod.

Although many Mexicans would find refuge in San Antonio during
and after the Revolution, eventually becoming permanent residents, for
Guzmán and Vasconcelos, guided in their wanderings by "good taste"
and a strong sense of the inviolability of authentic Mexicanness and correct Spanish, Chicanismo spoke to them in Nimrod's voice. In their
life both heeded Virgil's advise and continued their respective journey
without wasting more time on useless dialogue with the repulsive, condemned giants who inhabited the nether regions, of which San Antonio,
Texas, has the misfortune of representing the clearest manifestation.

Why are Chicanos so repulsive and despicable for Mexicans? Why,
despite a few exceptions, do Mexican writers tend to view us negatively?
In brief, because we undermine the protective wall of national separation between Mexico and the U.S.A.; we deconstruct the fictions of
exclusivity necessary for Mexicans to go on seeing themselves in terms
of a solidified absolute. We are a threat because we short-circuit their
national self-project, so they must reduce us to less than equals.

If we borrow a construct from the Moscow-Tartu school of semioti-
cians, cultures or ethnic groups perceive space as divided by a boundary
into at least two parts: one, internal and organized, the space of *We*, a
structured area opposed to the other apparently disorganized and un-
limited external space of the *They*—that is, as seen from the insider of
the We-space. Jurij M. Lotman's examples of this opposition include:
our nation/foreign nations, initiated/laymen, culture/barbarism, intelli-
gentsia/ masses, and cosmos/chaos (105). Ironically, Lotman's formulation echoes Mircea Eliade's sacred/profane structure, leading us back,
then, to my own of the space of Chicano literature, which I now extend
to explain the concept of Chicanos in Mexican literature.

From the Mexican *We* perspective, Chicanos have ventured beyond the limits of internal space into U.S. chaos, where they wander like lost children or frightful monsters. Lotman would say that Chicanos have an inverse orientation, a *We* who focuses itself around the center of a space previously regarded as external; that is to say, that as a group Chicanos supposedly seek to assimilate to, or appropriate to themselves, the values or properties of an alien *They*. For the Moscow-Tartu school, the boundary belongs to either the inside or outside group, always marking "the break in the continuity of space, with the property of inaccessibility" (Lotman, 111). Therefore, the exceptional group that crosses the boundary struggles against, and puts into doubt, the inherent structures of the world; that is, it betrays the cultural fiction of inviolable unity, exclusivity and cohesion so dearly protected and maintained by the group that remains back inside the old zone, so often called the motherland.

To the primary, unitary text of Mexican nationalism—those texts, literary and non-literary alike, that depict or represent Mexican identity as a reality in clear opposition to other national groups—Chicano culture is, in Lotman's terms, a secondary text in that it represents a violation of the tabu against crossing the forbidden boundaries established by the primary cultural texts. Chicano texts claim the right, through *de facto* existence, of exploring the zone declared as foreign in the Mexican primary texts. And, to the chagrin of the Mexicans, Chicano texts do so while simultaneously claiming a right to remain in some way connected to the Mexican tradition, although no longer only Mexican. Thus, the Chicano text is superimposed on the Mexican cultural text as a violation of limits. In other words, Chicanos represent an ominous possibility of deconstruction through escape. The internal culture of Mexico depicts this as betrayal and prefers to force the traitors into the role of seeking complete assimilation to the *They*.

However, Chicanos, especially since the mid-'60s, refuse to fit these patterns. We insist on being, not those who have crossed an absolute boundary, but the active producers of interchange and synthesis between the would-be binary opposites. We construct the alternative, if nothing else on the ideal plane, of transcendence. On a lower, practical level we represent the disturbing revelation that the solid wall of the border belongs to both sides—or even more horrifying for Mexicans and Anglo Americans, that it is actually an expanding organism with the perturbing capacity to absorb, discriminate, reject, retain and/or synthesize portions from the living space of either bordering group without having to limit ourselves to one or the other. And if language is culture, our manipulation of it into hybrid forms is a metaphor of the boundary turned open, productive frontier, never static and thus continually in synthetic process never fully achieved. Chicanismo calls for a definition of culture as process, open ended process, not as a static code of permanent characteristics. This, of course, threatens those on either side.

Octavio Paz perceived this threat when he began his study of Mexican culture, *El laberinto de la soledad*, with an essay on the Pachuco (see note 2). Paz wanted to portray Mexico as the binary opposite of the U.S.; this explains why several times in the book he offers simplistic contrasts to prove his point. The Pachuco, however, horrified Paz because he was a hybrid who rejected the established national alternatives which Paz needed —and seems to still need—in order to orient himself and his text in the world. Paz had to reject the Pachuco solution to preserve his own existential integrity. He was obliged, then, to attempt to destroy the Pachuco as a viable alternative. This he achieved, at least rhetorically, by interpreting Pachuco dress and behavior as a desire to be absorbed into the U.S. system, if only as a criminal. Paz turned the Pachuco into an isolated shouter of unintelligible protest who finds his ultimate place—and meaning—in society as a prisoner, perhaps still misunderstood, but at least chained within the institution, and, therefore, accepted to the extent of now residing inside it. Paz turned the Pachuco into one more avatar of Dante's Nimrod.

Paz' desperate desire was to force Pachucos into Lotman's category of inverse orientation, because to entertain the possibility of the fluid continuity of intercultural space would deconstruct the fictional *We* of Paz' psychomythological historicism. Paz first had to firm up the exterior walls of nationalism in order to eventually plunge into the ahistorical universals of Jungian archetypes. The stark reality of the hybrid, semi-foreign Pachuco patrolling the ramparts is too much for Paz to accept—but not too much to ignore when he could use the Pachuco for his own purpose. Like Dante's Nimrod for Virgil, the Pachuco gives Paz the opportunity to lecture his fellow traveler, the reader, on the potential evils of attempting to become more than what you are, especially if to do so one must venture beyond the borders, or limits, traditionally set by the society one has been born into. The Tower of Babel story has a moral fit for immigrants who plan to build their new homes in a manner which might transcend their old ways, or surpass their old world limits, or even worse yet, leave the inhabitants of the motherland behind. The moral is that god punishes those who attempt such feats of self-transcendence. Paz uses the moral to scare Mexicans into following him back into the national labyrinth to find themselves, even if that encounter will be with another monster awaiting at the heart of the voyage—at least, Paz would say, it is Mexico's own monstrous self, and not the Nimrodian giant called a Chicano.

Dean MacConnell's depiction of modern anthropology's relationship to alien cultures fits Paz', and many other Mexican authors', reaction to Chicanos. "Once reallocated in an alien culture," says Mac-

Connell, "at the edge of their own world, their discipline requires ...
a textual preservation of the core of cultural values, key symbols, and
central themes they find there. Operating in this way, anthropology has
built a bulwark around our civilization, a cultural equivalent to the Ma-
ginot Line or the Great Wall" (150). The imagery is appropriate. Paz
reads Pachucos as aliens and notes their values and symbols. He does so
not only to record them, however, but also to set them up as a warning
against Mexican inauthenticity, an example of the fate awaiting those
who wander beyond the limits of Mexicanism. In so doing Paz reaffirms
Mexican core values and symbols and himself as their authentic voice,
dug in behind the Cactus Curtain.[3]

Yet Chicanos more accurately represent what MacConnell calls the
new approach of ethnosemiotics, "specifically a reversed polarity for
anthropology which aims in the direction of a synthesis of center and
periphery, [which], if accomplished on a historical and concrete cultural
level, [promises] not merely the possibility for adaptation and survival
but for transcendence, that is, the potential to develop new forms of
society" (151). New forms, synthesis, central value for the peripheral
being, transcendence—an enumeration of revolutionary terms and thus
threatening for those who defend the old forms of centralized society,
who will go to any lengths to prevent the transcendence of their status
quo.

The possibility that the periphery might influence the center was
hardly entertained by Guzmán and Vasconcelos. They dismissed Chicanismo as an aberration only deserving of humor or scorn. The decades
between 1920 and 1950, with the advent of mass media, rapid mobility
and a surging Mexican immigration to the U.S. made the possibility a
frightening one for Paz, who designed his book as a retreat, first into
Mexicanness, and then universalism. Yet the periphery had already influenced the center in a decisive manner during the Revolution.

Friedrich Katz' *The Secret War in Mexico* has revolutionized our conception of the Mexican Revolution by highlighting the key role of Mexico's northern states as an area of U.S.-Mexican interaction. Vasconcelos denigrated this phenomenon by calling the northern strategy *Pochismo*, that is, the ideology of inverse orientation.[4] Yet, years later, but before Paz' *Laberinto*, Agustín Yáñez, in *Al filo del agua* (1947), his novel-
istic analysis of Mexico on the brink of the revolution, depicted as one
of the catalysts the return of "norteños," who were actually Mexicans
who had been living and working in the U.S. These workers, as Katz has
noted, no longer respected traditional Mexican customs. Their behavior and language defined them as different, yet they were still Mexican—
should we not say Chicano? Their presence became one of the main
factors in the collapse of the Mexican government.

Carlos Fuentes, writing a decade after Yáñez, created an updated norteño in the character of a *bracero*—a documented migrant worker—in his novel *La región más transparente*. The character's language, spiced with Anglicisms, and his aggressive behavior make him a threat to society. Coming from the lower economic class, he is a grotesque caricature of Guzmán's Samuel Belden, who, in spite of his peculiar speech patterns, was respectable and even likable in the way a friendly animal would be. Fuentes' bracero is none of this, being entirely offensive in behavior and language. While Belden represented a subtle threat to the grammatical reflection of social hierarchy, the bracero is a physical menace to all social structures. Yet both represent essentially the same phenomen: the Mexican-U.S. synthesis. Both are eternally condemned by the respective authors to literary infernos of negative imagery. Guzmán at least allows Belden to serve the purposes of the Revolution, while Fuentes kills off his bracero instead of letting him play out any positive role in changing society. Fuentes cannot see the possibility of any such role for these hybrid creatures. Like Paz' Pachuco, Fuentes' bracero finds his place in suicidal behavior. What Fuentes' and Yáñez' characters share, however, is the Chicano's characteristic of synthesis, of Mexican/U.S. hybridism, which places Mexicanness in doubt. They have crossed the tabued boundary, survived in the chaos of hell, and returned to tell others about the possibility of change—not necessarily improvement on all fronts, but change. In passing, one might note the irony in Fuentes' case, in that he himself is a prime example of the positive possibilities of that hybird process, having been brought and educated during a key part of his life in the U.S, like a Chicano. He, too, is a product of living in the intercultural space of which Chicanos are the inhabitants.

Chicano visibility in the U.S. itself has acted like a Yáñez norteño, producing an increase in references to Chicanos in Mexican literature since the mid-1960s. *La frontera plural, estancias de un amor indocumentado* (1979), Miguel Alvarez Acosta's novel, promises much in the title, but good intentions aside, it adds little to Mexican understanding of Chicanos. If anything it betrays the author's less than profound comprehension of the differences among the several geographic areas along the border, each with its distinctive Chicano subculture. And in the end, Acosta claims that to be Chicano is to want to be Mexican, which makes the Chicano an inferior Mexican. Fiction by Federico Arana, David Ojeda, and Luis Casas Velasco satirizes Chicanos, seeing little of value or sincerity in Chicanismo. Casas Velasco's *Death Show* (1981), a grotesque parody of Horatio Alger fiction, offers as a metaphor of the Chicano synthesis a restaurant chain featuring cannibalistic meals in the guise of Mexican pre-Columbian rituals.

More positive voices have spoken, however. Vicente Leñero's references to Chicanos are succinct, yet highly significant. In his parody of the New Testament, *El evangelio de Lucas Gavilán* (1980), one possible explanation for St. John the Baptist's strange behavior is that he has spent time working with Chicanos—he has learned about God in the desert and in the enlightening company of Chicanos. Christ himself saves money because he wants to go north to be with the Chicanos. Chicano culture, then, is depicted as both the rite of passage that produces Christian radical insights, as well as that part of humanity most in need, or perhaps most deserving, of God's presence.

José Agustín's satirical foray in the U.S., *Ciudades desiertas* (1981), can be read as a journey into Chicano territory as well. Near the end, through the eyes of a Mexican who has settled in New Mexico, Agustín offers the most accurate description of the regional subcultures on the Chicano Southwest. Yet Agustín also calls on the traditional leitmotifs of language and food to give quick, encapsulated summaries of Chicano culture. In Iowa, the Mexican protagonist finds a Chicano couple who "ya casi había olvidado el español y servía una barbacoa aceitosa y hecha con carne de cerdo" (110). In the Southwest itself we are told that things are much better. One can find all the tortillas one desires and even speak Spanish, although it may be "de pueblito, vaciado con truje, ansina y sus mercedes" (172). Yet the narrator finally realizes that he, as a Mexican, cannot adjust to the New Mexican synthesis. He must return to Mexico and his Mexican woman. It is highly significant, in this context, that the novel ends with one of the most blatantly macho, male chauvinistic scenes in recent Mexican fiction. The sojourner returns and, like Paz and others, through the semiotics of macho aggression and possessiveness reestablishes the clearly drawn borders of reactionary Mexican society.

Two short works begin with epigraphs taken from Chicano literature. The first, Florencio Sánchez Cámara's "Poly y el emparedado," is preceded by Alurista's poem "Mis ojos hinchados." The story is narrated by Pedro Vidales, the "primer mexicochicano en azotar las calles de Chicago con sus huaraches" (107). In the Chicago ghetto Vidales battles Blacks, Whites and everyone. He marries a Polish woman and has a son who later attends college. Although he remembers Mexico as a glorious land, he knows that life there is impossble for the poor. And from all this he has gleaned an important philosophy of life, one that deconstructs the old national dichotomies: "todas las sangres salpican del mismo color. Esa fue mi cultura política" (108).

This quick historical overview brings us back to Francisco Segovia's poem, the second contemporary work to utilize a Chicano epigraph. Now we are better prepared to listen to the text itself, with its use of food and language motifs.

> Los dientes de sal
> como espinas secas
> del robalo
> la oniónica cebolla
> con los añales atados a la frente
> y el ajo gárlico
> ancestro
> de los ejércitos de árabes.
> La oliviada aceituna griega
> La gárlica rabia parda, curtida
> La violada lengua de la almeja
> en los duros arrozales del desierto ...
> Pero nadie va a tener un paladar
> para probarlos.

We could leave it at face value, or more specifically, at Mexican face value, as one more negative commentary and rejection. Certainly the last verses imply a reaffirmation of Virgil's wisdom as conceived by Dante. Yes, Segovia echoes his high culture predecessors.

However, I propose that we reread it, this time from the center of the Chicano periphery. Let us begin with Nimrod's arrogant Tower, the apparent source of this lesson in negativity. It reminds me of Alurista's use of Icarus in *Floricanto en Aztlán* (poem 12). Like Nimrod, Icarus wanted to reach the heavens and soared higher than his fellow humans, almost to the sun before ultimately failing. So both mythological figures attempted what in human terms is the impossible. And although their stories can be used to teach a lesson of containment, from another perspective they represent the noblest urge to rise above human limits. To accept ground level, to settle for the mundane, has never satisfied the human spirit. Read from this alternative interpretation, Chicanos represent the desire to transcend; that is, we represent the best, not the worst, in human endeavors. Moreover, the threat of chaos, raised by the Babel allusion, makes little sense to us now, living as we do in the midst of chaos itself in the guise of order. And perhaps the attempt to transcend is fated to fail, but after Camus, Adorno, Borges or Musil, even assured failure must be read as the quintessential human situation, but always with the mandate to attempt the impossible with as much class as one can muster—a lesson José Montoya's "El Louie," at the heart of Chicano literature, bespeaks eloquently.

Segovia's verses allow even more interpretation. Chicanos are compared to Arabian armies, an image followed by the introduction of the Greek olive. Should we not read this as a reminder that the Moorish invasion of Europe, while produing a threat of chaos with respect to the

Christian kingdoms for centuries, also brought about the eventual creation of a new order and society on the Iberian peninsula, one that we
now call Spain, and through the Arabic interaction with the Latin-based
languages of the old order, helped produce what we now know as Spanish. The invasion from the periphery of the European world dramat-
ically changed that world forever, intellectually, spiritually and politically. It was through Arabic texts that Greek civilization was passed on
to Europeans who had no direct knowledge of it. And that process took
place in the interlingual society of medieval Castilla. In this light, the
Chicano Nimrod may threaten violence and change, but also promises
a renovation of humanistic values, a reorientation of the dominant, but
decadent, central powers towards the common, lost origins of the high-
est ideals. After all, the sole reason that Nimrod cannot be understood
is because he speaks the original human language. It behooves the rest
of humankind to listen for echoes of itself.

Finally, we arrive back to the question of language. Segovia, with
Virgil and Dante, seems to condemn Chicano culture through the accusation of unintelligibility. However, the irony is that both Dante and
Segovia undermine the surface message by creating examples of that
speech which prove highly successful as communication. "Raphel maí
amech zabí aalmos," Nimrod's words, ring with echoes of the angelic
spirit—*Raphel*—of the soul or perhaps trees—*álamos*—and whatever
else the imagination, freed from the restraints of signifying specificity,
wants to attribute to the pure sounds. Segovia, while not as heavenly in
his inventions, offers such phonetic and gastronomic delights as "el ajo
gárlico" and "la oliviada aceituna." His interlingualism is minimal, and
certainly far from natural or authentic, yet it proves the process to be viable. And in the final analysis, Segovia contradicts himself—and Dante.
It is Segovia's palate that savors the linguistic possibilites opened to him
by the monster Sánchez. Segovia has tasted Chicano food and come
away changed. His poem is a dialogue with Nimrod, even a translation
of sorts offered to his fellow Mexicans. Perhaps Segovia intended none
of this—probably not. Perhaps he really does side with Dante's Virgil—
probably so—and seriously believes that Chicano culture will appeal to
no one—surely wrong. But Segovia has chosen to speak to, and even
for, Nimrod. And once having tasted la auténtica lengua of transcendence, can any mere Mexican seguir the same?

Missions in Conflict. Essays on U.S.-Mexican Relations and Chicano Culture
(Tübingen: Gunter Narr Verlag, 1986): 55-64.

8 Chicano Literary Production, 1960 – 1980

As always in my work, in the following essay the term Chicano refers to all people of Mexican heritage living permanently in the United States. Some are monolingual in English or Spanish, but most find themselves on a sliding scale of interlingualism based on a Spanish/English mixture (Bruce-Novoa, *Chicano Authors*, 28-29). A thorough study of the phenomenon of a hybrid culture produced by the contact between the United States and Mexico would trace its origins back into the conflict between Spain and England during the period of Europe's en-counter with the Americas, but here my focus will be limited to the contemporary period of this process we now call Chicano culture, starting in the 1960s.

In the early '60s, with the rise of the Black Civil Rights Movement and Martin Luther King, Chicanos began to demand the same consideration from different sources of socio-political power. Admittedly, Chicanos borrowed from the Blacks much of the rhetoric and tactics they utilized, and, in a similar way, Chicanos also organized around local issues as a base for a generalized struggle. Unlike Blacks, however, Chicanos have had little success in channeling regional interests into support for a national movement. Chicanismo remains highly fragmented and regionalized, bound loosely by a shared sense of Mexican heritage and U.S. residency, more so than by a deep recognition of racial cohesion, a political ideology or even a pragmatic agenda. The Spanish language, often considered by outsiders as the mother tongue of Chicanos, although a basis for mutual sympathy, is so diverse in its usage due to regionalism and to great disparity in levels of proficiency that it can also function as a divisive factor. From the start we are dealing with a highly diversified cultural production with no accepted monolithic standards of performance, although at certain times different centers of producers have exercised more influence than others. Some try to occupy the center, while others revolve at some distance, and yet others burst out beyond the limits of the space or come speeding in. The topography changes with each variation in any of the objects. And public interest is another factor that can change the dynamics of the space, giving more or less gravity to different elements over time. This is, of course, just a metaphor, but such a paradigm from systems theory will serve us well in our discussion of the space of Chicano literature.

The Chicano struggle for civil rights, known perhaps too optimistically as the Chicano Movement, catalyzed increased cultural production of the community on the one hand, while it provided the means of distributing and consuming it on the other. In the mid-'60s, each of the major political organizations had a newspaper that included literature of some sort (Ybarra-Frausto, 84-86, 89-92). The staff of, as well as the contributors to, these publications were for the most part workers, so it can be said that the literature of this early period was truly a proletarian one, with strong emphasis on political and labor themes. Stylistically, it utilized traditional, popular and oral forms. Its purpose was mainly communication, the emphasis was not on *how* but *what* was said. Quickly, however, this writing gave way to that of more specialized authors with some degree of exposure to, if not training in, literature. Then, in 1968, when the university campuses became the arena of Chicano struggles for equal participation in the system, the literature shifted towards a closer approximation of academic forms and values— or at least there arose a great preoccupation with the academic forms and values as they related to Chicano literature. This situation persists today, despite the continual resistance by some individuals to the cultural and societal mainstreaming of our literary production.

At least two major founding blocks of contemporary Chicano literature came from the initial period of political, pre-academic activism: Luis Valdez' Teatro Campesino and Rodolfo Corky Gonzales' *I Am Joaquín*. The former began as an organizing and propaganda arm of César Chávez' United Farm Workers Union. Valdez, a university trained actor/playwright, persuaded field workers to act out situations from real life for the entertainment and consciousness-raising of their fellow workers. From 1965 to 1967 the short skits, called *Actos*, focused on farm labor problems. The Campesino utilized agitprop and street theatre techniques: simple costumes, popular humor, satire, slapstick, simplistic political rhetoric and stereotypes. What distinguished their works from the general panorama of U.S. street theatre was that they spoke not only *about* oppressed workers, but *for* a part of that class doubly oppressed because of their mixed race, Mexican origin and Spanish language. Valdez' *Actos* spoke the interlingual language of the Chicano people, and the actors were actually workers. Yet, as it grew in popularity and influence, the Campesino ironically was slowly becoming less a workers' theatre for and by workers than a professional acting troupe of ex-workers performing plays about farm workers for non-farm workers. This is not a criticism, simply a statement of fact. By 1967 Valdez ← broke with the U.F.W. in order to expand the scope of the Campesino's activities, first into urban topics, then into student issues, and by 1970 into the anti-Viet Nam war movement. Valdez was reflecting in his and his troupe's evolution the multifaceted community they wished to represent, which in no way can be taken as an abandonment of commitment, but exactly the opposite. In addition, we should remember that by the turn of the decade, Valdez and the Teatro Campesino had started a whole movement of its own, Chicano theatre, whose evolution I will pick up later.

The same year Valdez began the Teatro Campesino, Rodolfo Gonzales founded the Crusade for Justice, a community action organization in Denver, Colorado. His stand was militantly separatist, advocating the reclamation of land for the Mexican/Chicano people on the basis of historical rights, violated after the U.S. invasion of Mexico in 1846, and on the moral right of laborers to own the means of production they work, in this case the land. Like Valdez, Gonzales utilized drama to publicize his political and cultural stand, writing and acting in *The Revolutionist* and *A Cross for Maclovio*, plays which unfortunately remain unpublished. His enduring contribution to Chicano literature, however, came in the form of an extended historical poem, *I Am Joaquín*, first published by the Crusade in 1967. It swept through Chicano communities like a popular manifesto, and it is still considered the best crystallization of the early cultural nationalism which influenced so much of Chicano thought and rhetoric in the 1960s and early '70s.

Gonzales drew from Mexican history to teach Chicanos a centuries-old heritage of struggle for justice and property ownership that has gone through many phases, the most recent of which was called the Chicano Movement. Although the poem lauds the miscegenation process that produced the Mexican nation, it also calls for strict racial separation from, and militant opposition to, Anglo American society. It stresses a tradition of shedding blood for the struggle, glorifies it and extends that tradition into the need for contemporary militants prepared to shed more blood to continue the struggle. Anglo Americans are portrayed as racists who refused to mix with the Mexicans when the U.S. invaded and stole the territory of the Southwest from Mexico. Mexicans, true to their tradition, offered the invaders an opportunity to participate in miscegenation, but when the Anglo Americans refused they lost the chance to create a unified U.S. people. Now, the poem's logic argues, Chicanos must fight against being absorbed into a society which demands one forget who they are in order to assimilate. While its resonance has diminished over the years, Gonzales' poem continues to echo in Chicano literature (Bruce-Novoa, *Chicano Poetry*, 48-68).

Valdez and Gonzales set and/or reaffirmed some precedents for Chicano writing. Their works were openly didactic and political, with a strong undercurrent of moral justification. Like Blacks, both men used the popular traditions of their people and spoke in common language. They avoided anything but the most simple analysis of social problems, often relying on folk wisdom. In their works life assumed a Manichean simplicity: *We* (right and good) versus *They* (wrong and evil); but the We was subdivided also into the real WE, that is, those Chicanos who supported the political Movement, and the sell-out We or *vendidos* who accepted the society as it is. Both Gonzales and Valdez stressed that the future lay in racial and ethnic solidarity. Gonzales utilized more historical data than the early Teatro Campesino, but Valdez, like most Chicano authors, soon incorporated retrospection into his work. History became essential as an explanation of the present and a storehouse of traditional wisdom that could provide survival tactics. *I Am Joaquín*'s pattern of seeing the present through a series of retrospections and the past in terms of present problems continues to appear in Chicano literature. History became an obsession to Chicano authors. However, both Gonzales and Valdez knew that history was and is still written mostly by the oppressors to justify themselves, so Chicanos must rewrite history from their own prespective if they want to change the present and future. History is a text that empowers or enslaves. The voice of the Chicano community has been silenced, its images distorted or erased in mainstream cultural production, so Chicanos must speak and create themselves for themselves. In great part, Chicano literature has been an attempt to rewrite U.S. history from our point of view.

In opposition to the Anglo American emphasis on the individual, Valdez and Gonzales stressed the community. Their works were presented, not as the personal expression of one author, but as the collective voice of the people channeled through a servant of the cause. This populist rhetoric would dominate for some ten years and still today has many advocates.

About the same time as *Joaquín* appeared, a group of intellectuals at the University of California at Berkeley initiated the academic arm of what by the end of the decade would be called the Chicano Movement. They, however, still called themselves Mexican Americans, and their first aim was to revaluate, from their perspective, the sociological studies related to the Mexican American community. To publicize their efforts they started Quinto Sol, a publishing house with its own journal, *El Grito*. It became the center of Mexican American intellectual and—although the sociological emphasis always persisted—literary production for the next seven years. In the journal would appear for the first time at a widely distributed level such future hallmarks of Chicano literature as Tomás Rivera, Rolando Hinojosa, Rudy Anaya, Estela Portillo, José Montoya, Alurista, Miguel Méndez, etc. But before Quinto Sol began full scale literary production, another change would occur to make it viable.

1968, when all over the world students were protesting for countless reasons, Chicano students, first at the high school and then at the university level, took militant action to force their schools to initiate programs relevant to their communities. They demanded ethnic studies similar to what had been implemented for Blacks across the country. When in the summer of '69 they met at the first National Chicano Youth Conference, hosted by Rodolfo Gonzales in Denver, the student movement took on a tone of cultural nationalism from the Crusade for Justice. Its promise and potential was that through the students the regional struggles might be united in a transregional manner never achieved by the political leaders. A central goal became higher education as a foundation for a new Chicano nation to be called Aztlán, a term foreign to Gonzales' manifesto, but introduced by student groups from California. The document produced by the conference delegates was titled *El Plan Espiritual de Aztlán*, an idealistic statement of nationhood through a common cultural heritage. On a more realistic level, the sudden influx of Chicanos into the universities produced a demand for Chicano related courses and materials. Now there was a market for books, so someone had to supply the products.

The fledgling Quinto Sol rushed to fill the demand, publishing an anthology of literature, *El espejo/The Mirror*. Significantly, it was subtitled *Selected Mexican-American Literature* (1969)—the Quinto Sol editors had been caught unprepared for the shift in militant student circles to the term "Chicano," as Gonzales was caught the same year by the unexpected rise of the term "Aztlán." The students were affecting changes on their older counterparts, forcing them to keep up. Quinto Sol's anthology and its subsequent increase in space dedicated to literature in the journal reflect that sudden increase in demand for literary reading material. At the same time, authors outside the Quinto Sol stable began small presses to publish their own books as the above mentioned Gonzales had done earlier in 1967: Abelardo Delgado (Barrio Publications, 1969), Ray Barrio (Ventura Press, 1969), Luis Valdez (Cucaracha Press, 1971), Ricardo Sánchez (Mictla, 1971). But distribution was, and still is, a major problem with Chicano books—they never have been readily available, even when in print, and going out of print was and is common. The fact is that when Chicano students began demanding courses about their own literature, there existed very little, and what was available was extremely difficult to find. Even *El espejo* consisted of literature the editors had to search for. Unlike Black literature, which had had a Harlem Renaissance and almost a century of literary production more or less known to specialists, Chicano literature was undiscovered—buried in archives, library collections, newspapers, memoirs, unpublished manuscripts, awaiting researchers who have come along since the 1960s—or simply non-existent. This gave the early years of the Chicano civil rights struggle a sense of urgent project—Chicanos not only would rewrite history, they would create a new literature. Quinto Sol led in promulgating this atmosphere of creation by instituting a prize for the best new book of fiction.

Before the first Quinto Sol winner was announced, however, major publishing houses moved to capitalize on what they perceived as a new market. In addition to economic motives, ethnic publication would allow them to satisfy political and social demands from governmental Affirmative Action guide-lines to open opportunities to minorities. In 1970 Doubleday published two titles: Richard Vazquez' *Chicano* and a paperback edition of José Antonio Villarreal's *Pocho*, which had gone relatively unnoticed when first published in 1959. Ray Barrio, Ricardo Sánchez and Rodolfo Gonzales had their books republished in commercial editions by prestigious presses, and anthologies began to appear from mainstream houses. Several universities started publication series for Chicano material, the most notable and enduring being UCLA, with its journal *Aztlán*. All of this activity, along with the sudden appearance of Chicano mural projects and a certain degree of mass media coverage, gave the impression of a great flowering of cultural output during the first half of the 1970s. And while Philip Ortego's attempt to compare this production with the Harlem Renaissance by calling it the Chicano Renaissance was excessive (Ortego, 1971), this period was probably the most intense moment we have experienced with respect to publications; never again has there been so much interest at so many levels of production.

Before moving on to the mid-'70s we must consider a few more works that shaped the literature. While Gonzales looked back into Mexican history for heroes and an ideology based on the violent blending of European and Native American cultures, Alurista, a young poet from Southern California, devised another vision of the Chicano past and future. His was the ideology of Aztlán that fired the imagination of the young Chicanos at their conference in 1969, competing with the nationalism of Gonzales and finally melding with it—although actually Alurista's third worldist tolerance was incompatible with Gonzales' racial separatism. Yet at the time there seemed to be a fusing of the two ideologies. Alurista had focused on the pre-Columbian period, drawing from Nahuatl sources—mostly derived from Leon-Portilla's writings—mixed with a strong dose of Carlos Castañeda's counterculture social science-fiction, which many took seriously at first. Thus Alurista offered an Amerindian poetic philosophy as an alternative to the European orientation. He proposed to save the urban Chicanos by reorienting them back to nature through their pre-Columbian heritage based on the harmony of all life. His concepts were in tune with 1960s anti-Western culture sentiments of the youth, but they also appealed to Chicanos in search of a mythological underpinning for a new nation.

Other authors felt uneasy with these historical or mythological models, especially with their rural character. They sought more contemporary heroes and settings, particularly since by 1960, 80% of Chicanos lived in cities. The most popular of these urban models was the Pachuco whose battles with the U.S. military in Los Angeles, California, during W.W.II were legendary in the Chicano community (see note 2). Pachucos represented more than the rejection of Anglo American society, they also turned their backs on traditional Mexican culture, openly flaunting in their dress, behavior and speech a synthesis of Mexican and U.S. customs. For this reason Chicanos in the '60s saw them as precursors of their own Movement.

Of the works about Pachucos, José Montoya's "El Louie" is still the archetype, and as I have stated elsewhere, it also serves as an excellent paradigm of Chicano literature in general. The poem begins with the disappearance of Louie, the leader of a Pachuco gang, a death which threatens to strip the group of its temporal, spatial and ethnic orientation which Louis represented. The poem retrieves Louis's images from the past, displaying them for readers. Louie's life, based on a Camus-like existentialism of performance with style and class despite the absurdity of life, appears as a counterpoint to his death by heroin overdose. His lifestyle is offered as a positive example, while his death serves as a warning against contradictory self-destructive activities that eventually overwhelmed his ability to improvise responses to life-threatening problems. While realizing its goal of saving a communal hero from oblivion, more significantly the poem becomes itself what Louie was: the centering experience for the community of readers. Chicano literature is a ritual of communal cohesion and transcendence in the face of constant threats to existence.

Montoya wrote "El Louie" in his native interlingual speech: "Hoy enterraron a Louie / And San Pedro o san pinche / are in for it." Like Valdez in the theatre, Montoya violates the sanctuary of monolingual literature in the U.S. with the spoken language of the people. Thus his poem is proof of the viability of hybrid culture, which Pachucos had incarnated.

What Montoya did for Pachucos, Raul Salinas did for the barrio. In "A Trip Through the Mind Jail," Salinas begins with the disappearance of his neighborhood, then rescues its images from his memory to reconstruct a homespace which is ultimately the poem itself. This (re)creative act countervails the threat to his existential cosmic orientation. The barrio offers both positive and negative lessons, but principally it demonstrates survival by creating art from life, and death, just as Montoya had in "El Louie."

Time after time Chicano literature will save the past from silence, while simultaneously offering itself as the new source of orientation in the present. It asks readers to take the lessons to praxis in society beyond the space of literature, and is therefore didactic. Changes it might inspire would be political, its aim being to better conditions for the community.

During the first half of the 1970s, these models, repeated in numerous variations, held sway. Although important works appeared, they were always compared or contrasted to those considered the central, authentic works. Sergio Elizondo's *Perros y antiperros* had no problem; it seemed to synthesize all of the models into a historical and mythological voyage through the Chicano homeland. On the other hand, Ricardo García's *Selected Poetry* proved too esoteric for most Chicanos who still wanted readily identifiable social themes and narrative devices. García's reliance on lyric techniques, metaphor, imagery, and his emphasis on personal rather than communal content seemed non-Chicano in the context explained above—too mainstream at a time when Chicano literature was limited to alternative, ethnic cultural preoccupations. García was ahead of his time. Finally, falling somewhere between these two, Tino Villanueva's *Hay otra voz poems* moved from the personal lyric to culminate in a declaration of community service through poetry. Poems from the last section were greeted as Chicano, while those from the first were used to attack the author as too mainstream. But Villanueva's Chicanismo was strong enough to convince even those who misunderstood his personal poetry.

While poetry had diverse models by the early 1970s, the novel tended to fall loosely within one pattern, that of the *Bildungsroman*, usually featuring a boy destined to become a writer (Bruce-Novoa, "Portraits"). Such a pattern can be found in Villarreal's *Pocho*; the first two Quinto Sol prize winners: . . . *y no se lo tragó la tierra* by Tomás Rivera, and *Bless Me, Ultima* by Rudy Anaya; Ernesto Galarza's *Barrio Boy*; and Oscar Zeta Acosta's autobiographical novels, *The Autobiography of a Brown Buffalo*, and its continuation *The Revolt of the Cockroach People*.

Even Rolando Hinojosa's *Estampas del valle*, the third Quinto Sol prize, suggested a similar possibility, though it became apparent only after several sequels. In each work, the narrator or the protagonist searches for a lost orientation in the world and finds it through retrospection. Acosta treats the topic satirically, debunking both the American Dream and the Chicano Movement, but still the basic structure and development are present. As in the poetry, these works pose the question of community survival, some very directly like Hinojosa's and Rivera's works, others more subtly, like Villarreal's and Anaya's. In all of them writing itself is offered as one solution to the threat to Chicano culture. Certainly the works attack social injustice and advocate, to some extent, political responses to real problems—though not as blatantly as the poetry—but they also take seriously literature's capacity to provide the people with orientation, meaning and pleasure.

While in poetry and prose patterns were being solidified at the start of the '70s, in theatre Luis Valdez was already breaking with the Acto genre on which his Teatro Campesino had built its reputation. His influence had been enormous. All over the country groups of Chicanos practiced Actos in the Campesino style. Valdez had begun the annual theatre festival to bring these goups together and teach them techniques, as well to give them the opportunity to perform for and learn from one another. By 1972 theatre had become the most dynamic genre in Chicano literary production.

Valdez' Actos had, as stated above, evolved to encompass urban and youth themes, but the Acto did not lend itself well to the longer plays Valdez had in mind. He had seen Chicano ideology develop Manichean opposition to outsiders without considering the negative elements inherent in Chicano culture itself. To deal with these he envisioned a new type of play, as he explained in the introduction to the published collection *Actos*: "Our belief in God, the church, the social role of women— these must be subject to examination and redefinition on some kind of public forum ... Not a teatro composed of actos or agitprop but a teatro of ritual, of music, of beauty and spiritual sensitivity. A teatro of legends and myths. A teatro of religious strength" (3). His *Mitos* were to be long rituals aimed at molding the spiritual character of the people. Valdez drew from the pre-Columbian philosophies, similar to Alurista's approach, and mixed them with Christianity in a sort of archetypal anthropological theatre. This advocacy of myth and religion, introduced with the first full-fledged Mito, *La gran carpa de los rascuachis* (1973), provoked immediate controversy (Yarbro-Bejarano). Once again those who demanded that Chicano literature remain within the limits of realism and social relevance claimed that myth or lyricism were non-Chicano. Marxists accused Valdez of deluding the people by displacing the real social struggle into an ideal plane. Valdez was suddenly seen as having strayed dangerously into escapism.

By the mid-'70s these conflicts were splitting TENAZ, the organization Valdez had founded to bring the teatros together. At the 1974 teatro festival in Mexico City, Valdez was viciously criticized for his use of mythological and religious symbols and message. Surrounded by the heavily marxist Latin American troupes, the ideological differences among Chicanos were exacerbated (Bruce-Novoa, "Report"). The following year, the teatro festival in San Antonio, Texas, although now free of Latin American pressure to conform to their political orientation, was racked with similar ideological tensions. In addition to the mythological content of the mito Valdez' group presented, the Teatro Campesino was advocating a retreat to nature and communal living, which produced an incredulous reaction from urban oriented members of TENAZ, even those who did not oppose Valdez' mythological views. Those dedicated to questions of political power struggles were especially offended. Valdez and the Teatro Campesino pulled out of the festivals after that year. Valdez, however, was even then starting his move beyond community and street theatre towards the commercial mainstream and eventually film.

However, as the Campesino drifted into spaces where other Chicano groups could or would not follow, another group appeared to compete for predominance. Under the directorship of Jorge Huerta, the Teatro de la Esperanza (Santa Barbara, California), developed documentary plays, the best of which, *Guadalupe*, competed favorably with the Teatro Campesino's *Carpa* for the best play at the 1974 festival. In 1975, when the Teatro Campesino presented a preliminary and still rough version of *El fin del mundo*, Esperanza's *Guadalupe*, polished to perfection, was clearly the best play at the festival. Documentary theatre offered an alternative to mythical orientation, one that appealed to the political pragmatists.

For most Chicano theatre groups, however, anything beyond a short Acto, in any style, has proved too difficult. They are nonprofessionals with little time to develop the skills necessary to perform anything but the simplest agitprop skits. Furthermore, many of them do not see theatre as more than a useful appendage to political action.

1975 marked a change in Chicano literature. Conflicts similar to those that divided TENAZ surfaced in other areas as well. Quinto Sol, the major publisher for the first seven years, was torn apart, not over political disagreements, but personal conflicts. Ideological splits did, however, fragment the critics into what some observers have classified as the following tendencies: nationalists, Marxists and a third line usually called formalist, although the critics included here followed diverse methodologies not strictly formalistic (Salazar Parr). More significant than differences was the decision by major critics no longer to praise works solely because they had been written by a Chicano. Standards, different for each tendency, were applied, and some works were found wanting. The question of craft, skill and talent—previously dismissed as the values of bourgeois elitism—began to be discussed openly, as were doubts about the ideology of many writers. This brought critics into conflict with some artists and deepened the differences among artists themselves. While these critical trends produced controversy, they also opened new possibilities for the literature by breaking down the rigid sociopolitical molds into which much of the literature had been forced.

On a national level, the economy had begun to slip into recession. Conservative trends manifested themselves in attacks on minority programs. Retrenchment in governmental agencies produced cuts in support for cultural projects. Affirmative Action enforcement, which had begun to decrease after the election of Nixon (1968), continued to decline in the '70s. In addition there was to be a general drop in social awareness and a growing cynicism among the youth. All of this negatively affected cultural production in the second half of the decade, especially at the university level.

On the positive side, new books expanded the genres of poetry and fiction, challenging the concepts of Chicano literature. Miguel Méndez' *Los criaderos humanos* was a harsh political satire, but stated in a highly esoteric lyricism, showing that political message need not be expressed simply and clearly to be effective. In fiction, Ron Arias' *The Road to Tamazunchale* and Alejandro Morales' *Caras viejas y vino nuevo* opened new ground. Neither is a *Bildungsroman*. Gone is the nostalgia for youth and the idealization of the barrio, as is the attempt to speak for the community—both works are highly personal visions of reality. Also, both authors openly display influences from the mainstream—Arias from Borges and García Márquez (to say nothing of Goethe and Cervantes), and Morales from Luis Buñel and La Onda writers of Mexico. Neither worries about relating to the Chicano movement. There are few if any political messages here. Both use fantasy as if it were an essential part of reality. This can be seen as the start of a shift away from simple, obtrusive sociopolitical writing that had dominated since 1965. A freer, more open literature was being demanded by artists.

The criteria for classifying a work as Chicano was rapidly moving away from content to settle strictly on the author's heritage—and even then that heritage did not have to be on display in the work. This coincided with my own call for just such an openness to the total community in my first essays. While this allowed us to include formerly ignored writers, such as John Rechy, the gay novelist, it also provoked attacks from

critics dedicated to hard line sociopolitical aesthetics, both of the nationalistic and Marxist schools. Yet no amount of critical feuding could
prevent the evolution in the cultural production that the artists wanted
and achieved.

The most significant change, however, was not generic, thematic
nor stylistic, but much more fundamental and radical: it was sexual.
In the 1975-76 period, Chicanas, who had been excluded almost entirely from the first ten years of publication, began to appear in notable
numbers. Estela Portillo, who had won the Quinto Sol Award (equivalent to second place) the year in which Hinojosa had won the prize,
had to wait three years longer for her book to appear. Quinto Sol had
first tested public reaction by allowing Portillo to edit an issue of *El
Grito* (7, 1 [1973]), the first of any major journal dedicated to Chicanas.
Rain of Scorpions, her book, did not get into print, however, until after the Quinto Sol ownership was embroiled in a court battle among
its co-directors, and Octavio Romano needed new material for his new
Tonatiuh International publishing company.

Other Chicanas had to take matters into their own hands and publish their books themselves, just as the men had had to do earlier—the
difference being that the women faced exclusion not only by mainstream
publishers, but also by presses started by Chicanos for the publication
of Chicano literature. Ironically, those Chicanos had to be forced to
treat Chicanas as equals. Most notable of the first flurry of Chicana
texts was Bernice Zamora's half of *Restless Serpents* (1976), a feminist
manifesto written in thoughtfully crafted poems that proved instantly
that Chicanas could write as well as, if not better than, Chicanos.

The questions that Zamora, Portillo and other Chicanas raised about
the oppression women suffered at the hands of men within traditional
Chicano culture brought cries of protest from Chicanos. The women
were accused of betraying the political struggle by criticizing the behavior of Chicanos, just as those men who wrote other than political
works were accused of selling out. The women reacted by declaring
their solidarity with the Chicano movement's ideals of political change
and liberation, but persisted in their criticism, which was well founded
and undeniable—except by those who dared to hide or smooth over reality. And feminism grew with each new piece by a Chicana, even when
some of them disclaimed the term. Despite the animosity that arose,
Chicana publications had the positive effect of sensitizing the artistic
community to its rampant male chauvinism. Since the mid-'70s conditions have improved slightly, although the problem is far from resolved.

1976 brought the publication of four titles by established authors:
Anaya, Hinojosa, Ricardo Sánchez and Alurista. In the case of Hinojosa and Sánchez, the books were continuations of their earlier works,

with little to differentiate them. Of the two, however, Hinojosa's continued expansion of his basic thematics seemed more justified, since his project had been defined almost from the start as a long progressive novel. Anaya and Alurista seemed to be moving into new territory, but actually each was exploring possibilities found in their previous works. None of them succeeded in surpassing, or even equalling, the levels they had set earlier. Seen now from the distance of almost a decade, it seems that with these books the first period of Chicano literature had reached a stasis, like a wave spending itself in a last burst of foam.

The new thrust, both thematically and technically, came, as I said above, first from women: Zamora's book, previously discussed, and Isabela Ríos' novel *Victuum*. The latter is a biography of a woman from birth to cosmic consciousness, spoken in dialogue without narration. The novel has received little critical attention, which in part attests to the originality of its structure, but also to the flaws in the realization of the project. We might say that established Chicano criticism, still dominated by male critics in the mid 1970s, was not capable of understanding Ríos' writing, and that a feminist criticism equipped to give it a fair reading would not come into existence until the 1980s, beyond the scope of this essay. However, one cannot ignore the collapse of the novel in the last chapters, with the apparent disintegration of the writing, as if the author no longer cared to maintain the effort. For whatever reason, the novel ends badly. At best it can only be considered an interesting attempt to create a Chicana voice different from that which Chicanos have established.

Also in 1976 there appeared two new literary magazines: *Mango*, published in San José, California, and *Cambios/Phideo*, published at Yale University. They manifested the character of the other group who brought change, a group whose appearance was as logical and inevitable as that of the women: the younger generation. The editorial staffs and contributors were young writers, mostly students. The editors, all three poets, were to make names for themselves later: Lorna Dee Cervantes, Orlando Ramírez and José Saldivar. Eventually the three would collaborate in *Mango*, founded by Cervantes. Later, the best of the younger generation of poets, Gary Soto, joined them as chapbook editor. All four advocated more craft in writing, implicitly criticizing older writers for their lack of attention to technique. In addition, they recognized that the rhetoric of the initial phase of contemporary Chicano writing seemed spent of its power to move the audience, and was in need of renewal through a new approach to language. Not that they opposed writing with a message, but they wanted it done with fresh images, not clichés. They avoided the hyberbole of early Chicano writing, preferring to return to basic personal experience. Since 1976 all of them have gone on to achieve success in their writing, especially Soto and Cervantes.

Gary Soto is the epitome of a new trend within Chicano literature. While the ethnic element is not missing from his work, he writes more for a general public than for solely Chicanos. His poetry is well within the mainstream of U.S. poetic style: concise metaphors, elimination of prosaic or narrative elements, brief illuminations of emotions, conversational tone. He publishes predominantly in mainstream magazines rather than in Chicano outlets. Also, Soto is the first major Chicano writer trained by a major U.S. poet, Philip Levine. Not only has Soto entered the mainstream, but he was groomed for it by someone who could open doors previously closed to many Chicano writers. Young Chicano writers more and more often would like to follow Soto's example.

Towards the end of the 1970s it appeared that Chicano literature was losing its focus. It became more difficult for critics to agree on what defined a Chicano work. In addition, research into the past found that many assumptions about the absence of written literature in the Chicano community, the supposed context for what thus seemed the unprecedented emergence of Chicano literature, were simply not true, nor were the claims of uniqueness or isolation for U.S. literary influences. In every direction the literature was expanding rapidly. There even appeared the first in what is now a group of works written by Chicanos who deny the validity of the Movement's ideals and Chicanismo itself. Nash Candelaria's *Memories of the Alhambra*, with its denial of Mexican heritage and ridiculing of the search for cultural roots, its advocacy of assimilation and rejection of ethnic distinctiveness, was a precursor of Richard Rodríquez' infamous *Hunger of Memory*, published in the early 1980s. Yet somehow, instead of destroying Chicano literature, these works have enlarged its space, enriching it and forcing an acceptance of new possibilities of its character, simultaneously having the effect on the culture itself.

In one of those shifts of gravitational force during the last few years of the 1970s, Luis Valdez drew attention back to theatre. He wrote *Zoot Suit* and directed it for two major Los Angeles theatres, playing to full houses. In 1979 he took the production to New York, where, however, the run was short and unsuccessful. Despite this setback, Valdez attracted the eye of Universal Studios and was contracted to turn the play into a film. *Zoot Suit* combined docudrama with musical theatre, both of the New York and Brechtian type. Based on the 1942 Sleepy Lagoon incident, it focuses on the leader of a Pachuco gang who is arrested and convicted of murder, along with his gang members. Valdez managed to condense the proceedings concisely, conveying just enough information to demonstrate the injustice and prejudice of the times. The case pre-dated the infamous Zoot Suit riots, so Valdez had returned to one of the original figures and historical events in the code of early Chicano mythology, one which the literature had already given ample treatment. Valdez could borrow from that literary tradition, taking from precursors like José Montoya and Raúl Salinas, in ways that previous writers had not been able to do because the material simply had not existed. This proved the vitality of the process of building a literature which could then serve as inspiration for future writing. In the hands of a genius like Valdez, this material was taken to new heights, and the interpretation he gave the Pachuco image stands as one of its best and most effective treatments.

While Valdez' achievements were undeniable—*Zoot Suit* had broken the barrier of commercial theatre—he again provoked controversy in Chicano circles. Critics who had attacked the Mitos now accused Valdez of having abandoned his own concepts of anti-commercial theatre by supposedly selling out to mainstream society and turning his back on the people. However, as other critics understood, the political message of the play was clear, perhaps even too obvious. And Chicanos had filled the theatres in California. *Zoot Suit* was the logical evolution of Valdez' career, one more step in his investigation and remolding of Chicano culture. As always Valdez had jumped outside the defined limits of Chicano literary space only to force it to expand out to him. Valdez proved at the end of the 1970s that, just as in the mid-'60s, he was the most dynamic and consistent producer of bench-mark works within Chicano literature.

As the '70s came to a close, there was a combination of pessimism, cynicism and hope. The decrease in social awareness among young Chicanos disturbed veterans from the 1960s and early '70s. The young were increasingly cynical about the claims of the Movement and its literature. The promises had not come true, but worse, for many of the younger generation, the goal had shifted from changing society to gaining a comfortable position in it. The priority became the acquisition of practical knowledge, and less with the concerns of identity—as if self-knowledge were somehow not practical. Students no longer insisted on having classes on their literature, preferring to enroll in standard literature courses, or none at all. The hope came from the surge in women's writing and the success of Valdez' play. There was also the promise of a new expansion into major length film, not only by Valdez, but by Jesús Treviño (*Seguín*) and Moctezuma Esparza (*The Ballad of Gregorio Cortez*). The first years of the '80s were marked by the release of these films.

More significant for literature itself was the activity of young writers who showed continued interest in producing Chicano literature, if not always within what critics of the sociopolitical school accepted. These young writers—for example: Soto, Cervantes, Orlando Ramírez, Laurence Gonzales, Alma Villanueva, Sandra Cisneros, Cherríe Moraga, etc.—along with younger critics, showed better preparation for their craft than the older generations. These writers held the potential to bring a revived impetus to the literature and new dimensions in technique and content. As of this writing, 1984, it must be admitted that no spectacular breakthrough has appeared other than the relative success —artistic more than financial—of Valdez' film version of *Zoot Suit*. The literature continues to grow slowly, still waiting for master craftswomen and men. While the old clichés certainly are dead, and the enthusiasm of the 60s is a fading memory, nothing as powerful or moving has arisen to take their place.

Les minorités en Amérique de Nord (1960-1980) (Bordeaux: Presses Universitaires de Bordeaux, 1985): 115-132.

II

9 The Space of Chicano Literature Update: 1978

> No se trata de otra cosa que de la imposi-
> bildad del Ser para terminar de manifes-
> tarse libre o independientemente. Su es-
> encia se encuentra en la realidad y lo que
> percibimos de ella son sus signos, sus re-
> flejos, que muy pronto desaparecen devo-
> rados por la contingencia.
>
> Juan García Ponce, *La apari-
> ción de lo invisible.*

> *But that same image, we ourselves see ...
> It is the image of the ungraspable phan-
> tom of life; and this is the key to it all.*
>
> Herman Melville, *Moby Dick.*

> *Only from nothing are there infinite
> possibilities—all simultaneously possible.
> Only in nothing can you find everything.*
>
> María Medina López, unpub-
> lished paper, 10/20/74

Introduction

In 1974 a group of Chicano critics gathered to treat critical
approaches to Chicano literature, the critic's role and, indirectly, the nature of the material.[5] I introduced my concept of "The Space of Chicano
Literature" as a response to chaos, later published in the symposium

proceedings and, almost simultaneously, in Spanish in Mexico ("Literatura," 1975). That essay then was expanded and updated for the Corpus Christi Canto al Pueblo Conference (1978). This second version is presented here because it includes more applications of the theory.

From the start Chicano literature has suffered imposed definitions, mostly from people seeking to use literature for non-literary ends, expurgating anything (or anyone) not amenable to their dictates. In 1973 I appealed for open perspectives in "Freedom of Expression and the Chicano Movement." Yet we are subjected still to calls for criteria based largely on extraliterary concerns. This may be all well and good when, as sociologist or anthropologist or politician or *patrón* or high priest, one evaluates a literary work's utility in the light of socio-political goals, but it fetters literature. Fortunately, it is negated by the growing number of Chcanos who explore wider and wider realms of experiences. To deny their writing is impossible, so those who would like to control it often resort to the ethnic slur, impugning the author's Chicanismo, as if solid criteria existed for measuring authenticity. Others insist that our literature must "protect" the community. We are asked to judge books according to the damage they may do, a moral standard with its baneful corollary: negative literaure should not be read. They desire a Chicano Index of Forbidden Books and Excommunicated Authors. This would be humorous, if cases were not already on record. This paternalistic attitude ironically is prevalent among those who claim to be "just plain folk," yet they would dictate to the authors, critics and, worst of all, the community what readings are acceptable—literary totalitarianism, *a la Chicana*.

In 1974 I again decried such extraliterary shackles and drew the comparison with the word *Chicano*, with its many truncating definitions. To repeat, I propose that *Chicano* remain undefined; that it, and thus the literature, is *nothing*, in the sense in which María Medina López speaks above, a *nothing* in no way negative, one which may manifest itself in many facets, but which perversely resists final definition, maintaining the ability to reformulate its totality from within, in spite of the best—worst—efforts to ossify it for whatever reason. I hope my concept of literary space continues to offer an alternative to approaches which would limit our literature.

Finally, a word on the origin of this approach. I freely acknowledge influence from many authors, particularly Juan García Ponce and Octavio Paz, the most significant literary essayists Mexico has produced in the last thirty years. One lives and perceives according to the body's sensibilities and the structures of the mind. I do not disguise nor apologize for mine. Yet Chicano literature is the source for my concept. Only in the reading and the sharing of the reading experience in the classroom did a paradigm repeat itself from within, surely because García Ponce has taught me to read phenomenologically, but, also, because the books, varied as their surfaces are, contain that paradigm. The implications of its presence for non-literary fields may be far reaching, but it is not for me to chart their significance there. Truly it would be more appropriate for our social scientists to do so. That they probably will not is just another indication that Chicano academics do not differ that much from those of other groups—and social scientists hardly ever read literature seriously, if at all. My purpose then? To address the question of the literature itself, and, *ojalá*, to lead readers directly to it, or back to it, with an expanded ability to enjoy, appreciate and understand it. This is my concept of the critic's role, perhaps not as grandiose as social guruism based on literary analysis, but I am more than willing to leave to the works themselves the function of leading readers to the outside world.

Literary Space

It is a truism that modern people find themselves isolated in the world, stripped of transcendental absolutes and condemned to ultimate death to which they are led by the apparently incontrovertible flow of consecutive time. Even spatial relationships, the distance which always separates bodies even in close contact, only underscore their particular individuality as *this* person and no other. In one of the most perceptive studies of the human condition, *Death and Sensuality*, George Bataille utilized the terminology of continuity and discontinuity to explain the dilemma:

> We are discontinuous beings, individuals who perish in isolation in the midst of an incomprehensible adventure, but we yearn for our lost continuity. We find the state of affairs that binds us to our random and ephemeral individuality hard to bear. Along with our tormenting desire that this evanescent thing should last, there stands our obsession with a primal continuity linking us with everything that is. (15)

Discontinuity is the social order, founded on work and time, and the concept of the individual which rigidly defines us as separate from others. Continuity includes those spaces in which human individuality is violated and depersonalized, resulting in the dissolution of the normal order, the interruption of temporal flow and the unity of all particular beings in spatial simultaneity.[6]

Juan García Ponce, who in his essay "El arte y lo sagrado" (1968, 77-100) avails himself of Bataille's exposition to explore the sacredness of art, concisely reviews Bataille's spaces of continuity—childhood, death, eroticism, love and mysticism—whose common characteristic is the violation and disappearance of the individual's particular discontinuity through/in a type of death, permanent or momentary, and union with another being, the world and life. The process rescues us from time and returns us to the transcendent unity of impersonal continuity. Sacredness "is the revelation of continuity through the death of a discontinuous being to those who watch it as a solemn rite ... what remains, what the tense onlookers experience in the succeeding silence, is the continuity of all existence with which the victim is now one," Bataille tells us (22). Despite eroding absolutes and the chaotic discontinuity of the socio-temporal order, through/in the experience of the sacred, "tal vez es posible recuperar el sentido del mundo y vencer el miedo" (García Ponce, 1968, 88). I could not improve on García Ponce's exposition of these ideas in his essay, to which I remit those desiring further explanation, because here it is yet another space of continuity that interests us.

García Ponce treats explicitly a continuous space only alluded to by Bataille:[7] art, which sacrifices man and the world.

> El artista de que se trate, sea el poeta en su relación con la palabra o el pintor en su trato con las imágenes, despoja al mundo tanto como a los seres de su apariencia, de su particularidad, para convertirlos en palabras o en imágenes ... en imagen. Sin embargo, esta muerte es una nueva vida. La realidad es devorada por la obra, por la imagen, para que ésta nos la muestre como otra vida. Pero ésta es una vida muerta a la que precisamente se ha sacado del tiempo, despojándola de su discontinuidad, dejándola fija para siempre fuera y dentro de la vida al mismo tiempo. En este hecho se encuentra el secreto y el poder de permanencia de la obra de arte. En ella el sacrificio vuelve a repetirse una y otra vez ante la mirada del espectador atento. (1968, 95-96)

In this way art holds life's fleeting images, to which García Ponce refers in the first epigraph, rescuing them from devouring contingency and offering them for our contemplation. In these images we can find our reflection permanently held so we can encounter the essence of our being in a graspable form. This sacred act renders the world meaningful. Armed with meaning we can resist the chaos which threatens us. Literature becomes a space for responding to chaos, and more, the response itself.

Objection: The images are particular, personal, and not impersonal; and literature, unlike painting, is not simultaneously experienced, but, rather, sequentially, discontinuously. How can such material and experience give rise to a totally simultaneous space? Paradox.

Response: Art works utilize discontinuous prime matter in their attempt to convey continuous experience. Visual arts are thought to be experienced at a glance, while literature or music cannot be.[8] Yet one experiences the visual totality of a painting only as an aura around a particular focal point. Stand too close and the aura will not cover the canvas, and in many cases tones will separate which the artist intended to be seen as one color. If we consider sculpture, the problem is compounded by perspectives impossible to simultaneously perceive. However, in the relationship of experience to object, these limitations are transcended by the onlooker, who, armed with recall, can in some way meld the perspectives into one image. On still a higher plain, that of the object itself, all these perspectives are simultaneously proffered and possible, and each creates a point of tension in its role as one of a total sum of elements. The object is the sum of all its tensions. In written matter the image on page 11 is not on 220, but in the reader they can coincide; in the work as image of itself, they exist in simultaneity. In literary space, things are sacrificed, stripped of material existence and given a new representational form in words, becoming impersonal and atemporal. Writing's permanent, fixed nature is exactly the means of killing them, thus saving them from sequential time. But as atemporal objects they cease being the particular objects in order to become surfaces of all the possibilities of its kind. Borges sums up the paradox in "El aleph," where total simultaneity is possible to experience, but impossible to capture in language. Yet, and yet, we come away from the story with the image of the aleph. The vitality of paradox is that it does not resolve itself, forcing continual movement from the discontinuous to the continuous, the movement of eroticism, the movement of life.

What this means is that our images are revealed outside of ourselves and outside of contingency in the Other, which is the world tranfixed in art outside of time, though experienced in it. We unite with the Other in art. Octavio Paz, in speaking of the image in poetry, explains the process:

> La imagen transmuta al hombre y lo convierte a su vez en imagen, esto es, en espacio donde los contrarios se funden. Y el hombre mismo, desgarrado desde el nacer, se reconcilia consigo cuando se hace imagen, cuando *se hace otro*. La poesía es metamorfosis, cambio, operación alquímica, y por eso colinda con la magia, la religión y otras tentativas para transformar el hombre y hacer de "éste" y de "aquél" ese "otro" que es el mundo. El universo deja de ser un vasto almacén de cosas heterogéneas ... La poesía pone al hombre fuera de sí y, simultáneamente, lo hace regresar a su ser original: lo vuelve a sí. El hombre es su imagen: él mismo y aquel otro ... La poesía es entrar en el ser. (1967, 113)

Thus, art offers humankind a possible space of sacredness, the creation of which, as well as the participation in, constitutes a response to the world's divisive forces.

Chicano Literary Space

Chicanos, in their condition of a societal extreme which continually demonstrates in a more acute fashion the state of the center, have suffered extremely the alienation of the discontinuity of modern life in that even the ephemeral reflections surrounding them are not theirs, but those of the majority which categorically excludes them. We can, of course, find ourselves in art which achieves universality; that is, the basic human quality of continuity such pieces reveal will reflect our humanity. However, the surface image remains a particularity, and until recently those surfaces—and a page is as much a surface as a canvas—excluded us in a dual fashion: 1) it was not a Chicano particularity being sacrificed and universalized, which prevented many Chicanos from focusing their attention; 2) the surfaces were not readily available to Chicano artists. Our general sense of alienation from Anglo American society was reinforced in the arts.

When the Chicano civil rights struggle began, we sought art to which we could relate, and for a time we clung to Mexican art, trying to negate Anglo influences. Though this confusion persists in some circles, we have begun to create our own art instead, and Chicano writers, in spite of would-be dictators on both the right and left, are exercising their freedom to explore their full reality. However, no one would deny the predominance of the Mexican and the U.S. influences; yet we are neither, as we are not Mexican American. I proposed, in 1974, that we are the space (not the hypen) between the two, the intercultural *nothingness* of that space.[9] For those reluctant to accept this sense of nothing, I offer a compromise: read the above as "the intercultural possibilities of that space." We continually expand the space, pushing the two influences out and apart as we claim more area for our reality, while at the same time creating interlocking tensions that hold the two in relationship. In reality, there are not just two poles, but many. Neither Mexico nor the U.S.A. is monolithic. Each is pluricultural. Thus the synthesis is multiple and plurivalent, not bipolar at all. This means that we are not simply bicultural, but intercultural.

Each Chicano work opens a space for itself, while adding to the total of Chicano art, as well as Art itself. No Chicano represents all Chicano art, yet each work manifests, in the particular, the impersonal totality of it. Each addition, traditional or innovative, has a legitimate place, and each participates in continuity. Chicano art is the space created by the tensions of all its interrelated particular manifestations. Criticism enters as well, although it can be studied as a field itself, with similar characteristics. Some artists courageously work the frontiers, daringly traversing them to force expansion, while others prefer safe, previously charted areas. What was once sufficient—mere presence—becomes less acceptable, and quality rapidly assumes its rightful place. Nevertheless, the space is the sum of all these products and producers in simultaneous relationship, creating one unit. We may concentrate on one, or the group of most outstanding, but they are only particular surface examples of the space itself.

Objection: Oral tradition seems to be discounted here in favor of concentrating on written literature.

Response: Perhaps, but I nowhere exclude oral tradition. It has its place, surely, as film, recording, television, comic books, rock concerts all have theirs, though none has been explored to the depths as have literature and painting. Also, it is painfully clear to those who work with the younger generations that the oral tradition is not as healthy as we would like to pretend. This fact is central to much Chicano literature and its preoccupation with the loss of culture.

Application

Chicano authors confront discontinuity, as all artists do, but, in the most representative works, this conflict is the essential theme—time and again Chicano literature focuses on the threat to the existence of an individual, the family, the community, tradition, or whatever. The threat is responded to by the salvation of the images of the threatened party, and the ordering of them in the meaningful structure of the aesthetic object. The theme appears in the deep paradigm of Chicano literature: threat of chaotic discontinuity ⟶ recuperation of vital images ⟶ unity in continuous literary space. Here I propose simply to demonstrate the presence of this theme and the paradigm in key Chicano works, those likely to be found in most survey courses of the literature, reserving detailed analysis for book-length studies or articles on single works.

If one poem could center Chicano literary space, it would be "El Louie," José Montoya's elegy to a dead pachuco (see note 2). It begins with the disappearance of the physical substance of his discontinuous being: "Hoy enterraron al Louie." Death, which can facilitate the sacred, manifests itself in the cadaver, but the poem begins from the disappearance of that surface, plunging Louie, his group and time, of which he was a prototype according to the poem, into the invisibility of death. Left unchallenged, moreover, Louie's last, degrading image—his solitary death—threaten to envelop his memory. It falls to the poet to retrieve the other, disappeared life images from time and death by giving them a new surface, a new body, in which to display themselves visibly. That reconstituted body is the poem itself, which opens a space for Louie's life and death to be replayed continually, displaying his dynamic presence and his search for value and meaning in a life limited by a society that offered few doors to pachucos. It is no longer Louie, but the image of Louie depersonalized into permanence. The paradigm is clear.

Threat	$\longrightarrow$	*Recuperation*	$\longrightarrow$	*Response*
Louie's death strips group of meaning and identity.		Selection and display of Louie's life images as vital and central to group.		Poem as affirmation of Louie's life as "remarkable!"

The Chicano images and code are recovered in the poem, which, however, refuses to ameliorate the foreboding future. The result is a response to the threat, but not a falsification of the situation.

"To a Dead Lowrider," by J.L. Navarro, resembles "El Louie" in that it starts from Tito's death, recalls his image, then returns to how he died. However, the paradigm and similar content are transformed into quite a different surface. The focus here is exterior, creating the image of a misunderstood misfit, even among the narrator's group, an irrational, though splendid beast lacking valid social values. "A strident bull. Everyone moved for ... never much cared ... never knew what for ... didn't care." Even his speech is "another language" to the narrator. The poem posits a possible tragedy at the outset—"It *seems* a tragedy the way he died" (emphasis mine)—but finally, when the *seems* gives way to direct affirmation, the tragedy is reduced to "a shame the way he died." Navarro debunks the pachuco by shifting from a heroic to ironic, even pathetic mode within the poem. Life images are rescued, but apparently devoid of positive meaning other than mere presence. The poem refuses to justify a purposeless Tito, admirable as a bull is admirable, but slaughtered meaninglessly. Yet the same poem turns the life-death process into a ritual, a bullfight, for the reader, and this allows for a minimal, qualitative step at the end—not for Tito, but with respect to the narrator-reader relationship. The poem repeatedly addresses the reader, creating at the beginning the structure of an "I" talking about "he" to "you." The "you" does not "remember" Tito, a loss which separates the interlocutors, perhaps representing the Chicano community's disunity due to a loss of historical consciousness. By the end of the poem, the "I" addresses the "you" as "carnal," signifying a newly forged brotherhood.[10] The mutual experience of the ritual saving of Tito's image—pathetic as it might be in the poem's terms and still misunderstood—produces the change, constituting a response to chaotic discontinuity on at least two thematic levels.

Navarro, a Californian, asks if the reader remembers the pachuco, and, from another extreme in Chicano space, a Texan constructs an answer. Tino Villanueva's "Aquellos vatos" (42-43) is written as a pachuco's response to someone asking Navarro's question. "Simón, we knew him," it begins, and proceeds to enumerate nicknames, with quick identifications. However, the poem is not simply a response to casual forgetfulness. A second threat arises in the form of the school system. Villanueva's internal, metaphoric references that function like a vast network throughout his book make difficult the analysis of single poems, but let it suffice to say that school represents a key socializing agent which forces acculturation in exchange for success. "Aquellos vatos" focuses the struggle around different codes of animal names. The pachucos' vital, dynamic world takes the exterior sign of animal nicknames; the school, on the other hand, attempts to teach culture and identity "by reading 'See Spot run,' and by going to the zoo on a Greyhound bus with Miss Foxx" (43). School threatens to displace the pachuco subculture and the Chicanos' by extension by forcing a redefinition of the exterior signs. This clash of two cultures over words can also be read as a struggle between the oral tradition and the established written code.

Raul Salinas' "A Trip Through the Mind Jail" (55-60) shifts emphasis from human disappearance to the barrio's, the spiritual center of the pachuco's world. "La Loma / Neighborhood of my youth / demolished, erased forever from the universe." The center's destruction flings his order into chaos. The poem then states, "You live on, captive in the lonely cellblocks of my mind." The poet is about to liberate the devoured images from the invisibility of mere memory and fix them in the poem's space. The trip through the barrio establishes two internal orders: 1) of place names, signposts of the barrio map; 2) the temporal charting of the narrator's peer group's development, erecting markers of specific experiences. The second is played out on the background of the first, and together they represent the lost barrio and life images. The narrator writes from a jail cell, and the trips's significance is revealed when he states explicitly the use of poetry to resist chaos.

> i needed you then ... identity ... a sense of belonging.
> i need you now.
> So essential to adult days of imprisonment.
> You keep me away from INSANITY'S hungry jaws;
> Smiling/Laughing/Crying. (60)

The barrio's order responds to prison's chaos. Destroyed in the real order, the barrio resurrects itself in literary space. The writer, though, cannot escape jail, but by metaphorically equating himself to the barrio—the barrio was captive in the cellblocks of his mind—he authors a prison break of sorts, which provides him with a sense of cosmic place needed to survive. Exterior, social reality does not change, but the poem's reality responds successfully to its threat.

Perros y antiperros, Sergio Elizondo's first book of poetry, also constitutes a geographic rescue operation. After stating the conflict in dialectical terms—natural man vs. synthetic man, poor vs. rich, we vs. they—the *they* are identified as invaders of *our* territory. He then embarks on a journey through the Southwest, recuperating images of that territory and its people. The poem slowly arrives at the images of two heroes in Chicano mythology, Joaquín Murrieta and Quetzalcóatl, linking their spirit to that of the Chicano movement. The book then closes with an ironic debunking of the glories of the American Dream. Elizondo draws the contrast between cultures, favoring one, degrading and ridiculing the other. Thus the loss of land is somewhat ameliorated by emphasizing our preservation of humanness, but more significantly, the poems recapture territorial images by turning them into objects defined as ours.

I Am Joaquín, the best known Chicano poem, begins with the narrator lost in "modern society," confused, scorned, suppressed and destroyed. The first thirty verses develop the chaos theme, introducing the conflicting choices open to Chicanos: acculturation with spiritual loss but a full stomach, or the spiritual wholeness of cultural separatism but suffering hunger. The options seem dim as the threat looms—an overwhelming "Giant called progress and Anglo success" (10). Joaquin retreats into the secure space of his people, then makes a sweeping, though rapid, voyage through history, from pre-Columbian to modern. Several times along the way, the terms of conflict are restated, as when the poem's persona states that he weeps to see his children disappear into the death of mediocre existence, forgetting their ancestors, which in turn stirs in him the determination to convey to them a sense of his—and thus their—identity (82). The poem follows this structure of the recognition of a threat of acculturation, followed first by a simple yet direct affirmation of existence —"I am Joaquín"—which then gives rise to the struggle aimed at passing the self image on to future generations. The affirmation of identity is the sum of all the images gathered, which by the poem's end allows Joaquín to reject modern society's chaos and project his image into the future as an undeniable capacity to endure (100).

Whence the new assurance in the face of what at the outset seemed overwhelming odds? Not from outside reality which has not changed. The strength derives from contemplating his reflection in the recovered images. Regained confidence and pride can be willed to his sons, lending them strength to counter-attack oppressive society. Those images are displayed and offered to his sons through/in the poem, an atemporal space in which they can survive. In their related tension those images are Joaquín, the Chicano Everyman, who is both one and all Chicanos, thanks to literature's impersonalizing process. He is each successive image in its singularity, while in the poem's totality, he is all the images at once, a solitary, completely simultaneous image: Joaquín. It is no accident that the title is *I Am Joaquín*, for the book is Joaquín, and Joaquín, the book. Where does this miracle happen? In the poem's space, to which we can turn, even though exterior reality resists its affirmations. The structure is clear:

Threat $\longrightarrow$	*Recuperation* $\longrightarrow$	*Response*
Modern society as a devouring giant.	Selection and display of Mexican and Chicano historical images.	The poem arrives at revolution depicted as a sleeping giant arising to confront the menacing giant and allow a future for Chicanos.

One can agree or disagree with the political concepts of *I Am Joaquín*, but we cannot deny its well programed structure that thematically and technically utilizes, and thus exemplifies, the miracle of literary space.

Whereas *I Am Joaquín* brings the past to the present to arrive and stop at future-projection, Alurista's work concentrates on the future from the start, but his goal is to realize a better future now. Those who know Alurista only from anthologies may find this statement odd, for he is often characterized as the high priest of pre-Columbian mythopastiche. However, a careful reading of his works in their totality reveals a now-centered Alurista, consciously utilizing history in the atemporal space of myth, a constant present, and with the purpose of providing Chicanos a spiritual logos which would empower them with practical but human abilities to deal with real situations now.

Floricanto en Aztlán begins with an epigraph taken from Carlos Castañeda's *The Teaching of Don Juan* in which fear is the enemy that defeats man before the battle begins. The quote also alludes to the struggle as a quest. Alurista constructs his book to analyze the reality of Chicanos' fear of the Anglo American, represented as "the man" or "mr.

jones," and to spur them to action in quest of a future without fear, a future to be realized in the action itself. The first poem is a question: "when raza?" Taken at its simplest, it signifies, when will we achieve freedom? The poem urges that we do so now, for "our tomorrow es hoy." Yet on another level we should note that *raza*, here and at other times, is not set off by the commas of direct address, though this "oversight" does not hinder understanding it as direct address. However, Alurista's poetry is always calculated, sometimes deliberately to the sacrifice of smooth flow, so the "error" must be read for, if not strictly intent, at least effect. It achieves a shift in meaning to, *when will there be a raza*?, implying that without freedom we remain a divided group, without self-identity. The quest, then, is to find the communal ties. Our inactivity and our submission to the man prevents that from happening. Yet, though the man is rich, his greed and intolerance have alienated him, seen in the loss of his shadow (poem 4), while the shadow of the Chicanos' ancestors protects them. The key to the struggle is "to will our [still authentic] manhood into eternity / to perpetuate / and live for ever / in our LIBERTAD" (poem 3). That is to say, activate ourselves into what we know we are. "We have to Raza / nuestra voluntad" (poem 7), again drops the comma, verbalizing the noun. *Raza* = to realize, to activate. *Raza* becomes the praxis of its own logos.

The book accumulates Chicano cultural images, especially the barrio's, caught in instants which manifest their cosmic significance in the quest. In the collection's center, the poet announces the birth of la Raza to its rightful place, the sun, the fearless life source. This is particularly significant in that the sun has been portrayed ambiguously as the Chcianos' oppressor when he works for the man or feels trapped in the barrio, but also as his mythical heritage. Now the future is born to clarify the image.

The dialectic with the man is constant, but after the birth of the Raza and the centering of the cosmos, Alurista strikes his distinguishing chord: a colorful, multihued identity symbolized as "el sarape de mi personalidad" (poem 10). This affirmation leads to the birth of the future in the center of the present—the center of the text and of the solar system—which in turn produces the security of-and-within the affirmation. They feed off of each other. Yet Alurista knows the danger of arrogance, for it has dehumanized the man, so he insists on the sarape's multiracial substance, including the Anglo. In "other in the quilt" (poem 61), he insists on, not superiority to the Anglo American, but equality. This is humanity as tolerance, but only possible after the affirmation produced by a process of activation of la Raza as self-awareness ⟶ self-assuredness ⟶ unselfish human praxis. The acceptance of the man, however, does not change him, and as the book ends the Raza is defying the man's complaints, celebrating life in frenzied movement to the accompaniment of mariachi music. The collection's last verses restate both threat and response: death is negated and responded to by affirmed life. The end echoes the start, responding to the initial question of when? *When* truly becomes the book's now. Alurista offers a programmed survival manual in response to disappearance which could result from apathy and oppression, both perpetuated by fear. His is a courageously open and human dream of survival.

The first prose example reemphasizes that not always are the conserved images positive. Chaos can overtake the characters, as in "To a Dead Lowrider," but even those images partake of continuity, and their contemplation serves a positive purpose. A prime example is "A Rosary for Doña Marina," Octavio Romano's story about family dissolution and the protagonist's self-inflicted loneliness. Images of destruction and death are sharply etched by Doña Marina's ritualized hand movements, essentially repeated, though specifically varied, as when gutting fish (mirrored metaphorically in the abortionist's hands to which she delivers her niece), cooking, tearing the heart out of a shattered watermelon, chopping up her cousin's bed or snipping his image from old photographs, and, of course, fingering her rosary. The story holds the separate images so they can reveal their singular significance: self-destruction. Beyond that, however, the story utilizes its space to transcend Marina's tragedy and save her, at least partially.

Upon realizing she has destroyed the family, Marina prays for the Virgin to see, hear and help her. Her prayers are answered, however, by the reader, who hears her story, sees the reasons for her suffering and helps her by reactivating the life images of her family. Marina lives in the reading. The *for* of the title and the small circles between segments assume special meaning: the story is the rosary; the circles, the beads; and readers pray it. Marina's hands, furthermore, mirror ours by analogy; her movements, ours. Our hand movements as we read the book—turning pages and perhaps running our fingers down the lines, extracting the heart of the material—are they not similar to those images irrevocably captured in the text? Do we not share Marina's potential for error and destruction? Doña Marina is sacrificed, and we, the spectators, touch our own vulnerable discontinuity held in the moment it manifests itself in epiphany, a sacred ritual of continuity, as Bataille and García Ponce have explained.

In *Memories of the Alhambra*, Nash Candelaria's aging protagonist, José Rafa, feels tradition slipping away and flees to Spain in search of his ancestry. He finds death instead. The threat in *Memories* is multiple. For José, his father's death, with which the novel opens, draws into question the deviation from New Mexican cultural norms he has permitted in his own family. This crisis provokes José's voyage to Spain. For Teresa, José's wife, his disappearance strips her of the life center she thought she dominated, won through constant struggle. For Joe, their son, José's flight forces him to emerge from his comfortable, middle-class, interethnic home and confront once again his father's family and all it implies. In each case the character has recourse to memory to explain their present situation. The flashbacks retrieve the images thrown into doubt by José's flight and eventual death. In the end the novel reconstitutes a family history as a unit, for better or worse, when it appears to be disintegrating. The response to the threat of chaos is clear. Once again, the family suffers fragmentation, but the text salvages it from disappearance.

Ron Arias created yet another old man facing imminent death in *The Road to Tamazunchale*. Fausto, after passively waiting at home for six years to die, suddenly decides death should be an active adventure and sets out to create his. Fantasy images are played off against the reader's tendency to set reference points of reality. Fausto's imaginary world is juxtaposed to the "real existence" of his niece Carmela, as in the opening scene, when Fausto offers her his flayed and folded skin in the palm of his hand, and she asks him if he wants more Kleenex. Yet careful reading uncovers, at the level of language, the overlapping of reality and imagination—both characters refer to "tissue." Skin and Kleenex metonymically fuse in shared synonym, giving us fair warning that not all is as clear-cut as it appears on the surface. As the novel progresses the reality pole is undermined time and again. If Carmela represents the real world, as do also her boyfriend and Fausto's friend Mario, than how can Mario steal the boyfriend's car that really does not exist, a 1957 Impala.[11] How can Mario converse with Fausto's dead wife? The examples are many, and the answer is that all of them are characters in a novel. Of course! How simple. Yes, but the author is Fausto, the book-salesman, who, too weak to leave his home, ventures back into active life through his most familiar spaces, books and memories, which he mixes freely. Fausto's response to disabling illness and pending death is to construct an account of his last days as if it were a novel; literature from literature, with a dash of reality—although in the memory there is no real difference. This explains and justifies the many obvious literary allusions employed. At the point of death, when no future is possible, only the past can serve as substance and goal, and Fausto's past was selling books in his barrio and coming home to his wife and niece. How fitting that his death be a lived, written novel, composed of those elements.

With *Tamazunchale* we move to a group of novels in which the protagonist's experience is an apprenticeship to writing, and the text is the proof of the lesson well learned. The group includes *Pocho*, by José Antonio Villarreal, ... *y no se lo tragó la tierra*, Tomás Rivera, and Rudy Anaya's *Bless Me, Ultima*. I have analyzed *Pocho* at length elsewhere ("Pocho as Literature"), so here I will concentrate on the other two.

... *y no se lo tragó la tierra* is a novel-like narrative composed of fourteen short narratives and thirteen vignettes. The apparently disjointed structure reflects the protagonist's chaotic disorientation in the first story, which also introduces elements of his conflict.

> Aquel año se le perdió ... se le perdían las palabras ... empezaba con un sueño donde despertaba de pronto y luego se daba cuenta de que realmente estaba dormido ... Siempre empezaba todo cuando oía que alguien lo llamaba por su nombre ... y luego hasta se le olvidaba el nombre que le habían llamado. Pero sabía que él era a quien llamaban ... Se dio cuenta de que él mismo se había llamado. Y así empezó el año perdido.
>
> Trataba de acertar cuándo había empezado aquel tiempo que había llegado a llamar año. Se dio cuenta de que siempre pensaba que pensaba y de allí no podía salir. Luego se ponía a pensar en que nunca pensaba y era cuando se le volvía todo blanco y se quedaba dormido. Pero antes de dormirse veía y oía muchas cosas ... (1)

Chronological and visual perspective are confused, undermining reason and shaking his sense of identity and place. Fear results. Chaos centers on the loss of a year, which is then disassociated from its temporal definition and tied to language. Insanity seems imminent. Only the discovery of literary space will save him.

The stories and vignettes relate a series of experiences, fraught with fear and danger, in which death and oppression constantly threaten. Realizing life's ephemeral quality, the boy undertakes a series of negations of socio-religious beliefs. We might expect this to release him from fear, but in the last story the boy is again hiding from the world. Fear that a teacher will beat him for not knowing words—the keys to identity and the ability to structure the world into meaningful order—has driven him under a house, where he recalls fragments of incidents we have already read. He wants to save the people from dispersion and does so through recall. When he emerges from under the house, his disorientation has dissipated, because he has discovered the process of creative memory:

> ... se dio cuenta de que en realidad no había perdido nada. Había *encontrado. Encontrar* y *reencontrar* y *juntar. Relacionar* esto con esto, eso con aquello, todo con todo ... Eso era todo. Y le dio más gusto. Luego cuando llegó a casa se fue al árbol que estaba en el solar. Se subió. En el horizonte encontró una palma y se *imaginó* que ahí estaba alguien trepado viéndolo a él. Y hasta levantó el brazo y lo movió para atrás y para adelante para que viera que él sabía que estaba allí. (169, emphasis mine).

Life images need not be lost, and more, they can be ordered into meaningful form.

When the boy makes this discovery, the images and words are still in his imagination, but if left there they will fade again behind the opaqueness of everyday life. That is the meaning of his statement: "apenas estando uno solo puede juntar a todos " (169). In order not to lose them again he must fix them outside time and the mind: in art. The projection of the self image as the Other in the last scene—a counterbalance to the voice calling him in the first story—proves he has learned the lesson, because it is essentially the artist projecting images outside himself, with which he interacts, establishing his own place and meaning in the world. It is his first creative act after discovering the unifying process of organizing ideas into coherently related images.

The ultimate proof of the boy's apprenticeship as artist, however, is the novel itself, with its written, logical texture, not at all like flow of consciousness—though analysis will show that the segments link and flow through a system of repeated themes and motifs. Yet the text affirms itself as written because the boy is the author. I repeat, as I have many times over the last years, that this is not a naive nor gratuitous game of asserting the autobiographicalness of the novel; it is the serious game of asserting literature's reality. The need to display the loose images in a coherent manner, relating and unifying them, is thematically central to the work. Readers are essential to the creation of the space, their glance activating the total image. The text must be written to achieve the boy's goal of gathering the people together in one place. Besides, the utilization of words proves his victory over fear, while insuring against the nihilism resulting from his negation of religious order. Thus the necessity of writing the novel is obvious, the literary act being central to the success of the plot.

Bless Me, Ultima narrates Antonio's apprenticeship to writing at the side of a curandera. During the two years covered by the novel, Antonio stands between childhood and the rational world of the adult, the fulcrum of their opposition. Antonio perceives his world as divided into opposing factions: his father's roaming, plainsmen Mares family vs. his mother's stable, farming Lunas; day vs. night; doubt vs. understanding; good vs. evil; death vs. life; Catholicism vs. the naturalistic belief in the Golden Carp. The underlying conflict seems to pit linear against cyclical time, and in its center we find Antonio, seeking understanding and fearful of isolation. To his side steps Ultima to guide him safely through.

During one of Antonio's frequent prophetic dreams, the conflict assumes the aspect of a "cosmic struggle of the two forces [water vs. land, Mares vs. Lunas, etc.] would destroy everything!" (113). Ultima appears to dispel the chaos, explaining that the elements are actually harmonious. "The waters are one, Antonio ... You have been seeing only parts ... and not looking beyond into the great cycle that binds us all" (113). Near the novel's end, Antonio experiences the same revelation in a conscious state while watching the Golden Carp. "Questions and worries evaporated, and I remained transfixed, caught and caressed by the essential elements of sky and earth and water. The sun warmed us with its life giving power, and up in the sky a white moon smiled on us" (227).

The path to continuity is difficult, however, and Antonio must survive encounters with evil, witchcraft, murders and family disintegration. One goal guides him: understanding, promised by two social agencies, church and school. Yet neither seems to satisfy him, though he does learn the magic of letters in school. Unfortunately, the promise of infused knowledge to be gained with First Holy Communion overshadows his progress in reading, but it leads to disappointment. This, in turn, decides him in favor of the cyclical order of the Carp, forgetting Ultima's admonition against such dichotomies. Antonio will have to learn again her lesson that the world is one, harmonious unit.

The acceptance of the natural union of forces is symbolized by Antonio's father's repairing of the windmill, a circular object being torn apart by the linear winds. Repaired, the windmill harmonizes with the wind for the good of man and nature. The importance of his act is heightened by its narrative position directly after the scene in which the older brothers decide to leave and dash the father's hopes. He faces chaos by restoring order: even though the menacing chaos of his sons' departure cannot be changed, the windmill over which he has some control can be brought into harmony with nature. Antonio, too, will face the same menace in the form of death, and his response is the same, although applied to other elements.

As the novel draws to a close, the hierarchical order Antonio structures around Ultima is obliterated by her death. From some time in the future, Antonio the narrator recalls the murder with a powerful, disturbing image of fragmentation: "That shot destroyed the quiet, moonlit peace of the hill, and it shattered my childhood into a thousand fragments that long ago stopped falling and are now dusty relics gathered in distant memories" (245). Thus the novel seems to end on a note of discontinuity, after advocating continuity. But this is really the start of the story of the writing of the novel, and it is there where Antonio realizes his destiny.

Ultima's death stirs in the reader's memory—another case of literary simultaneity—Antonio's promise to her at their first meeting: "You will never die Ultima ... I will take care of you" (11). Between the promise and Ultima's death, which frame the narrative, Ultima teaches

Antonio the harmony of all things. When he is unable to prevent her
death, however, his childhood shatters, opening a gulf between apprentice and mentor, producing the need to find a way to keep his promise
and affirm the truth of her teaching. It is as if Ultima's death were part
of a final test of Antonio's dedication.

To return to childhood is impossible, so Antonio goes forward to
the point where he sees his childhood as a unit of past time, albeit fragmented. From that perspective he starts to utilize the tools—pen and
paper—he had chosen as a baby when offered objects of destiny, re-
trieving the fragmented images from where they lie and placing them in
order around Ultima's presence, yes, but without eliminating the conflict. He has learned that it all has a legitimate place, so he tells it all,
taking the center for himself. As when the world centered in him as a
child, it does so again in the world's representation, the language of the
narrative. With faith in the truth of his apprenticeship, he begins writing, knowing that harmony will result. The space he opens is analogous
to the one Ultima taught him to see, and in reality they are identical,
for the novel is essentially a lesson in reading. Antonio must learn to
see beyond linear façades and divisive circles to the great cycle encompassing both, and more: she taught him to see the world as one image,
a poetic way of reading reality. It is then that we understand the many
misreadings of events in the action as well as the use of irony which
leads us to misread, until the final misreading, when Antonio thinks
that his childhood still lies in "dusty relics gathered in distant memories." Antonio-the-writer, who sincerely makes that statement, must go
a step further and become Antonio-the-reader to understand that his
childhood is no longer distant nor fragmented, but quite near at hand,
only a reading away.

Antonio becomes a reader, but so do we, and in that moment Ultima
teaches us the sacred act of reading carefully, totally, beyond discontinuity. Yet it is in Antonio's language that she appears, and we realize
that the oral tradition has sought the printed page once again, utilizing
Antonio's pen to convey its voice. The lessons traditionally learned at
the old peoples' side are now preserved in literature's permanent space,
perhaps because in the outside reality lurks the danger of their silence.
And it is then that we correct yet another misreading: Antonio has become more than a writer, he is the conveyor of tradition, the curandero
of his people with old medicine in a new bottle, the faithful apprentice
to Ultima and a blessing to his people.

My last example is perhaps the most difficult to treat: John Rechy,
author of six controversial novels at the time of this writing, among
them, *City of Night* (1964), *Numbers* (1967), and *The Sexual Outlaw*
(1977). Rechy writes about the gay hustler and a world of chaotic, mul-

tiple, chance encounters, continual movement, and the constant threats
of momentary rejection, police and social repression, violence of all
sorts, and relentless aging. Alternatives promising more peaceful, secure life, such as monogamous relationships, marriage, going straight,
are considered, but his protagonists reject them as mediocre existence
of low intensity. They opt for the danger and excitement of the sex hunt.
This choice to remain in what to outsiders appears a chaotic, senseless
life is disturbing for the average reader, but one must remember that its
rewards in the realm of intensity are presented in the texts as superior,
and, therefore, worth whatever "sacrifice" required. (In this, Rechy's
gay world reflects the Chicano minority world, which is also considered
by outsiders an anachronic enclave of stubborn holdouts.) Yet it is undeniable that the characters often yearn for a sense of permanence and
place, a secure identity, and, ultimately, an understanding of the meaning of their life in the face of the constant danger of negation and exclusion. For the majority of characters, there seems little hope, but, as we
might expect by now, for the protagonist-narrator there is the response
of the text.

City of Night starts with a statement written from the perspective of
the completed experience to be related in the novel.

> Later I would think of America as one vast City of Night stretching
> gaudily from Times Square to Hollywood Boulevard —jukebox-winking,
> rock-n-roll moaning: America at night fusing its darkcities into the un-
> mistakable shape of loneliness. (11)

This perspective recalls the boy's at the end of ... *y no se lo tragó
la tierra*, or Antonio-the-reader's as we imagine him reading the novel,
or Montoya's at the end of "El Louie," or our own in the presence of
the complete image of these works. The artist holds chaotic reality, for
himself and us, in the ordered image, allowing meaning, ungraspable
during the fleeting experience, to be apprehended. Only in the rescued, structured and visible offering of those images—the aesthetic object aesthetically experienced—does contingent reality reveal its meaning. This does not mean that life should become just books, and Rechy's
work ironically draws the distinction between those who give themselves
completely to life and the writer who withdraws at times. What it means
is that art is necessary.

As others we have seen, Rechy knows literature is a response, but
not an escape. He refuses to ameliorate the image; life takes the "shape
of loneliness." Revealed meaning may be itself a threat to so-called stability. On this Rechy is most disturbing for readers. As all outstanding
eroticists, he advocates a surrender to the most intense areas of experience, where the rational order dissolves into impersonal, uncontrolled

exerience itself, but without ignoring the danger it implies to mind, body and identity. Johnny Rio, of *Numbers*, invents a game to justify hustling by rationalizing a structure for what seems chaotic:

> Having limited the anarchy by choosing 30 as the symbol of his triumph ... He was battling against chaos, and all that matters is that a symbolic "reason" has again emerged to save him from disintegration. Now that the game has a winning score, the horror of counting toward no limit ... is actually gone. (191)

Rechy's world again reflects the human condition. Arbitrary structures—religion, political movements, cultural tradition—respond to chaos, but carry with them limitations which, though providing peace of mind, sooner or later restrict even their creators, or crumble on their arbitrary foundations. When Johnny returns to the hunt after reaching the limit, "his mind flails anxiously awaiting that 'reason' to rescue him from the edge of chaos and surrender" (244), but it does not materialize, because no reason exists outside life itself in all its dangerous intensity. Exterior absolutes long ago fell from the sky.

Yet Rechy does more than simply disappear headlong into experience; he writes (perhaps another form of surrender), and in his writing the apparent chaos is revealed as hidden, highly structured, complex and at times beautiful order—reflected in the novels' skillfully achieved design and the intricate choreography of the action, especially the hunt scenes—and the real threat to the characters lies in possible expulsion from that life. His protagonists alternate between total immersion and aesthetic recreation from a distance, a movement itself reflective of life as movement seeking to preserve and contemplate its own flow without stopping it, life as subject-object, as life-death. This movement produces the first person narrative of *City of Night*, with it underlying bad faith of the withdrawn observer-participant, and the swing to third person in *Numbers*, with its affirmation of total surrender. Neither is final, because though Rechy is the hustler, he is also the writer, and his authenticity can only be found in the harmonizing of his own image.

Rechy, the writer-character, is threatened by the discontinuity rending his own image. The novels attempt to respond, but only in his latest book does the form capture the reality he seeks. In *The Sexual Outlaw* perspective shifts from third to first person in rhythmic flow, the observer becoming the object of his glance, the actor becoming the camera. In the text the image manifests its discontinuous dichotomy; in the reading it activates into movement; in the total image which is the novel, which is *The Sexual Outlaw*, the discontinous poles fuse into the image of the outlaw—in society, a hustler, and among hustlers, the potential writer. The space of that image is the literary creation called Rechy.

Rechy is the extreme writer of Chicano literary space, but, paradoxically, at the very center of the issue, not only because his works employ the deep paradigm, nor because thematically they respond to disintegration, albeit in their own way, but because he raises questions seemly implicit in many of the others. His works deny the validity of limiting, simplistic answers to life, stripping the façade from social structures to show their arbitrariness and the vulnerability of their participants. He includes the structures of his own minority, and, by extension, those of others. Does literature reflect a stable order outside of itself, therefore serving the secondary function of exemplifying *a priori* absolutes? Or is it an independent order itself, part of life, but not subservient, whose function is not to maintain arbitrary orders but to undermine them for the freedom of man, a freeedom perhaps fearful, on the surface chaotic, but with its own order? He questions the reality of so-called reality and the validity of old structures in modern life. Yet he rescues images in literature because his faith is in the writing process; ultimately this is the sole structure a writer can offer readers. What these questions mean to Chicano literature is for us to explore in the future, but they can not be ignored, as Rechy can no longer be ignored. He throws the gauntlet into the center of our literary ponderings, and its presence radiates disquieting, though—personally—welcome, vibrations through the ranks of the quest: "Because within the hunt is the core of the mystery. The search is the end. Not the answer—the riddle. The ultimate life-hunt, without object. Everything is found in nothing" (Rechy, *Sexual*, 300).

As an extreme, Rechy somehow proves the norm. Chicano literature is a response to chaos, but at its best it rejects limitations, perversely working from and returning to the space of nothingness, for *only from nothing are there infinite possibilities—all simultaneously possible. Only in nothing can you find everything.*

The Chicano Literary World 1974 (Las Vegas: New Mexico Highlands University, 1975): 22-51; revised for Canto al Pueblo, Corpus Christi, 1978.

10 Charting the Space of Chicano Literature

One of the outstanding characteristics of traditional societies is the opposition that they assume between their inhabited territory and the unknown and indeterminate space that surrounds it. The former is the world (more precisely, our world), the cosmos; everything outside it is no longer a cosmos but a sort of "other world," a foreign, chaotic space, peopled by ghost, demons, "foreigners" . . .

Mircea Eliade, *The Sacred and the Profane*

Chicano literature is an ordering response to the chaos which threatens to devastate the descendants of Mexicans who now reside in the U.S.A. The space this response opens is an alternative to both Mexican as well as U.S. spaces, while at the same time being a synthesis of those two zones that border it. However, the creation of this new space requires that its center be fixed "here" among us, and for that reason, despite the synthesizing process, there is a continual charting action to mark clearly separation and differences. I need not repeat here the similarities between this aspect of Chicano literature and Mircea Eliade's concept of the sacred. Suffice it to say that the literature functions as a ritual capable of cosmicizing the space inhabited by Chicanos in the midst of what for us can assume the aspect of chaos—U.S. culture—despite its appearance of order. Chicano literature charts a territory for the faithful, for its own, a territory in which the faithful find the meaning and reason for their existence. Like a circle in perpetual expansion, this territory grows with each work; like an organic cosmos, it has a dynamic order which readjusts itself with each new creation. Without denying the volatility of Chicano literary space, which can easily render obsolete any attempt to map its topography, I offer here some transcending motifs, keys to understanding its nature.

From the start there was an acknowledgment of the need to retreat from an inherently repressive social milieu. The two protagonists of the novel *Pocho* (1959) in the end must withdraw from U.S. society, to which their family has been assimilating over its twenty years of residency in California. The goal of both is personal integrity. Juan Rubio, the father, abandons his family to live with a young girl who recently has arrived from Mexico. Through this personal subterfuge he returns to the Mexico of his machista customs and to his lost youth, all without returning physically to Mexico. His wife has come to represent the U.S. customs that degrade Juan's self-concept as a Mexican man. At the same time, Richard Rubio, Juan's son born in the U.S.A., feels that his mother forces him to become responsible for the family in, ironically, a very Mexican fashion, and he abandons it to escape the repression of both U.S. and Mexican traditional values in his environment. Richard delivers himself to war's chaos to feel alive through the danger of death and to be able to write the text about his life. In *City of Night* (1963) the narrator protagonist repeatedly flees from work in order to reenter the intense life of the homosexual hustler. The author, John Rechy, brands not just U.S. society as repressive, but all societies. Yet in the end, Rechy, too, advocates a momentary retreat from street turmoil in search of repose in which the Apollonian author replaces the Dyonisian hustler. The Teatro Campesino's first Actos denounced the farm owners and proposed that the workers' pull out of the fields and into the union, itself a type of protective circle.

With the advent of the Chicano political movement, these withdrawals became a return to the popular traditions—almost always Mexican traditions preserved by the old people, but unknown to the young. *I Am Joaquín* (1967) set the standard during those first movement years. To save himself from the chaos of U.S. society, Joaquín withdraws "to the safety within the circle of life—Mi Raza" (13). Although the poem's voice tries to speak for all Chicanos, it obviously favors the parents when it declares that the children are disappearing "behind the shroud of mediocrity" (83). This fearful possibility produces the didacticism of so much of Chicano literature: "My children . . . must know who I am" (83); Joaquín's words could stand as the epigraph to many works that appear during that period and even still today. Joaquín insists that Chicanos have participated in U.S. history uselessly, and that the only response can be a withdrawal, like in the poem itself. That is to say, *I Am Joaquín* returns to history to find that corridos contain the necessary traditions of survival, that they are oral history generalized and aestheticized through music and the retelling by the anonymous people. The poem itself imitates the corridos, and succeeds in capturing an oral version of history. However, although it might seem a return to Mexicanness, the author carefully distinguishes—draws a line between—the Mexicanness of Mexico and that which is "ours" on this side of the border. As I have shown in *Chicano Poetry*, during the first historical flashback in *Joaquín* there is a pause in which woman appears in an ahistorical manner, with a mythical presence that fixes her outside time. This pause separates Mexican from Chicano heroes, while simultaneously linking them through the same woman's maternal quality (57-58). Like Juan Rubio in *Pocho*, Joaquín returns to Mexicanness in the U.S.A., which implies—despite the poem's highly exclusionary (read racist) attitude and separatist ideology—a new synthesis, a Chicano reality formed from and in continual contact with Anglo Americans.

The withdrawal to the circle is a cosmicization ritual, or at least its necessary start. Once out of chaos, people can begin to order the world to suit themselves according to their own traditions. To achieve this, Chicanos find history indispensable. It must be learned and repeated, preferably out loud, but if that is not possible, then in print. From the start it is understood that to make the world meaningful we must name it from our perspective. To do that we must find the storehouses of oral history. *I Am Joaquín* chose the corridos; other works look in other directions.

That the young no longer listen to their elders and so do not know the oral tradition also worries Miguel Méndez. In "Tata Casehua" he condemns the young, attributing to them the white man's blue eyes; but he criticizes the adults more severely for living in isolation, without forming a true community (*Peregrinos de Aztlán*). Méndez posits a withdrawal to the voice of the ancient ones who await, forgotten in the silence. He declares himself the people's servant and guide, a Chicano Virgil utilizing the word to transform the desert Sahuaro trees into exemplary statues from the history, mythology and literature that are the legitimate, although unknown, Chicano inheritance (*Los criaderos humanos*). To deserve the role of guide, the protagonist of *Los criaderos humanos* retreats from the world to make a pilgrimage to the mythological world where he witnesses the revelation of the causes of social chaos. As a guide enlightened by poetic vision, he can save us the suffering of the pilgrimage and lead us directly to our tradition. That is, the visionary poet substitutes a more positive retreat. The goal of Méndez's readers' withdrawal should be the founding of the nation of Aztlán, independent of both the U.S.A. and Mexico—a country which itself would be one more retreat from present repression.

Alurista declares the need to escape from capitalism. *Floricanto en Aztlán*'s opening situation is that of the Chicano family exploited and bled by capitalist work. Alurista proposes to rescue pre-Columbian mythology, Mexican history and the barrio, zones in which Chicanos supposedly can develop freely in the present. Oral tradition for Alurista, however, signifies much more than what the people commonly know. He includes in it his idiosyncratic version of Nahuatl philosophy, Carlos Castañeda's pseudo-anthropology, and music in all its forms, from jazz to classical. Of course, Alurista has had to extract those elements from books and records, but in this Alurista's poetry reveals its didactic function—literature researches the sources of a new oral tradition. In the last analysis, literature itself is both the space to which one withraws and, simultaneously, the voice of the cosmic ritual. Moreover, Alurista, unlike Gonzales and Méndez, sides with the young and trusts in the affirmation of a new sysnthesis. To a rigidly Mexican past, Alurista opposes an openly third-worldist future: "La esencia de mi Raza es fundamental / basic / to the chromatic wheel of humanity / free to compound in secondary colores / retaining the basic texture / our woolen skin of color bronze" (poem 10). But first, he would explain, the people must define themselves as free Chicanos. In existential fashion, they must come to a conscious understanding of who and where they are, and that requires a withdrawal from capitalist society.

The boy protagonist of ... *y no se lo tragó la tierra* flees from school to hide beneath a house. The social and familial world is chaotic, and he does not understand why. He constantly finds himself suspended between rejection by the Anglo American system and the impossibility of accepting Mexican superstitions and rigidity. Compounding his confusion, his family always pushes him towards the Anglo American choice. Beneath the house, withdrawn from society, he can think, organize his experience and affirm himself as the center of a new order, projected through the creative word arising from the people and directed back to them. This word expresses the child's intercultural state in that it negates the inacceptable extremes and affirms the synthesis process. Only the retreat to a solitary place makes it possible. Rolando Hinojosa is less explicit, but in his first three books we begin to realize that the narrative voice has assumed a distant perspective explained by the fact that some of the characters went to the Korean War. These young men, like Rafa, have the patience and desire to listen to the old men. Hinojosa's books are testments of a generation about to disappear; and the books become substitutes for them, awaiting future generations in search of themselves.

In "Homing" Ricardo Sánchez recalls his home in the barrio, setting of the evocation of a a series of images of the Chicano world as a space between two countries. By the end we see that Mexico and the U.S.A. form a plot to wipe out his native, inbetween country (1976, 144-148). Yet Sánchez shows that the true familial space is the love of relatives, which changes any house into a home, and that national space is the friendship among people committed to revolution and to publication as a revolutionary act. Thus, one can retreat from chaos to create a space beyond the reach of national powers.

Sergio Elizondo observes that young Chicanos are obsessed with everything Anglo American, creating of it a false center for the world. Elizondo writes *Perros y antiperros* in order to orient us with respect to the history of the fragmentation of the U.S. Southwest at the hands of the Anglo Americans, aided by Mexicans. His poems seek to set off clearly the ethnic spheres, marking the differences and, finally, locating Chicanos in their proper space somewhere at a distance. Significantly, he denounces the purely Mexican in several poems ("Buenos hijos de la Malinche," "Machismo, chismo, chismo," "Del Nueces al Bravo," "Sueño"). Chicanismo will unite the best of the Mexican spirit with the historic and on-going experience in the U.S.A, tempered in the continual conflict—contact—with the Anglo American. To achieve the goal Elizondo goes to history, then pours it into lyrical images in popular rhythms. The result is the stylized, but always authentic, voice of the people.

Tino Villanueva points out the need to pause—the second section of *Hay otra voz poems* is titled "Pausas de ayer y hoy"—which equals a withdrawal from the personal and social nature of the first section, "Por ejemplo, las intimidades." The pause makes possible the introspection that produces the poet's declaration of himself as the voice of "Mi raza," the title of the book's last section. The works of these authors, like that of many others, are, as Villanueva says, the "other voice" of the people, silent in the past, but which now wants to speak. But before speaking, it must first withdraw from chaos and chart its own space, a space where Chicano silence can reveal itself an eloquent voice, and where Chicanos themselves can learn to listen and learn.

Perhaps by now readers may be asking themselves if this withdrawal from the social setting is justified. In the "Introduction" to *Chicano Authors, Inquiry by Interview* I outlined the oppression suffered by Chicanos in their dealings with courts, police and even organized religions (24-27). The history of that experience can explain Chicanos' aversion to social participation and the tendency to retreat to alternative spaces. Below I will add a few other areas of the same confrontation.

Like other minority groups, Chicanos have dreamed of taking advantage of the undeniably superior benefits of the U.S. education system (in comparison to the Mexican system). Juan Rubio (*Pocho*) wants his son to study, so he refuses to take him out of school to follow the harvests. In ... *y no se lo tragó la tierra* the children have to study to better themselves, and the elders convey to them a respect for teachers as their second parents. The mother in Nash Candelaria's *Memories of the Alhambra* insists that her son graduate from the university, although her husband doesn't agree; she even gets a job to help him with tuition, once again defying her mate's will. Inés Tovar's grandparents "cut out honor roll lists whenever their nietos' names appeared." Antonio's mother (*Bless Me, Ultima*) trusts that school will convert her son into a leader of his people. Tino Villanueva summarizes well this general trusting and hopeful attitude: "Estudia para que no seas burro como nosotros, our elders warn," and "Los niños en seventh-grade piden lápices con futuro" (39, 35).

However, rejection generally turns these illusions into disillusions. The same children in Villanueva's poems encounter "Maestros que ni ven, ni oyen, hay otra voz que quiere hablar" (37). One of The Teatro Campesino's actos is titled *No saco nada de la escuela*; and El Teatro de la Esperanza's masterpiece, *Guadalupe*, documents official racial prejudice in one California school district. Oscar Zeta Acosta recalls being prohibited from speaking Spanish during recess (1972, 187), a situation well known to many Chicanos, especially in Texas. The child from *tierra* is expelled for defending himself against a group of Anglo students who attack him solely because he is Mexican. Raúl Salinas tells us that in Austin all Mexicans were expelled for supposedly having head lice (56). In "Jesse" José Montoya reveals the paradox of the minority athlete who receives a university scholarship, but must not approach the attractive daughters of the Anglo American coaches (1972, 7). Ricardo Sánchez summarizes concisely the illusion/disillusion conflict: "I looked ... toward school authorities, and in return, they looked down at me" (1973, 151).

Traditionally, Chicanos disillusioned by education are offered the alternative of military service as a way of bettering themselves, and literature also deals with this topic. It, too, almost always ends equally in disillusion. *I Am Joaquín* shows that Chicanos have fought and died in U.S. wars without having won social equality. Sergio Elizondo says the same thing, emphasizing the case in Texas of Chicano Medal of Honor winners being refused burial in Anglo American cemeteries. Alurista denounces military service as genocide, a conspiracy to get the non-white races to exterminate each other. He insists that if we are to fight and die, it should be to defend the barrio and our own race from the enemies here in the U.S.A. (*Floricanto*, poem 97). The Teatro Campesino's *Soldado razo*, has the same message. In *Bless Me, Ultima* the war drives a Chicano crazy, which in turn leads him into a form of suicide by forcing the men of the community to kill him. In *tierra* military service becomes synonymous with "lost in action," a euphemism for death. In summary, with few exceptions, in Chicano literature military service signifies being duped and exploited.

The counterpart of military service is incarceration—the *pinto*, or convict, experience is a theme of major import in Chicano literature. Despite its apparent negativity, its significance is, however, paradoxical. Like school, prison signifies the rejection of the Chicano by society. Raúl Salinas and Tomás Rivera underscore the irony that school rejection can turn into acceptance by that other school known as reform or correctional school. The threat of jail is found in works as different as *Pocho, City of Night, I Am Joaquín, Estampas del Valle, Chicano, Canto y grito mi liberación, Floricanto en Aztlán,* "Aztec Angel," "Aquellos vatos," "To a Dead Lowrider," "El Louie," *The Road to Tamzunchale,* and more. The paradox stems from the fact that jail also is a form of retreat from the world—prisoners find themselves isolated from society, although in this case far from the family circle. In this situation, some prisoners resort to literature as a way of reintegrating into life: they recognize that society, even when it seems free and open, is also a prison. Jail produces an existential lucidity. This is the essential perspective of Ricardo Sánchez, whose work is replete with limits, barriers, threats that make life a continual struggle for survival (Bruce-Novoa, *Chicano Poetry,* 151-59). Salinas, in his "Trip," sees the barrio as another kind of jail; then after getting out of prison, realizes that freedom is an illusion. Pintos teach us a valuable lesson, learned during their forced retreat from the world: there is no sure escape from the threat of chaos, because every space is in danger, even that which we think of as our own.

This lesson reveals a disagreeable fact, but one impossible to dismiss: violence and instability predominate in Chicano life. We can further extrapolate another conclusion: the security of the ethnic circle stems, not from some utopian peace, but from the mere fact that it is "ours." In *Chicano Authors* (24-25) I pointed out that the Chicano family often appears in literature in the process of fragmentation. Clearly, our circle too often has been violent and destructive. Without repeating that previous exposition, we can list some works in which Chicanos oppress, atttack, or even kill each other. They include: "El Louie," "Aquellos vatos," "The Trip Through the Mind Jail," *Bless Me, Ultima, Restless Serpents, Heart of Aztlán, Estampas del valle, Generaciones y semblanzas, The Autobiography of a Brown Buffalo, The Revolt of the Cockroach People, Rain of Scorpions,* ... *y no se lo tragó la tierra, Canto y grito mi liberación, Caras viejas y vino nuevo, Memories of the Alhambra, The Militants, Los Vendidos, This Day's Death; Noches despertando inconciencias,* among many others. It should not surprise us, then, that *I Am Joaquín* proposes the bloody sacrifice of those brothers who choose not to side with militant nationalism. In terms of the pre-Columbian philosophy preferred by Chicano poets, *Joaquín*, as other Chicano works, is essentially Huitzilopochtlian in its ideology of fratricidal war for the benefit of the race.

In contrast, however, there are works that attempt to create a loving center, best exemplified by Sergio Elizondo. First came *Perros y antiperros*, a tribute to the loving family as the nucleus of the Chicano movement, and then some of the most beautiful love poems in Chicano literature in *Libro para batos y chavalas*. Bernice Zamora creates an image of the natural harmony and equilibrium possible between the sexes in "Anton Chico Bridge" (58), although it must be read in the context of the rest of *Restless Serpents*, which tends much more towards a feminist attack on male chauvinism—a well-deserved one, I might add. Ron Arias offers us an exemplary loving family in *The Road to Tamazunchale*, while Alurista tenders women equality: "in her arrogant walk to pace and have to run behind no more" (*Floricanto*, poema 41). Yet this is not, unfortunately, a dominant tendency in Chicano literature.

The above considerations about family, women, and love require the mention of the specific violence perpetrated on women: to this point in time, the image of women in our literature, still dominated mostly by male authors, is a lamentable tergiversation when it appears, which is altogether too infrequently. The general lack of female images is as lamentable as the distortion of it when it does surface. In *I Am Joaquin* the woman is portrayed in the traditional black shawl, passive, silent, man's witness and companion, the ahistorical storehouse of tradition. Much of the literature paints her in the same manner. Not even the curandera Ultima, admittedly a dynamic figure, belies this fact, because she is actually asexual, representing more her shamanistic function and the oral tradition. Ultima's own categories of women's social roles is not liberating: pretty ones serve men as wives or prostitutes, while ugly ones become witches, and nothing inbetween. Some poets, like Leonard Adame, Gary Soto, and Rafael Jesús González, have written tributes to grandmothers or old women, nostalgically idealizing them, but they still do not differ much from the stereotype in *Joaquín*.

Some Chicana writers counterpose more authentic images of women which, significantly, imply a withdrawal by women from the male circle, even when the males are Chicanos. Alma Villanueva revels in images of menstrual blood, and when a man sculpts her figure, she rejects it, despite its beauty, because "I can no longer be the woman who's been thoughtfully created by man" (36). She could be dialoguing directly with *Joaquin*. Lorna Dee Cervantes creates the image of an all-women family of three generations living together in which the youngest learns the valuable lesson of being able to love a man without depending on him for her own survival (*Emplumada*, 11-14). Estela Portillo's female characters repeatedly resist male domination, Chicano or Mexican, freeing themselves even if they have to abandon the family or break the law. Up to now, Bernice Zamora has offered the most developed treatment of the topic in *Restless Serpents*. She begins by analyzing a traditional male centering ritual, but infusing it with a feminist dialectic by showing that women were excluded from participation. She goes on to catalogue further exclusions and repression, while slowly building up an alternative female voice invested in the androgenous ritual of aesthetic creation. However, although these images are positive, they still are too few to successfully alter the general image of the women in Chicano literature. And until a much larger body of female generated self-imagery is produced, that general image will continue to be unacceptably false.

When Chicano authors have searched for heroes to populate their literary space, they have chosen the following archetypes: Pachucos, the Farm Worker, the Shaman and the writer himself. Through literature the Pachuco assumed the status of the first Chicano who openly withdrew from both the purely Mexican tradition as well as the assimilationist model of the Mexican American, while representing at the same time a new synthesis of cultures that can only be called Chicano. From "El Louie" (1970) by José Montoya to Luis Valdez' *Zoot Suit* (1978), the Pachuco presents a paradox of negative affirmation, of creative destructiveness, the admired model that also sparks aversion. And as with so many themes in Chicano literature, this motif can be found in *Pocho* (1959), when Richard Rubio feels drawn to the Pachucos, while acknowledging himself incapable of being completely one of them. Richard's attitude prefigures that of many Chicano authors: "Obessed with a hunger to learn about them [Pachucos] and from them" (149). Time and again the figure of the Pachuco will be invoked to teach a lesson about being Chicano, without, however, the negativity being ignored or glossed over in the best cases. Life and society destroy Montoya's Louie, true, but there was also something inherent in his character that contributed to that end.

The most interesting thing that emerges from these works is a dynamic process of converting the common and usual, the mundane and prosaic, into an aesthetic object of personal and cultural value—what Montoya calls "class." Pachucos conducted and dressed themselves with it, and, most significant for writers, they reveled in it in their speech. Chicano literature takes them as models, and poems like "El Louie" prove the vitality of their process when they approriate it for their own realization.

The migrant farm workers represent the cultural element that more than any other has maintained the provincial Mexican ideal, the customs rooted in the traditional rural life—or at least this is how they appear in many works. Through the efforts of The Teatro Campesino at the start of the political movement, the farm worker became the prototype of the Chicano committed to popular revolution. For a time many urban Chicanos indulged a nostalgia for a rural experience few of them had ever known—Chicano authenticity was exemplified by the farm worker. With time and other works, the farm worker's image has become more realistic. Although almost no one has noticed, in *Bless Me, Ultima* the Mares family, once free wanderers of the plains, are depicted as migrant farm workers whose travel is now dictated by the harvest seasons; they have become second class workers of the soil compared to the Lunas, who own their farm. To Tomás Rivera goes the credit for having sketched a just image of migrant farm workers as morally and physically strong people, with human values, but also with some traditional, repressive superstitions and customs—and most of all, the will and capacity to survive.

The enfasis on oral tradition and the need to withdraw to a more defined and secure space produces another exemplary character: the shaman, or elder with magical powers. The old Yaqui in Miguel Méndez' story "Tata Casehua" knows the tribe's true history. Silently in the desert, like a guru, he awaits his heir. When he arrives, Casehua submits him to trials before finally initiating him into the knowledge of the past, the mysteries of the desert. Ultima fulfills a similar function in *Bless Me, Ultima* for the young Antonio. Alurista creates the presence of an amorphous knowledge of the pre-Columbian past, a form of priestly voice within the voice of the poet himself, and that voice speaks to us as an ancient teacher. But in the final analysis, in all of these cases, the real hero is the author in the role of guide and/or curator of knowledge.

In *Chicano Authors* I pointed out that the theme of the author's apprenticeship was central in Chicano literature. Books like *Pocho, Bless Me, Ultima, ... y no se lo tragó la tierra, City of Night*, both of the Oscar Zeta Acosta autobiographic novels, *Canto y grito, Hay otra voz Poems, Restless Serpents*, and even *The Road to Tamazunchale* deal with the development of the writer. And since all of them also represent the response to the threat of chaos, we can understand how that response depends essentially on the writer's existence. Writers create the space where they can serve as observers and participants in life. They structure the cultural vision. When they chart a space for themselves and for their people, they officiate at the basic ritual of cosmicization of sacred space, the creation of the Chicano world. When a people finds itself in a diaspora, the warrior priests are the authentic heroes. Their words are the very action and material which chart and create the space of and for the literature.

It is important to state, however, that this space can only encompass words. That does not mean that it is less real than the life which we call, with blind security, *real life*, the one made up of matter and time. No, literary space is real, just as real, although in another way. Literary space is itself a withdrawal from physical life to the realm of images, a space set off from the contingent world by its permanent essence. That is why it can offer another alternative; that is why it can be the voice that awaits, with the treasure trove of traditions always present in an always present time. And that is why it is capable of serving as a cosmicizing ritual. The people come to literary space to retreat momentarily from the chaos that is profane life, be it Mexican or U.S. or whatever. By virtue of its otherness, literature is a withdrawal, a retreat, but, I repeat, not an escape. Readers always return to their material, contingent, social, dangerous life. Few have been trapped between the pages of a book. Yet, if they enter this space with an open attitude—if they read well—literary space can transform them, sending them back to the social world with a new vision and a capacity to change the world. The realization of change is the work of people, not literature, which must maintain its space. Its border is the page of a book, the words of a song, the edge of a screen. Readers extend the reach of that space and expand its influence when they fulfill themselves as the products of their reading in this life—and once again we become aware of the didactic nature of literature. Whether or not Chicano readers have taken Chicano literature's lessons into social praxis is a topic for sociologists or political scientists to discuss in their own forums. But undoubtedly, with respect to literature itself, the charting of its expanding space must go on.

Published in Spanish as "El deslinde del espacio literario chicano," *Aztlán* 11.2 (Fall 1980): 323-338.

11 Surviving Our Decade

When invited to address the plenary session of the 1987 National Chicano Studies Conference, I agreed immediately, then only later thought about the assigned task: to discuss the general topic, "Will Chicanos Survive Their Decade," from the perspective of my field of expertise, literature. From the outset, even before being invited to speak, I had felt that the topic was mis-stated. First it was based on a media concept, "The Decade of the Hispanic," with no choice on our part, so at once it becomes suspicious. Moreover, notwithstanding the obvious appeal of the rhetoric of crisis and apocalypse, few seriously doubt the Chicano people's survival past the 1980's into the last decade of the century. The real question, therefore, is more one of "how" than "will," less "whether" than "whither," with the appropriate corolary of what form the culture may assume in making the necessary adjustments in the day-to-day process of survival.

Although many of our colleagues in the supposedly more scientific disciplines accuse us in literature of practicing mystifying rituals, I willingly disclaim any special access to knowledge of the future. Humbly I can offer only limited observations of a more retrospective and contemporary nature and attempt to extrapolate what perhaps could be the extension into the future of some pattern of recent development. A final caveat: my comments certainly should be taken as a venture into the genre of essay, justified by the nature of the mandate under which I write, an essay based on my work in the general field of cultural production and the specific area of literature. Although I have opinions about the synecdochical validity of the observations for Chicano Studies itself, I leave specific application to the specialists in those fields other than mine. Yet if we can say that we have created a true intellectual discipline, then each part of it could be expected to reflect the rest in microcosmic fashion.

The common lament among veteran activists of the '60's and early '70's is that the Chicano Movement, if not completely dead, appears moribund. Things just aren't the same, we repeat. We miss the enthusiasm, the sense of direction and cohesiveness of the early years, and above all the feeling of creating something new, with the promise that those efforts would change society. In literature one often hears that the political message has disappeared from the recent works, or that there is no longer a firm ethnic base in what is being written today. However, although I plead quilty to lapsing into this Chicano version of '60's nostalgia, my sense is that these accusations should not be taken as statements of fact, but rather as symptoms of disappointment among those who would have liked to see us maintain the same spirit of those years, especially in the light of the depressing resurgence of many of the sociopolitical ills the Movement first attacked. The futility of that desire is obvious and needs no commentary. Yet it is time that we speak to those changes and try to understand them, if not in a positive light, at least in some pragmatic and even utilitarian way that can, thus, be applied to our situation in general.

We tend to date the changes in Chicano literature in the mid-seventies. Up to to that point it could be said we were in the period of idealistic figuration in which we desired to read ourselves in terms of A Movement, A Nation, with all the unity and coherence implied. Influenced strongly by the Black civil rights struggle, we attempted to imitate the pattern of community unity through racial and ethnic identity and opposition to the predominantly white social structure Blacks were successfully presenting to the country. It was then that we portrayed our activity as that of binary opposition—we versus they—in cosmic, heroic struggle. In this effort, literature was the supreme genre: "Stupid America" we yelled with Abelardo, "Yo Soy Joaquín" we entoned in deadly serious fashion, drawing the battle line clearly, forgetting that the true context of literature is the printed page, a space from and in which the complex pattern of real life can be simplified, edited to receed into the background like the weave of the paper fibers, necessary but invisible so as not to distract from the words, an illusion of the art of print communications.

Some historians and social scientists practiced a similar literary tactic in those early confrontational calls to guerrilla warfare against the colonizing enemy in our midst. Such works as the essays in *El Grito*, Camarillo and Castillo's *Furia y muerte: los bandidos chicanos*, and Acuña's *Occupied America* were thrilling, provocative texts. No one who read or heard them in in the heat of the Movement's first surge will forget the sense of unity and purpose, although few if any can remember agreeing on exactly what that unity was based on. It was a sticky question likely to produce debate, so it was more popular to end a rally with a poem to remind us of the clear-cut question of survival in the face of the enemy. This Manicheanism, of course, prepared us for the possibility of couching our present disappointment with less than full victory in the terms of a tragic fall and apocalytic menace. Epic heroes don't compromise, as colonized people should not give up resistance—they take to the hills and fight to the death.

The scenario, which I have used myself, is that around the mid-seventies the first group of writers seemed to reach a point of stasis, and, although we did not realize it at the time, the publishing house which deserves the credit for so much of the impetus of those early years, Quinto Sol, was passing into history, and along with it disappeared the centering function it served in Chicano intellectual circles. In theatre, however, Luis Valdez was anything but static, having already introduced the Mito, which can be taken as a move towards a more universal genre than the specific-problem oriented Acto. Yet even that move seemed to disorient many through its ambiguity, appeal to the spiritual, and apparent rejection of the Acto form, which in the late '60's had become synonymous with Chicano Theatre per se. At the same time, there began to appear new writers with different concerns, or at least different approaches to the old concerns. Chief among the signs of change we can put the following: the publication of women writers in significant numbers, depicting themselves and their preoccupations from a more independent perspective than many men, including Chicano publishers, were ready to accept fully. Simultaneously we began to read works by writers who down played the political content, while demanding greater attention to craft. In 1977 José Armas was shocked and angered by the young poet Orlando Ramírez's statement that you can say anything as long as you say it well. Ramírez would go on to win the Irvine prize for literature while Armas would fade slowly into oblivion.

If I can paraphrase what one of our leading historians told me in 1975, it was no longer enough to sympathize with the political cause and say the "right things," a writer had to develop the appropriate skills to be able to express well whatever had to be said. It is probably no coincidence that during those same years there began in earnest the debate over the literature within the field which is charged, rightly or wrongly, with judging the questions of quality, that of criticism; that is to say, we passed into a much more self-conscious phase in which not only was literature the object of more serious and systematic study, but also that same activity became itself the object of heated debate and study. I would add to this that shortly after there began to appear works by Chicanos that questioned those "right things."

All of these activities have in common a critical attitude with respect to what was being called Chicano literature at the time. One could call it a dialectical function, but, in the light of the general relativization of values that has been produced, Hayden White's term, "diatactical," is perhaps more appropriate. Each new work called into question the previous body of work, at least in the sense that through intertextual dialogue it demanded a reformulation of encompassing descriptions of the general field. Research into the characteristics of Chicano literature had the same effect. It became obvious that, just as in the political realm, there was no monolithic Chicano cultural production. Slowly, we also became aware of the naive assumptions we had made about ourselves. What should have been clear from the start was that any juxtapositioning of writers like Anaya, Villarreal, Rivera, Acosta, Valdez, Hinojosa, Villanueva, Portillo, Elizondo, Méndez, Alurista, Sánchez, Montoya and Gonzales—to name the early canonized figures, constituted an eloquent statement of the great variety of possibilities, ideological as well as formal, in Chicano literature. How much more apparent is this now, in the mid-eighties, with the addition of, for example, Sandra Cisneros, Ron Arias, Bernice Zamora, Gary Soto, Lorna Dee Cervantes, Alberto Ríos, Lucha Corpi, Laurence Gonzales, Cecile Pineda, Ernest Brawley, Sheila Ortiz Taylor, Cherrie Moraga, Arturo Islas, Jimmy Santiago Baca, etc.

What should have been obvious from the start, and what some of us tried to discuss from the edge, was the dialogical nature of Chicano literary space—an accurate reflection of the culture—even in the early period when so many still naively believed, still desperately insisted, our literature could be mimetically privileged and escape the rhetorical and tropic manipulations of discourse.[12] The mistake was in believing that our literature reflected reality, and then, logically, assuming that what was said in literature was somehow true. Well, yes, "somehow" it was, but not in terms of documentation. It was true in the sense of desire, of ideal, of utopian projection. That is why we turned to the space of literature where such ideals could be bracketed into independence and protected from the fragmenting discourse of life. And when the literature produced a pattern of discourse, in our enthusiam for the ideal, we read it superficially so as not to confront the questions it raised. By eliminating the facile political images that dominated works from the '60s, the new production is more difficult to read without considering its discursive nature, which in turn forces us to see the rest of our experience in the same terms. In this sense, the literature now being produced is much more realistic—if I can be permitted that dangerous abstraction—than the earlier writings. As a result, it is less pleasing to those who want to use literature as unequivocal exemplary writing. Ideologues do not want to cite a text that immediately provokes a dialogue about the validity of simplistic views of culture or life. Politicians do not want to end a rally with a poem that raises questions about the relativity of all texts, including speeches. And as more literature is produced, its dialogical nature becomes more and more apparent.

Not only has the bibliography expanded enormously by the appearance of new writers, but research has forced us to redefine the literature in terms of the past as well, adding numerous authors and works. In turn, this necessitates a rethinking of cultural definitions. In 1974, just before I first presented my concept of Chicano literary space in a forum outside of the classroom, I was told by the then foremost Chicano critic that I could not include John Rechy among Chicano writers. He was, I was informed in a whisper, a homosexual. Since then Rechy has been included in most of the comprehensive bibliographies of Chicano literature, while the critic has disappeared from the active circle of Chicano criticism. Another question raised by the work of several critics is how are we to incorporate into our view of ourselves the existence of a continually growing list of written materials from the past. For example, we have cultivated an image of ourselves as an oral culture cut off from the written expression of literature in Spanish. What, then, are we to do with the discovery of the pervasiveness in some Chicano urban and rural communities of newspapers, like *La Prensa*, *La Opinión* or *La Gaceta*, which published a continual stream of literary writing? It is not enough to dismiss them by claiming that they had no influence on the writing of today; we must begin to question what significance they had, and why, despite their presence and efforts, do they seem to have had so little influence. I might add in passing that at least in the case of Rolando Hinojosa, Tomás Rivera, and Américo Paredes, *La Prensa* probably did influence them in ways our critics have not yet begun to consider, much less understand. Of all this work, perhaps the most significant is Genaro Padilla's discovery of Chicano autobiographies from the nineteenth century. This opens a whole field of investigation in a genre we didn't know existed in our literature. We had always apologized for not having practiced this self-analytical art which since the early New England colonies has been a key genre among English writing Americans. Now we have it and that changes our self-image. However, it also infuses it with more problems for those nostalgic for the unitary voice. Padilla has found, among other things, the biography of a Chicano Texas Ranger. What bastion of the hated other can remain truly other when we have had even a *Rinche* among us? But extremes only reveal the commonplace in the center: we have always been a people of contradictions and synthesis.

In other words, Chicano literary space has expanded enormously over the last decade, becoming more problematic in the process. If anything, it has been forced, by writers and critics alike, to represent more faithfully the variety of experience in the wider Chicano community. The mere fact that our community now refuses to call itself Chicano, as we would wish, graphically demonstrates the discursive process at work. In the mid-seventies I noted that Chicano literary space lacked the perspectives of women and the middle class, a statement that could not be repeated today. Yet if we take into account the writing in the newspapers mentioned above, it was inaccurate even then, only possible due to the foreshortening of the objects within a naively delimited field of study many of us shared at the time. Certainly, with the presence of Richard Rodriguez and Nash Candelaria we now have strong voices of opposition to what we used to take for granted as a Chicano perspective, but somehow they really represent portions of our community which, whether we like it or not, we must take into consideration. They are neither solitary nor eccentric voices, but representative of the conflictive plurality within ourselves.

This realization—that our group is much more complex than what we thought back in the '60s and '70s—is at the heart of the great difference we complain about today. It is a challenge to us as observers and participants in cultural production to extend our vision to apprehend and comprehend the expanded space in equally comprehensive terms. We will survive in a more healthy fashion in direct correlation to our ability to incorporate these voices and to the ingenuity with which we mediate the polyvalent texts that will never let us conceive of ourselves as a monolithic We again.

This situation demands that we abandon the formulation of the space of our cultural production through the old dialectical rhetoric of simplistic opposition. Instead, I believe Chicano criticism is moving, sometimes in spite of itself, towards speaking more in terms of Hayden White's diatactical discourse—that is, one which is "as self-critical as it is critical of others ... [one which] will radically challenge the notion of the syntactical middle ground itself. It throws all 'tactical' rules into doubt, including those originally governing its own formation."[13] The effects of such a realization and the relativization of all absolutes, thrusts us into the ironic mode, which became apparent in the literature of the late '70s, and should have been part of our initial critical comprehension of the total space in dynamic tension. Certainly Oscar Zeta Acosta's satires were already practicing a severe debunking of the rhetorical positions, not only of mainstream society but of the Chicano Movement as well. Obviously there were intertextual battles over iconography and heroic figures. Can we forget the vicious battles over critical theory itself? All of this and more should have bespoken a debate about the proper tactical modalities for Chicano production.

Among the efforts of the younger group of writers appearing in the mid-seventies, as I have pointed out elsewhere, were two literary magazines, *Mango* and *Cambios Phideo*. Their unassuming titles, with their obvious and playful focus on food consumption as a cultural metaphor, symbolized their refusal to engage in the hyperbole of such earlier ventures like *Quinto Sol*, *Aztlán*, or *De Colores, A Journal of Raza Philosophy*. This reflected a turning away from the utopianism of the early Chicano Movement, a distancing from that rhetorical high ground, and a healthy questioning of both the tactics they represented as well as the reality of the achievements which had been realized. More and more, literature would come to reflect this attitude. Cynicism, perhaps, but a healthy one considering the state of modern life. Perhaps it is characteric of our post-modern situation, but it seems that at least for a while we are to be faced with a steady multiplication of voices that constitute a *de facto* rejection of hegemonic efforts, and a *de facto* appeal that culture be read, not in terms of a set of static characteristics from the past, but rather as a process of evolution towards a future.

If nothing else, I repeat that this is more realistic. I do not believe that we are less vital now as a culture, just less easily defined because we have been forced to accept that the great majority of our Chicano community does not conform to the program which relatively few participants in cultural production set out for us in the '60's. We may not like the willingness to assimilate or at least compromise that predominates in our community, but then we should look at ourselves and see just how much we have compromised in academia, and how much of our own work is essentially a product of U.S. society. Our cultural production makes no sense if lifted from the greater context of U.S. culture. Certainly it is not Mexican nor even Native American. I, for one, would have it no other way: I am still Chicano. And if we read the literature to draw lessons, instead of trying to dictate to the literature what it should be doing, we may find that survival means to accept what we are and make the best out of it. The Chicano Movement, like many of the dreams of the '60's may not survive, but the community, or better stated, our many communities certainly will. I just hope that we can keep up with them.

Previously unpublished

12 Canonical and Non-Canonical Texts

At the beginning of the contemporary Chicano literary movement, 1965-1975, any mention of a canon was clearly understood as a reference to mainstream literature, one which conveyed, to those of us involved in the somewhat romantic idealism of what seemed a revolutionary struggle, the image of the elitist Other, the body of works created by Anglo-American or European authors and sanctified by critics of the same class and cultural backgrounds. To state that we were excluded from the canon was to utter the obvious. Moreover, there was an ironic sense of worth associated with being outside the canon, almost a feeling of purity, because beyond the exclusionary ethnocentrism implied by *The Canon*, Chicanos infused the term with a criticism of the very existence of a privileged body of texts. Something in the process of selecting and eliminating works to create a superior core of definitive texts seemed less than egalitarian in a movement professing egalitarian ideals. Also, to those of us who were searching for any text we could call Chicano, the idea of excluding some appeared to be a luxury far down the road. And now, after having traveled what in terms of literary history is a short distance down any road, I presume to speak to you about the canon of the Chicano novel.

The fact is, however, that from the start Chicano literature has been subjected to a canonizing process, in all the basic denotations of the term. And Chicanos have been a party to that process, most likely the primary molders of it. First and foremost was the already mentioned need to find works by Chicanos, materials we could read, discuss, and, a matter of no little concern, compare to the other minority groups involved in similar projects. This comparative effort explains, in part, why, at a time when the number of works one would have found listed in a

Chicano bibliography was miniscule, our then leading critic, Philip Ortego, coined the expression *Chicano Renaissance*. Not only was this an obvious imitation of Harlem Renaissance, but also a reference to a line of supposed renaissances extending back to the elite category of European Renaissance. I do not mean to open up yet again the fruitless discussion of the virtues and vices of Philip Ortego's term, but only to show that we ourselves were involved early on in the canon game, even to the extent of hyberbolizing the small amount of writing we actually had.

That the emphasis, during the first years of the Chicano Movement, was on finding any and every text that could be utilized in literature classes, as well as in political consciousness-raising efforts, might lead one to expect that the earliest canons would have been liberally all inclusive. If one wanted to teach the Chicano novel in 1970, the choice of titles seemed to be dictated by scarcity: José Antonio Villarreal's *Pocho* (1959), Raymond Barrio's *The Plum Plum Pickers* (1969), and Richard Vásquez' *Chicano* (1970). Yet things were not as they seemed, and what appeared a matter of necessity was actually one of choice. Even in that time of need, few critics or teachers included in their bibliographies Floyd Salas' *Tattoo the Wicked Cross* (1967) or *What Now My Love* (1969), or Fray Angélico Chávez' *The Conquistadora* (1954), and probably only Raymond Paredes would have insisted on one or both of Josephina Niggli's novels, *Mexican Village* (1945), *Step Down, Elder Brother* (1947). Another Chicano novelist, John Rechy, had published three novels by 1970, two of which (*City of Night* and *Numbers*) had attracted international notariety among readers and reviewers, yet his were not taught in Chicano courses then and for the most part they are still excluded. While in the case of Salas and Chávez one might have justified their exclusion as a question of the substandard literary merit of the writing, this would have been much more difficult with respect to Niggli and Rechy. And in this consideration of literary merit, we should keep in mind the date, 1970, and those canonized texts which set the standard of the day. In the context of *Pocho*, *Chicano* and *The Plum Plum Pickers*, excluding Niggli or Rechy on grounds of bad writing was hardly defensible. No, the canon of the Chicano novel from the beginning, as all canons, has been as much a result—if not more so— of implicitly or explicitly expressed needs and ideologies as of formal excellence.

The pressing need at the start of the contemporary movement was one of identity, which has since become the favorite topic of Chicano criticism. But the identity involved in the political movement was not a question to be resolved through a call of the roll. The political identity was not allowed to be the sum of all possible parts of the community, but one restricted to those who fit into the ideological program. Identity was seen as a process of historical review carried out through an ideology of nation building which stressed several key points: retrieval of family and ethnic tradition, identification with the working class, struggle against assimilation, and the dire results if these efforts were not continued. Identity was not simply to be found, but to be forged, with careful attention to history and ideology. In some cases, as in much of the Movement poetry, this plan was obvious, while the novelists seemed to have been less affected by these ideological considerations. But canons are not the product of authors—although they supply the necessary raw material— rather of readers, critics and teachers, and in this instance those three groups coincided in large part with the politically involved Chicanos, at least people involved in the politics of the educational system, for to teach Chicano literature in 1970 was a political act. The texts chosen by those first teachers were by and large those that lent themselves easily to allegorical readings of the view of society that the Movement desired.

It is no mere coincidence that *Pocho*, the first of those three books that formed the core of the Chicano novel curriculum in 1970, and even beyond, centered around the question of identity as played out in the development of a boy and his immigrant father. *Chicano* expanded that plot into the struggle of the children and grandchildren of another immigrant. Both were family histories of a struggle to define oneself in the environment of the United States, define and survive with some sense of the old ethnicity. And *The Plum Plum Pickers*, although we can certainly justify it as the clearist of the three in the expression of the ideology of class struggle, can also be seen as the rendering in novel form of that part of the political movement which had become by 1969 almost synonymous with the new Chicano identity: César Chavez' United Farm Worker struggle. All three certainly were taken as metaphors of Movement concerns, despite their troublesome contradictions and negative outcome.

Rechy's *City of Night*, however, was another matter altogether. Although this novel had sold more copies than the three novels mentioned above put together, few Chicano critics were in a rush to claim it as a Chicano success story. The greatest stumbling block was the blatant homesexuality of the characters. Yet, sexual preference aside, Rechy had written the most searing denunciation of U.S. society of any of the Chicano novels written by 1970. Nor can we dismiss the novel for its negativity or pessimism, for *Pocho* (as usually read) and *Chicano* are no less pessimistic in their portrayal of the disintegration of the Chicano family. Nor is it acceptable to claim that Rechy's characters are too individualistic and thus lacking in the communal sensitivity necessary for a Chicano, because the same accusation can be leveled at Villarreal's and Vásquez' characters. What superficially distinquishes *City of Night* from the novels chosen for the canon is the lack of a narrow focus on ethnicity. Rechy does not convert ethnicity into a problem, nor even a necessary context. He neither asserts nor denies it, but rather lets it exist as one element in the protagonist's background. More significant, however, is another, much more essential difference: Rechy's novels deny the social values of stability, order, security and monogamy. His characters reject those familial values which Chicanos, especially in the early Movement, considered paramount. At the same time Rechy revealed the irony of homosexuality's close link with machismo, undermining the chauvinistic stalwart of the male dominated Movement. His ideology was diametrically opposed to that of the Movement and that of the community. At that time, and perhaps still, Rechy's extreme anti-social position could not be appreciated as a metaphor or allegory of liberation. His novels were simply ignored in favor of aesthetically inferior texts which, even though they did not bespeak Movement ideology, at least stated the problems in the rhetorical terms that the Movement wished to employ.

In 1970 there came into existence a concerted effort to create a series of canonized texts: El Premio Quinto Sol. As part of an overall project to create a Chicano consciousness, if not create a Chicano culture itself, the Quinto Sol publishers had taken on the task of stimulating the production of a Chicano literature. It was they who published the first anthology of Chicano creative writing at a time when there was almost none to be had. (As Tomás Rivera remarked to me years ago, Chicanos were the first people to have an anthology—Quinto Sol's *El espejo/The Mirror*—before they had a literature.) With the prize, Quinto Sol intended to repeat the feat with the novel, and the success of the venture is unquestionable. No one need be reminded that during the 1970's the three Quinto Sol Prize Winners became the most studied and, probably, the most read Chicano authors. To the satisfaction of some and the continual frustration of others, Rivera, Anaya and Hinojosa became the Chicano Big Three. More than a decade after the last Quinto Sol Prize was awarded, and despite the publication of numerous novels that have tripled the number available to readers and critics, one finds that most of the critical attention is still dedicated to these authors; they are the subjects of more written essays and presentations at conferences than any others.

Do not misunderstand me, I in no way deny the merit of the Big Three, nor take to task anyone—editors or conference organizers—for this situation, but simply call to our attention that this was the result, at least in part, of a planned creation of a canon, a plan that selected and, therefore, also excluded. Everyone in the field knows by now that

Rivera's "Pete Fonseca" story was turned down by the same Quinto Sol
editors who had awarded him the prize, not because it was any less skillfully writen—some even consider it his best story—but because it supposedly did not convey a positive image of Chicanos. The question was
one of identity, but the canonizers had a preestablished image of what
that identity was supposed to be. Those canonizers who gave us what
many consider the first truly Chicano novels also assumed the power to
deprive us of other material they deemed unfit. We know they practiced
exclusion in the case of that one short story by Rivera, but what we do
not know is which novels, if any, were rejected by the Quinto Sol Prize
committee. We would have to read them to know what was excluded
from the canon. As a matter of fact, it would be interesting to know
how many losers competed against the prize winners so as to know the
state of the field at that time. And if there were any other novels in the
running, what became of them? In this regard the canon has dropped a
veil of silence.

It should come as no surprise that two of the three novels awarded
the prize once again focused on the search for identity played out by a
young boy. The difference was that Tomás Rivera's ... *y no se lo tragó
la tierra* and Rudy Anaya's *Bless Me, Ultima* end in positive affirmations
of the Chicano community and its creative process, whereas their pre-
ceding counterparts were perceived as moving in the opposite direction. It is also no surprise that, like *The Plum Plum Pickers*, *Tierra* also
novelized what then seemed the epitome of the true Chicano, the farm
worker. And once again the texts lent themselves to the allegorical reading of the community development, although now that development led
through stages of growth to a point where a healthy and positive maturity could be projected into the future. Both novels mirrored the ideology of the Movement: find out who you are by learning your history and
the lessons inherent in the communal heritage. Those lessons, and the
very process of the search and retrieval, would teach survival techniques
and sustain life. Rolando Hinojosa's *Estampas del Valle* didn't seem to
fit this mold, yet it, too, was structured around the need for discovering
the oral tradition, the values, and vital processes of survival of the older
generations. And of course *Estampas* was only the first installment on
the now multivolumed life, from childhood to maturity and who knows
how much further, of the boys he introduced there. In short, Rolando
too was giving us the image we wanted of ourselves, an affirmation of
the process of our communal selves.

Another advantage in these three novels over the previous ones is
the apparent separatism. In all of them, despite the constant contact
with Anglo-American culture, the characters seem to exist in a separate space. All three novels implicitly posit the possibility of an alterna-

tive other space of Chicano existence in which the family and individual can survive as an ethnic entity. All three are rural and as such distance themselves from the contemporary urban setting of the majority of Chicano readers and the U.S. reading public in general. In addition, they seem distant in a temporal sense as well: the action appears to take place some decades in the past. Thus, none deals with the contemporary urban malaise, and so they permit, even foster, a nostalgic view of culture.

This period, however, also produced its troublesome novelist: Oscar Zeta Acosta, whose two novels coincide with the Quinto Sol Prize project (*The Autobiography of a Brown Buffalo*, 1972, and *The Revolt of the Cockroach People*, 1973). There are those who would rather not include Acosta in the canon. His intimate contact with the mainstream counter-culture produced the opposite sensation to that discussed in the previous paragraph. In Acosta's works the interaction between Chicanos and the great mixture of other groups that make up the U.S. people was too close and ultimately unavoidable. Certainly my Chicano students from Colorado, Texas, Arizona and New Mexico over the years have consistently expressed the view that Acosta's characters are less than entirely Chicano. And at least one critic, Raymond Paredes, has echoed this sentiment in print: "Acosta wants so desperately to retrieve his ethnic heritage. But the reader is struck by the superficiality of his quest and the flimsiness of the foundation on which he hopes to build his ethnic identity. In the end, Acosta's books seem indistinguishable from numerous other works that lament the destruction of ethnicity in America" (74). In other words, Acosta's novels should be set afloat in the mainstream where, it is hoped, they will drift off to somewhere well outside the Chicano canon. In the same article Paredes states that "Chicano literature is that body of works produced by United States citizens and residence of Mexican descent for whom a sense of ethnicity is a critical part of their literary sensibilities and for whom the portrayal of their ethnic experience is a major concern." The definition is general enough to be entertained at least, yet Paredes' exclusion of Acosta seems to imply further criteria. Acosta's concern for his ethnic experience was so major to him that he dedicated two books to exploring the traumas it had caused him. Apparently Paredes' added criteria is that one's experience may question ethnicity, but in the end must affirm it. This, of course, would eliminate the protagonists of *Pocho* and *Chicano* as well.

I suspect that, more than the flimsiness of Acosta's ethnic foundation, what bothers some Chicano readers is that Acosta draws into question the flimsiness of a Movement based on ethnicity in the context of a mobile and highly versatile society like the United States. His first novel

ends with a statement in which the narrator distinguishes between ethnicity as an accident of birth and political commitment as a product of
choice: "I am a Chicano by ancestry and a Brown Buffalo by choice"
(Acosta, *Brown*, 199). Brown Buffalo, as Acosta explained in the ac-
knowledgments to the book, was a political party. Acosta had prefaced
this distinction with an even more direct attack on the primacy of ethnic identity as a basis for healthy motivation in life: "My single mistake
has been to seek an identity with any one person or nation or with any
part of history" (199). In *The Revolt of the Cockroach People* Acosta
portrays the end result of his efforts to identify himself with the Chicano ethnic movement as, first, his being cut off from non-Chicanos
by the separatist (read racist) restrictions placed on him by his fellow
Chicanos—he is not allowed near a "Gabacha" who wants to congrat-
ulate him (230). Second, at the same time that he is forced into strictly
Chicano relationships, the plot of the text culminates in a fratricidal
court battle among Chicanos of different levels and persuasions: "Chicano defendants and defense attorney and prosecution. And there on
the bench is good old Chicano lackey, Superior Judge Alfred Alacran"
(202). He could have added that the case included Chicano witnesses
for both sides in the matter of the death of a Chicano reporter. Into
this microcosm of Chicano conflict, Acosta introduces César Chávez
and Rodolfo Corky Gonzales as representatives of opposite alternatives
of pacificism and militant violence, and he places himself between, the
link that holds them together, the source of a rhetoric that might lend
order to chaos and fragmentation. But in the end, Acosta is forced to
flee after attempting to bomb the Chicano judge's chambers, an attempt
that apparently kills a Chicano. This was not the picture of ethnic unity
Chicanos wanted to see.

As Horst Tonn, the German critic, has noted in his study of the Chicano novel, as early as 1972 Acosta was debunking the self-image of the
Chicano Movement (125-32). Perhaps what makes Acosta questionable
in the eyes of some canonizers was his recognition that, in spite of a
claimed and desperately sought-after bond of ethnicity, there were significant ideological concerns which fragmented the community whenever the realities of political action demanded confrontation with the
dominant society. Unity was approximated only during cultural celebra-
tions within a segregated space, such as the rally described by Acosta in
Chapter 13 (168-75). That rally could be a metaphor of what the canonizers at Quinto Sol wanted to achieve with their publications: a bringing
together of the Chicano community to celebrate the best of itself without concern for political differences and the emphasis on ethnicity. Yet
even into that moment Acosta managed to infuse conflict barely suppressed below the surface. And the conflict centered around the use of

the term "Chicano." It is seen as a dangerous term which, when finally uttered, releases tension and carries the people to an "orgy of nationalism ... (through which) the crowd melts into one consciousness and no man is alone in that madness any longer" (175). However, as the rest of the novel demonstrates, that kind of unity is untenable under the pressures from both exterior and interior forces.

Like Rechy, Acosta chose to plumb deeper than ethnicity. However, unlike Rechy, his novels treat readily identifiable Chicano subjects and figures, even to the extent that César Chávez and Rodolfo Corky Gonzales appear as characters in his second novel. In addition, he gives both of his books the facade of documentary reportage by presenting them in the form of the autobiography of a veteran militant—himself— of the Chicano Movement's most renowned urban struggle, that of Los Angeles at the end of the '60s and start of the '70s. So he cannot be excluded as easily as Rechy, whose seems marginal to Chicano political activism. Yet another consideration we must entertain with respect to the canon is that, with the presence of works like Acosta's that foreground "undesirable traits," readers then begin to find traces of those same traits in the canonized texts. Acosta's novels force us to reread those of Anaya, Rivera and Hinojosa in a different manner and find in them the same seeds of interior division. Ethnicity can never again be, if it ever truly was, the monological absolute, that some canonizers may have desired, after Acosta has stated clearly and openly what others had revealed more subtly. He remains a thorny presence for many, and a liberating one for others.

In 1974, when that interior tension surfaced among the Quinto Sol editors themselves, putting an end to the short-lived prize series, Miguel Méndez published what could be considered the successor to the Canonized Big Three. Méndez had appeared in the original *El espejo/ The Mirror* with the short story "Tata Casehua," generally considered one of the best pieces in the anthology, so it was almost natural that he should join the Big Three as a novelist. *Peregrinos de Aztlán*, like Acosta's novels, treats the urban malaise. It also focuses unmercifully on the divisions in the ethnic community. However, its saving grace for many critics who preferred to ignore Acosta and Rechy was that its protagonist was one of the underprivileged, the poor, the forgotten with which the Movement wanted to associate itself. Also, Méndez ended his text with an affirmation of unity through ethnic heritage—the harsh divisions in society could be transcended through a return to ancient pre-Columbian tradition. In other words, Méndez' text was more acceptable because, although it highlighted the urban malaise and the interior conflicts, it supported the Movement ideal of a utopian future through a recuperation of ethnic heritage. Acosta utilized similar elements to attack that ideal. The criteria for canonization was tied to political ideology.

As the interior differences in ideologies began to make themselves more and more obvious, the criteria for the canon became a debated issue. Critics used their publications to persuade us into applying different criteria than what had been used to establish the first canon. For instance, *Bless Me, Ultima*'s success has ired more than one leftist critic. The late Joseph Sommers would have liked to dismiss it for its escapist mysticism, preferring *Tierra*. The German Marxist Dieter Herms agrees with Sommers, but his preference for the canon would be *Bracero* (1972), a novel whose author, Eugene Nelson, is not even Chicano. Paredes seems to have had this question in mind when he ended his essay quoted above with a curious statement. His final point is introduced by a rhetorical question: "Can a sense of Chicano ethnicity be acquired by a person who is not of Mexican heritage?" (74). He goes on to offer the example of Chester Seltzer, an anglo newspaperman who published stories about Mexican/Chicano characters under the pseudonym of Amado Muro. Paredes mentions what to him must be the relevant rites of passage into Chicano ethnicity: he "married a Chicana ... and settled in El Paso ... immersed himself in Chicano culture and finally wrote about it with great understanding." Thus, the door is opened for those exceptional non-Chicanos to become Chicano writers, a possibility which Paredes accepts "happily" (75)—that is after rejecting the likes of Acosta and excluding John Rechy's major novels. And the Cuban American critic Robert González Echeverría, when questioned about Daniel James' impersonation of a Chicano novelist with his *Famous All Over Town*, replied that literature's purpose is to fool us, so he saw nothing wrong with "Danny Santiago" practicing the art. Of course, if we apply Paredes' criteria for admitting Amado Muro, Daniel James almost passes—perhaps he still has time to divorce his Anglo wife and remarry a Chicana.

The first attempt to systemize this particular thorny facet of a Chicano canon was Francisco Lomelí and Donaldo Urioste's coining of the term and category of *Chicanesque* writings for their annotated bibliography in 1976. It was to include literature about Chicanos written by non-Chicanos. This, of course, has not really solved the problem, rather only served to focus our attention more acutely on the unresolved nature of Chicano ethnicity. And Antonio Márquez, in his article on Chicanesque literature, would so like to grant John Nichols' *The Milgros Beanfield War* Chicano status, but painfully admits that Nichols just doesn't have the right blood (Leal, et al). Previously I responded to this position by pointing out that, although Márquez would like us to believe in the existence of a thematic and cultural criteria through which real Chicano works could be distinguished from Chicanesque ones, in his own discussion of Nichols Márquez can only eliminate him on grounds of not having been born of Mexican parents. Perhaps this argues in favor of Paredes' stand on learned ethnicity, but then we would be faced with another situation, intolerable for many Chicanos, in which our best novelist could well be John Nichols. As I suggested rather sarcastically in my review of *Decade* and the Márquez essay, maybe what we need is yet another category of "casi-casis," or "almost-almosts" in English, for those authors who cannot pass the blood test, but whose writing is culturally and ethnically Chicano (Bruce-Novoa, "Década," 13).

Our inability to submit authors to a *prueba de sangre* before nominating them for canonization can lead to embarrassing *faux pas*. La Casa de las Américas thought it was honoring another Chicano when it granted an award to Jaime Sagel(Sah HELL), aka Jim Sagel(SAY Guell), an Anglo-American who has performed the Amado-Muro rites of passage and then some—he actually has an advanced degree in Spanish and writes in an interlingual mixture of Spanish and English. So we see that the canon would expand or contract according to the whims or deeply felt concerns of the critic, if critics were the only ones in control.

These pressures are not all negative. They help insure that the canon, as it grows, better represents the differing views within the community. And despite the appearance of total chaos, there does seem to be some agreed upon criteria. Although critics generally still consider the Chicano novel to be a product of the post-1959 publication of Villarreal's *Pocho*, hardly anyone would now deny that before that date some novels were written in the United States by authors of Mexican heritage. These novels are considered precursors to the Chicano novel as such, but the titles begin to appear along side the others in Chicano bibliographies. Examples of these new entries are Eusebio Chacón's *El hijo de la tempestad; Tras la tormenta la calma* (1892) and Aurelio Macedonio Espinosa's *Conchita Argüello: Historia y novela californiana* (1938). These novels and others have been found in archives and libraries, where perhaps many more will turn up. Also, research has revealed that the Chicano community had access to novels in the major newspapers, some of which were written by authors living in the United States. The classification of these works is still to be resolved. The opening of the canon into the past has also sensitized critics to the historical presence of our literature prior to the contemporary period, so we can expect more discoveries and research into the nature of that writing. This may shed a different light on the canon as we conceive of it. Yet it must be noted that the extremely limited availability of these older texts prevents them from being more widely read or used in classes, so their active influence upon the canon is miniscule.

When referring to the contemporary period, most critics would rec-
ommend, and teachers require, the reading of the Big Three plus Villarreal. *Chicano* has largely gone by the wayside, its sociological stereotypes wearing thin over the years. And since works by non-Chicanos
have been relegated to the questionable status of Chicanesque, *The
Plum Plum Pickers* has been retroactively placed in the position of sometimes in, sometimes out, depending on how much one knows or cares
about Barrios' background and how liberally one decides to extend the
ethnic circle. Miguel Méndez, while respected by the critics, receives
less attention, probably because his highly creative and poetic use of
Spanish is difficult for many readers, even those who have no problems
with other novelists, like Hinojosa, who write in a more accessible idiom. Most critics tacitly agree to the existence of a category of important works which probably should be read, but that once again are not
considered entirely Chicano in that they do not address directly ethnic
issues. Examples are *The Road to Tamazunchale* by Ron Arias and the
aforementioned Rechy novels.

Novels by women, the few we have, are most often referred to in a
similar vein: novels that should be read to see what women have written about, but not as essential readings in the canon. Perhaps it is that
until very recently even the most generous reader was hard pressed to
overlook the faults in these novels. Yet, certainly Sandra Cisneros' *The
House on Mango Street* can be read as a novel, in a similar fashion as
Tierra, and it merits inclusion in the inner circle. And, although neither
author deals directly with "Chicano subjects" per se, Cecile Pineda and
Sheila Ortiz Taylor are novelists of the first order, surpassing in craft
many of the previously published Chicano writers.

This last point brings us to another concern. The break up of Quinto
Sol a decade ago has left a void not yet filled by any of the publishers who
have taken its place. Both Arte Público Press and Bilingual Press have
established excellent publication records, actually having published to
date more creative literature than Quinto Sol did, but their publications
still have not come to signify the same thing to Chicano readers. That is
to say, these new publications do not reach us with an *a priori* status of
canonized texts as the Quinto Sol Prize Winners managed to do. This,
of course, lies partly in the realm of merchandising: Quinto Sol devised
and carried out a canonizing strategy at a time when the Chicano consumer would accept almost anything offered and naively was prepared
to believe almost anything claimed about the books. Octavio Romano,
one of the originators of Quinto Sol, attempted to continue this strategy
when he began a new publishing house, Tonatiuh, in the mid-seventies.
However, the Tonatiuh Prize, unlike the Quinto Sol Prize which was an
almost strictly in-house operation, was set up with a national selection

committee, of which I was a member. The effort was undermined by a lack of cooperation among the judges, and eventually a winner was picked without the judges having read all the manuscripts. The fate of the winning novel, Abelardo Delgado's *Letters to Louise*, can serve as an example of the disintegration of the hegemonic control of Quinto Sol. *Letters to Louise* was never published as a book, but only as numbers of *Grito del Sol*, Octavio Romano's journal. It has received almost no critical attention and is never mentioned in the company of the three Quinto Sol prizes. By the time it reached the public, confidence in the Berkeley group—which had split into Tonatiuh and Justa Publications—had so diminished that the prize was no longer respected.

Similar canonization effort has not been attempted, so far, by either Arte Público or Bilingual Press, although the former has now established a literary prize in memory of Tomás Rivera and the latter has begun publishing a series called Chicano Classics. The Arte Público contest has not yet awarded its first prize, so how it will function is still to be seen. Bilingual Press defines the purpose of its Chicano Classics series as the reissuing of significant texts that have gone out of print. However, the fact that the first title in the series, José Antonio Villarreal's *The Fifth Horseman*, was never central to the Chicano canon nor a legitimate classic seems to allow us to see the series as more of a merchandising strategy than a real effort to save a "Classic." Certainly there are some novels we could consider classics that need reissuing—the Oscar Zeta Acosta books come to mind—but to republish a novel like *The Fifth Horseman* is not the act of salvaging a classic, but rather the attempt to create a market for a book that never established one in the first place. In that sense, Bilingual Press is repeating the canonization strategy of Quinto Sol. However, it has not worked, at least not with the first title.

Most likely the kind of hegemony sought by and granted to Quinto Sol a decade and a half ago cannot be duplicated, but not because the literature being published is inferior. Some Chicano works of fiction have garnered awards outside the Chicano establishment. Rolando Hinojosa's second book, *Klail City y sus alrededores* won the Casa de las Américas Prize in 1976. This certainly cemented his reputation as a leading Chicano writer established through the previous Quinto Sol Prize. More recently, Sandra Cisneros (*The House on Mango Street*) and Gary Soto (*Living Up the Street*) have won American Book Awards for fiction, yet neither has been received as instantaneous Chicano Classics. More than a question of the literary merit of new texts, the disappearance of the ability to create *a priori* Chicano Classics results from a change in the critical and reading public. It has more to do with an erosion of the centralizing energy of the cultural awakening that the

Movement released. Just as the criteria began breaking down once the bond of ethnicity was put into question, there has been fragmentation, or perhaps decentralization, in the production of Chicano literature. And decentralization brings with it the question of the relativity of values. Added to this is the questioning of the ethnic criteria for merit and the relatively new application of the criterion of craft. In short, the reception of a text is no longer guaranteed by the fact that it comes from a Chicano source. And finally, when the validity itself of the applicability of the term Chicano is under severe question not only in the community but also among writers, can we rightfully expect there not to be a questioning of what the value of ethnicity is in a text or even of which values are more or less authentic? Recent novels, such as those by Nash Candelaria, Arturo Islas or Alejandro Morales, put into question assumptions about the Chicano community, and in so doing expand the definition of the culture. This, however, is one more erosion of the cultural hegemony that allowed canonization to be a much simpler matter in the early 1960's.

Even more disconcerting is the relative absence of critical vehicles—journals, literary magazines, newsletters, etc.—in which the new literature is reviewed, evaluated, and yes, canonized. Not that there has ever been a wealth of such outlets in the Chicano community, but the canonization power of Quinto Sol made the process of review validification unnecessary. In the mid-seventies, when Quinto Sol began to founder, a series of novels appeared which still have attracted relatively little attention when compared to that given the Quinto Sol group. Francisco Lomelí has called this a lost, or ignored generation, including such writers as Alejandro Morales, Ron Arias, Isabella Ríos, Nash Candelaria and Aristeo Brito. In fact, this list could be extended up to the present. Little has been published about *The Rain God*, an excellent novel by Arturo Islas, or *Muerte en una estrella*, Sergio Elizondo's experimental novel, both published last year. More print has been dedicated to the questionable effort to keep Richard Rodriguez out of the Chicano canon than in assuring a place for some deserving authors. We need more active discussion to vitalize the canon with new material, or books deserving attention will be ignored. Even Juan Rodríguez' tendentious and openly biased *Carta Abierta* was better than the "abulia cerrada" which predominates now.

If we fail to critically discuss novels by authors we know about, it should be no surprise that little is done to discover others. Our rather incestual focus has prevented us from looking beyond the circle of recognized or recognizable Chicano writers to find new and possibly important authors. Some have gone unnoticed. Laurence Gonzales came to our attention only when in his third novel, *El Vago*, he addressed the theme of the Mexican Revolution. Yet Gonzales is a fine writer with years of experience and training, and a long list of publications in prestigious magazines. Another novelist who escaped even the eye of Roberto Trujillo in *Literatura Chicana*, the most recent Chicano bibliography, is Ernest Brawley who has three novels to his credit, each with protagonists who can claim at least a distant Chicano link. His second novel, *Selena*, narrates the life of a farmer-worker activist, and his third, *The Alamo Tree*, could be compared to Villarreal's *The Fifth Horseman* in its examination of the Mexican backgrounds of what is today the Chicano. The two woman I consider the best of the published fiction writers, Shiela Ortiz Taylor and Cecile Pineda, have not figured in any of the Chicana collections, nor to my knowledge have they been written about, discussed, or even mentioned in the Chicano context until now. Yet Pineda's *Face*(1985) is a fine novel, and Ortiz Taylor's *Faultline* (1982) is, in my opinion, not only the best novel written by a Chicana, but can bear comparison with the best in the canon, period.

But now I am practicing canonization, not criticizing the process, and though it is a legitimate and perhaps unavoidable function of criticism, any further indulgence of it is better left for another forum.

The Americas Review 14.3-4 (Fall-Winter 1986): 119-35.

13 The Topological Space of Chicano Literature

In 1974, when I first introduced my concept of Chicano literature as a space to be charted through successive mappings of the works in constant and dynamic relation, I had in mind the application of topology in two, different, although related, denotations. First, in its most common usage, topology is synonymous with topography, or the topographical study of a phenomenological field. I prefer to distinguish this denotation as topography itself: a detailed charting of an object and/or area in time and space. This involves the relation of works to each other, their relative effect on their field of presence, their changing configurations, etc. It can be as simple as tracing the chronology of appearances in the field, the delineation of the boundaries and the charting of the general area. However, although the topographical description is necessary for establishing the field of investigation, topography should not be confused with the second denotation of topology, or what I call topology *per se*.

Topology is a branch of mathematics that investigates the properties of a geometric configuration that remain constant when the configuration is subjected to transformation. It is in this sense that George Steiner utilized it in his essay "Topologies of Culture" (414-70). His comments prove useful for understanding topology's application to literature and the study of cultural production:

> Manifold transformations and reorderings of relation between an initial verbal event and subsequent reappearances of this event in other verbal or non-verbal forms might best be seen as topological ... The study of these invariants and of the geometric and algebraic relations which survive transformations has proved decisive in modern mathematics. It has shown underlying unities and assemblages in a vast plurality of apparently diverse functions and spatial configurations. Similarly, there are invariants and constants underlying the manifold shapes of expression in our

146

culture. It is these which make it possible and, I think, useful to consider the fabric of culture as 'topological'. The constants can be specifically verbal; they can be formal ... Defined 'topologically', a culture is a sequence of translations and transformations of constants. (225-26)

Although Steiner does not mention it, topology can be a creative instrument in cultural production. Since one of its functions is to find or create relations between or among works that otherwise might be classified as heterogeneous, the critic can utilize it to define into existence previously unknown units of whatever target material is in question. This interpretative practice also reveals commonality in so far as it implies the existence of one basic object of study, with multiple manifestations. This is apparent in its definition as a science of "properties of *a* geometric configuration." That object is culture itself, while the narrative of transformations through which it has passed could be termed its tradition or history. Thus, an end product of topological criticism is the proof of an entity called culture, which in turn proves the existence of producers of culture, that is to say, it provides proof of the identity of the people as producers. Ideologically, this binds cultural producers into a common effort, although admittedly, this may not actually be the fact. Criticism discovers or creates movements and schools by placing authors and works into a field of relationships. In this way, topology has served my purpose, not only of building Chicano literature as a cohesive corpus of cultural production, with all the values inherent in that status, but of supporting at the intellectual level the political struggle to establish the Chicano ethnic movement.

Up to the mid-seventies, attempts to characterize Chicano literature were narrowly, but vaguely, topographic. That is, they described individual works superficially, hardly ever entering into detailed analysis. Efforts to relate works on a broader spectrum usually took the form of attributing to them a radically anti-establishment political ideology. Yet, careful reading raised doubts as to the validity of that claim, as well as about the specific nature of protests and what they held in common. Certainly in the heat of excitement, anything that spoke positively of Chicanos seemed to share a common ideology. However, it was difficult to relate specific works when read in detail. We began to ask what a work like Tomás Rivera's ... *y no se lo tragó la tierra* really had in common with Rudolfo Anaya's *Bless Me, Ultima* or Oscar Zeta's Acosta's *The Autobiography of a Brown Buffalo*; what Rolando Hinojosa's *Estampas del Valle* had in common with Estela Portillo's *Rain of Scorpions*; or for that matter, what any of these prose fictions shared with major works in poetry, like Alurista's *Floricanto en Aztlán*, Ricardo Sánchez' *Canto y grito mi liberación*, or *I Am Joaquín* by Rodolfo Gonzales—not to mention the obvious distinctions among the works of poetry themselves. For example, while *I Am Joaquín* or *Floricanto en Aztlán* were both utopian in their projection of Chicano unity, they differed widely in the analysis of the situation and the proposal for action. Other writers, like Acosta or Sánchez, stridently questioned the Chicanos' ability to cooperate politically. Sánchez attacked Alurista and Gonzales for their ideology, although not for the same reasons, which in turn underscored the differences between those two poets. Content and setting varied tremendously from work to work. They were not all barrio experiences, nor even urban, but the rural ones were by no means all about migrant workers. What they were all about—although some radical political activists would have questioned this—was Chicano experience, but analysis imposed an adjustment to even that claim, or at least its formulation: it must be stated in the plural as Chicano *experiences*.

Through Steiner's statement quoted above, we can draw an analogy closer to the true condition of Chicano cultural production: "a vast plurality of apparently diverse functions and spatial configurations." Obviously, we needed something like topology to reveal the possible "underlying unities and assemblages" if we were going to talk of Chicano literature. This is exactly what my work was meant to provide.

I began by assuming a phenomenological approach: the works existed in a field of perception which had to be bracketed for analysis. Bracketing is never completely objective, but an effort had to be made to achieve as much objectivity as possible. My method was to study those works which were at the time—1974—the most read by the Chicano audience. The scarcity of published works, coupled to our relative ignorance about the historical backgrounds of publishing by Chicanos, limited the number of works in the field. Next I did close readings of the works, assuming that no matter how diverse they were among themselves, each expressed an authentic Chicano experience by virtue of having been written by a Chicano—anyone of Mexican descent living permanently in the United States. Immediately this eliminated two authors often included in early Chicano literature anthologies and academic courses: neither Amado Muro nor Raymond Barrio qualified because they were not of Mexican ancestry. The question also arose as to whether an author like John Rechy, a Chicano, should be included although most Chicano readers and critics did not recognize him as such. I chose to read him among Chicano authors to see what he had in common, and also to expand the literature with new texts. This clearly was an application of the principle that criticism creates the space of its production, and an author, usually not perceived as Chicano, becomes Chicano through the intervention of the critic, a strategy I continue to employ with other writers.

At the surface level, I began by identifying images or motifs that reappeared in different works. Limitations of space allow me to discuss only one example here. From the start of the contemporary Chicano movement, the farm worker had been a central figure, mostly because of the high visibility of César Chávez' United Farm Workers Union and the success of its propaganda arm, Luis Valdez' Teatro Campesino, founded in the mid-sixties. Through Valdez' early depictions of farm workers, audiences received a double message: on the one hand, the workers were exploited harshly by the capitalistic system of agribusiness—this was probably the image of greatest propaganda value with respect to the goal of promoting sympathy and support for the Union. Yet, on the other, there was a joyful, playful tone rising from the optimistic promise of relief from that exploitation through communal solidarity, the logical consequence of which was, again, the U.F.W. (Valdez, *Actos*). This image was most useful in bolstering moral in the ranks of the union membership and producing positive enthusiasm in Chicano communities. The first Actos—short, agitprop pieces that stated problems and answers in simplistic terms—not only reduced the farm workers to stereotypes, but also reduced their situation to manageable dimensions. All that was needed was unity, and at the center of a united Chicano community stood the farm worker. The appeal of this well-designed and dynamically staged propaganda was confirmed in the success the Teatro Campesino enjoyed, not only with Chicanos, but among liberal elements of the non-Chicano communities. Through that success the image of the farm worker was confirmed as an icon on the par with the mestizo head and the United Farm Worker flag.

However, the farm worker was not as central to community life for all Chicanos as the Teatro Campesino gave people to believe. This was evident to anyone reading another major piece of literature from the mid-sixties: *I Am Joaquín*, by Rodolfo Corky Gonzales, the leader of the Denver-based Crusade For Justice, considered by many the center of the Chicano cultural nationalism. In the original version of the poem (1967), there are only two specific references to farm work: "My knees are caked with mud. / My hands calloused from the hoe" (ll. 346-47), and "like the family / working down a row of beets / to turn around / and work / and work. There is no end" (ll. 419-44); eight lines out of five hundred and two, and none of them in strategically key or central locations in a poem whose detail and structure are, as I have shown elsewhere, carefully planned and executed (*Chicano Poetry*, 48-68).

How to explain this apparent divergence in centralizing imagery? Logically, the difference in emphasis is attributable to the authors of the texts. Valdez' affiliation with Chávez' rural and agricultural union demanded the foregrounding of the farm worker; Gonzales' leadership position of an organization with urban orientation relegated the same

problem and its people to a tangential position. Neither, however, excludes the other from being an authentic expression of Chicano experiences in divergent soiciopolitical and regional contexts.

Ironically enough, however, towards the end of the 1960's, these two
literary forces, Valdez' Teatro Campesino and Gonzales' *I Am Joaquín*,
would undergo permutations that exemplify the topological principle:
certain elements remain constant while the configuration is reshaped.
Without changing the name of "Teatro Campesino," Valdez cut official
ties to Chávez' union, feeling that he could better explore other realms
of Chicano experience if the group were not tied to a specific political
effort. Yet, while in the more urban oriented Actos that followed, the
farm worker was less emphasized, Valdez could not shake his perceived
link to the U.F.W. until the early 1980's, after writing *Zoot Suit*, a play
about a typically urban character, and staging it as a creative effort of
his own without the collaboration of the Teatro Campesino troupe.

At the same time, *I Am Joaquín* was suffering a transition in the opposite direction. First, Valdez and the Teatro Campesino made a film
of the poem in the collage/montage technique popularized on television
in the late '60s. Many of the photographs used for the montage were of
farm worker images. Then the text was reissued by a major New York
publisher, Bantam Books, with fifty-three illustrations and a photo of
the author. While the title page shows a barrio scene well in keeping
with the sense of Gonzales' urban-centered Crusade, the poem's first
segment (ll. 1-37), which orients readers by establishing key themes of
the historical drama to be resolved, has six illustrations, five of which
seem to be farm worker and/or agribusiness related. Photo number
three is of César Chávez himself, and is the only illustration to carry
a caption, which not only identifies subject and event, but gives a date,
thus foregrounding and privileging Chávez among the rest of the pho-
tos. Semiotically, the photographs create a hierarchy of values, at the
top of which stands—actually sits—César Chávez. This possession of
the visual reading is further supported, ironically, by the placement of
a photograph of Luis Valdez apparently leading a march and placed
strategically in the section when the poem arrives at a final thrust into
action. But we should remember that Valdez was perceived, as mentioned above, as an extention of Chávez and the U.F.W.

Highlighting Chávez within the text of *I Am Joaquín* came at the
expense of the poem's ideology and source. It semiotically centers the
farm worker in the readers reception field, and attributes that center to
a specific political group not affiliated with that of the author, Rodolfo
Gonzales. When we remember that Chávez' movement was insistently
non-violent, and that Gonzales' Crusade For Justice advocated the right
to violently defend the community—major sections of the poem, ac-

counting for much more space then the subject of farm workers, are dedicated to the tradition of violence and blood shed—then we can appreciate how radical this ideological reformulation was. Valdez' film version had begun this shift by excising what I have called elsewhere the "Blood Sacrifice" segment (*Chicano Poetry*, 61-63), a section accurately representative of Gonzales' political and cultural position. That this semiotic foregrounding of Chávez and the non-violent U.F.W. made the text more palpitable to the mainstream liberal audiences perhaps explains why the cuts were made in the film and illustrations were used by Bantam, but that is a question for another study.

Topologically, the farm worker remained a constant of both the Teatro Campesino and *I Am Joaquín* throughout the late '60s and early '70s, yet changed in relation to the phenomenological perception of each. While we might say that the latter is a text, and thus definitively set, while the former, as a living producer of images, can evolve, the transformations through which the latter passed served to make it, as well, an evolving producer of variable images. In geometric, metaphorical terms, the units of cultural production were being twisted into new shapes, effecting modifications in the way they were perceived. So while the element of the farm worker remained constant with respect to its mere thematic presence, in the Campesino the functioning value diminished, going from singularly central to one among many through deletion and deemphasis, while in *I Am Joaquín* it moved from extremely peripheral to almost dominantly central through addition and reinforcement.

Another poet, Tino Villanueva, himself a migrant farm worker in his youth, revealed his vision of the subject in the last section of his *Hay Otra Voz Poems*. While he paid tribute to Chávez' movement by mentioning him in a poem, his version of farm workers lacked any of the joy or playfulness of the Teatro Campesino's. His message was quite different; instead of the workers asking for solidarity in hopes of changing the system, they advised their children to escape from it through formal study. This element is missing in the two mentioned above, a lack that becomes conspicuous when we bring Villanueva into the field of relationships. Villanueva's migrant experience is privileged as the original source and catalyst of the poet's experience, and thus of central significance—unlike Gonzales' use of it—but the function differs from that in the Teatro Campesino's Actos, inasmuch as it is a source to be left behind, not maintained in an effort to better working conditions. Villanueva's farm workers' goal is to become something else.

A similar statement was made by Tomás Rivera in his novel ... *y no se lo tragó la tierra*. Although the migrant farm worker experience is essential to the book, serving as context for most of the stories that make up the collection, the desire is to transcend the state of farm work itself. There is no hope held out for better conditions, nor is their a utopian theme of union organizing. In fact, one can find a systematic debunking of almost all promises made by social organizations, including the Chicano family. The only hope held out for communal survival is through the personal efforts of the creative author, the poet or fiction writer. Although rife with alienation and contradictions, the school assumes central importance alongside the farm field in the text, because without the writing skills learned there, the field worker will not transcend to liberation. The only space in which the people can find peace and unity is in that evoked by literature, so it is incumbent on the child to focus his efforts in another area other than the fields, that of the school and books. Once again, although farm workers are central, their function within the work differs.

This limited review of the farm worker's image in these few works in no way exhausts the treatment of the theme. However, it suffices to demonstrate that at this level the topological study proves fruitful. It not only discloses common elements, but reveals the differences present from author to author, work to work. The ramifications of these differences would be part of the topographic charting of the space of Chicano literature.

My readings of the major works also revealed that at the surface level of content the following situation was consistently repeated: some element, with a key orienting function for the Chicano community, was threatened with disappearance. The element could assume any form, such as the leader of a youth group (José Montoya's "El Louie"), the barrio ("A Trip through the Mind Jail" by Raul Salinas), the oral tradition (Miguel Méndez's "Tata Casehua," Hinojosa's *Estampas del Valle*, Anaya's *Bless Me, Ultima*, Gonzales' *I Am Joaquín*), the protagonist's past (Villarreal's *Pocho*, Rivera's ... *y no se lo tragó la tierra*), the author's existence (Sánchez' *Canto y grito*), or the poet's survival as poet (Villanueva's *Hay otra voz Poems* or Abelardo's "Stupid America"). Whatever the form, it functioned like a traditional *axis mundi*: it created the sense of cosmos by ordering experience. Its loss, which could appear anywhere in the text's diachronic development, would throw the community into the opposite state, that of chaos.

Again at the level of content, the menace of disappearance was responded to by the recalling of the characteristics of the threatened central element. This lead me to postulate the presence of a common deep structure in the works, that is a topological constant in the form of a deep structure. At first I proposed the pattern in the following manner.

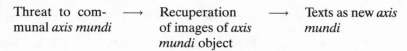

Threat to com- ⟶ Recuperation ⟶ Texts as new *axis*
munal *axis mundi*   of images of *axis*   *mundi*
                        mundi object

However, this seemed to imply that the defeat of the menace to the culture was simple to achieve, which hence made literature appear as an escapist panacea. So I restructured the chart of the deep paradigm to reflect a constant dynamic tension.

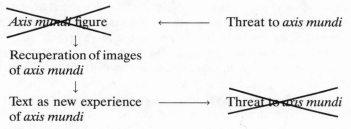

~~*Axis mundi* figure~~   ⟵——— Threat to *axis mundi*
          ↓
Recuperation of images
of *axis mundi*
          ↓
Text as new experience   ———⟶   ~~Threat to axis mundi~~
of *axis mundi*

In this new formulation, the *axis mundi* object appears under erasure, in manner a similar to Heidegger's and Derrida's use of the procedure (Derrida, xiii-xx). This means that the *axis mundi* is still named, though its signifiying function has been suspended. This renders whatever is placed under erasure powerless to function as intended, reduced to a memory of an absent function, a trace—as Derrida calls it—of something that, according to the belief system of those involved, it once should have been. This accounts for the feelings of impending loss, as well as the ability of the works to specify the representative figure in which the loss is encarnated.

The recuperation of *axis mundi* images cannot bring the object itself back—as representations, words can only mark the absence of what they name. However, the text itself is a real object, just as reading is a real experience, and together they can fulfill the same world-centering function as the threatened object. The literature counters the threat of disappearance of the *axis mundi* and resultant cultural disorientation by providing a new orientation ritual, one that represents the old *axis mundi*, but which is actually new. In this way the culture reveals its strength: its centralizing elements are retained through representation, while at the same time a new ritual of orientation is introduced. Through this new representation, the community can learn the secrets of tradition, the skills of survival, and, as is often the case, the fatal mistakes of the past. Thus, the text then shifts the power within its field of presence and puts the threat under erasure.

In *Chicano Poetry, A Response to Chaos*, I gave detailed analysis of the deep structure and its surface manifestation in major poetical works, so here I will illustrate my concepts with a two examples drawn from fiction.

In Rivera's ... *y no se lo tragó la tierra* the paradigm is obvious. The protagonist of the first episode is in a state of extreme alienation, to the point of losing touch with his identity and functions. While literally spinning around, he hears a voice call, but does not recognize it nor the name it calls; later he realizes it was his voice calling his name. The brief text contains a series of starting points, which relegates the ritual of an orienting beginning to the same ambiguity into which the character has fallen with respect to his identity. Rivera locates the *axis mundi* principle in the individual, and despite claims that the text's protagonist is the community itself, it is the individual who must recuperate his sense of centralized order for that community to exist as such. However, the relationship is mutual: the community must exist for the boy to know who, what and where he is. As we see in the stories and vignettes that follow, making up the body of what can be read as a novel, the community is in danger of losing its cohesion and disappearing into oblivion. The text leads us through a series of confrontations with traditional modes of social organization, but they all seem inadequate to the modern situation. Part of the problem lies in that the younger generation's activities contradict the older generation's belief system. The discovery of the tradition of the creative writer in service of the community provides the key to the boy's new identity. He will not loose himself nor his place in the world, because he now knows the secret of recreating his experience and that of the people around him in his imagination and recall. The boy cannot be lost if his community survives, even if survival assumes a representational form. The book itself is the praxis of the discovery, and it can be charted as follows.

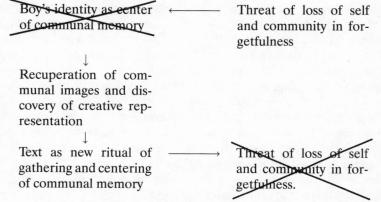

Rolando Hinojosa's *Estampas del Valle* resembles Rivera's text in that it too begins with an identity loss that bodes ill for the community.

In this case, however, the individuals in the initial vignette know who they are and how they relate to each other. A young man has come to ask an older one for the latter's daughter's hand in marriage. This simple action assumes ritual status when the older man recalls that he had come in the same manner to do the same thing. Continued observance of a traditional ritual proves the health of communal customs. However, when the old man wonders who his father-in-law dealt with when he played the suitor's role, we glimpse a potential breakdown in the oral tradition, a ritual as central to communal health as bethrothal. As the reading progresses, and we realize that at the heart of the testimony-like conversations making up the text lies the matter of geneologies, the original question assumes the significance of primal mystery. It must be answered. The text proceedes to enact numerous oral performances, creating for the reader the role of traditional youth, that is, a listener/rememberer, a future storehouse of tradition. And since in South Texas, of which this and all of Hinojosa's subsequent novels treat, geneologies are often the way one distinguishes between those to be trusted and those who have sold out to the Anglo Americans, the information gathered is of vital importance to communal preservation. Answering the first question symbolizes the community's ability to protect itself from further betrayal and displacement. Towards the end of the book, in typical oral tradition fashion—that is, while listening to information about subjects other than that which is directly sought—the answer is suddenly and matter of factly delivered, as if the oral tradition had it safely stored all the time. The text has sought it out by establishing a pattern of oral performances, and then sifted through testimony until the data appears. Thus the text affirms, in its methodology, the very existence and viability of the tradition threatened with loss at the start. Charted the paradigm looks like this.

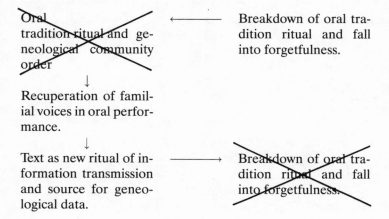

~~Oral tradition ritual and geneological community order~~   ←———   Breakdown of oral tradition ritual and fall into forgetfulness.

↓

Recuperation of familial voices in oral performance.

↓

Text as new ritual of information transmission and source for geneological data.   ——→   ~~Breakdown of oral tradition ritual and fall into forgetfulness.~~

Although these two texts share the topological element of the deep paradigm, the topographical characteristics of the paradigm's display differ. Whereas Rivera leads us to discover oral tradition as a function of the creative imagination of the individual in service of the people, Hinojosa spreads the tradition out into the oral performance of multiple voices of the people themselves. Rivera stresses the need for the individual artist to reproduce the images for a community no longer able to see itself in or through other social organizing rituals, while Hinojosa shows the community healthily practicing its oral memory. Geneology is of little or no importance in Rivera, while in Hinojosa it is the goal of the recuperative venture. This difference can be explained when we consider that Rivera's community is not involved in property disputes of a historical nature, while Hinojosa's work has evolved into a history of land claims closely interwoven with family relations. Ultimately the topographical study of the topological element reveals Rivera's to be the story of truly itinerant people, while Hinojosa's is that of dispossessed landowners with a long history of permanent roots. Despite their similarities, the close proximity of their geographical base in Texas and the perception of the same paradigmatic situation, they differ tremendously. If we so desired, we could use this textual difference to discuss the real-life difference in the authors, Rivera coming from more recent immigration into Texas, while Hinojosa's family counts themselves among the original settlers. Once the topological patterns are revealed, the possibilities for application are countless.

The same type of comparative/contrastive study can be made utilizing the topological approach at either surface or deep structure levels. Its main value lies in the creation of a unified, panoramic view of the literature, one which easily can be extended to include cultural production as a whole. No one topological element will link every work in the field, but a series of relations can be established, and eventually extended to explore ties with other ethnic groups, or with the dominant culture.

Revue Francaise D'Etudes Americaines 13.36 (April 1988): 264-79.

14 Chicano Literary Space: Cultural Criticism/Cultural Production

> Invention ... does not consist in creating out of the void, but out of chaos; the materials must, in the first place, be afforded: it can give form to dark, shapeless substances but cannot bring into being the substance itself.
>
> Mary Shelley, *Frankenstein: or, the Modern Prometheus*, x.

Almost fifteen years have passed since I addressed a gathering of colleagues and students in Las Vegas, New Mexico, at what was billed as the first national conference on Chicano literary criticism, to explain for the first time, outside of the confines of the classroom or the intimacy of a café, my approach to Chicano literature. My presentation on that occasion was "The Space of Chicano Literature," an essay that, like Frankenstein's progeny, has both led and followed me many places since its inception, at once my creation and creator, a whim, a fancy, a serious game of pursuit: much the unrelenting monster of my own invention.

It plagues me in the sense that, over a decade later and after numerous applications and reformulations of the concepts, "The Space of Chicano Literature" continues to be the most read of my essays, in many instances the only one people know, often solely through fragments quoted out of context by other critics. From the start, the difficulty the essay presents for readers has led to reductionist interpretations which confuse a general theory of space with my particular vision of the paradigm which informs Chicano literature. So as a framework for discussing my work as both social criticism, or, as I would prefer to

call it, cultural production, allow me to review the postulates inherent
in that now ancient essay and which have been refined in my later work.
At the same time I will attempt to clarify the chaos from whence it came,
and the elements I borrowed from it, to piece together my concept.

Literary Space

The space of literature is experienced as a phenomenological field
in which texts exist intertextually in relationship to other texts and/or
events which form and define their area of movement. Studies of this
space usually begin topographically, as descriptions of the distribution
of elements charted from some point, which serves as a landmark, and
bracketed within certain boundaries, depending on the viewer's interests. One usually starts with those in immediate proximity of a specific
work in need of explication, depending on the elements one chooses to
foreground—generic, thematic or other written texts by authors of similar interests and background, such as national, generational or ethnic.
This does not exclude other types, such as oral tradition, film, music,
history or the multiple facets of social interaction. Literary space is dynamic, constantly shifting, and has an insatiable appetite for anything
with which it comes into contact, continually devouring elements that
on first appearance seem extraneous and foreign. Criticism, by the way,
should be no less dynamic, since it is part of literary space.

Imagine, if you will, a model from physics displayed in computer
graphics, projected in perspective to give the appearance of transpar-
ent volume in three dimension. It should be in constant motion, never
static long enough to be defined into one form nor to allow a permanent
perspective. This space is generated by its inhabitants, the texts whose
characteristics bring them into relationship; if nothing else, the mere
fact of cohabitation relates them. Like stars, some burn intensely, while
others only begin to flicker or seem spent. The gravitational pull can
vary; clusters revolve around nuclei, but seen from a distance details
blur to give the impression of solitary points. Most newly arrived matter fits itself within the defined patterns of established nuclei, adding
weight and size, but altering little its character. There can even be cell-
like reproduction, or cloning, within a cluster. The space's general state
approximates that of the clusters. One can focus on areas of any size,
tracing borders to block off a space of action to be analyzed. There
are moments of more intense activity. Occasionally a comet-like shape
moves through. Or just outside what seems to be the space's outer limits a figure may appear, sometimes exerting irressitible pull, drawing out
and distorting the spatial form, causing readjustments and forcing new

considerations of relative values. At other times, the space itself forces realignments and even exclusions. The power of specifically literary entities can be enhanced or diminished by the activity of non-literary ones, but the relationship is mutual.

The critic's location with respect to the space determines how much or little she or he sees. A small cluster can seem the entire universe for some, while others desire or need to explore beyond ordained limits. If we peer into what seems a surrounding void, we discern similar systems. If we manage to travel even further, we may discover that, despite surface differences, basic similarities arise; on the other hand, we can find that, despite close outer similarities to some neighbors, there can be essential differences. The question of constant or common characteristics, despite the multiple variables of surface manifestations, takes us beyond topography to topology, from facade to deep structure. Yet this does not radically differ from the situation within the space, and we discover that the limits, however necessary for orderly life, are arbitrary and variable, often based on other than literary needs.

Critical studies freeze the space at a specific moment, or attempt to chart the movement of certain relationships over a set period of time. Either way, criticism must accept, and should acknowledge, its incompleteness; in no way can it embrace everything in the phenomenological field, whose total simultaneity and dynamic polivalence overwhelm the contingent observer. Therefore criticism, in an attempt to justify its limited scope, creates its own fiction of territory within which the critic and readers can travel in some orderly manner the length of the voyage. The same can be said of rhetorical strategies: they are terministic indicators allowing critics to function in a reduced field, more manageable and apprehensible. For example, the prevasive tendency to reduce experience to binary terms, or dialectical conflicts, is just such a rhetorical tool that, nevertheless, is yet another fiction which focuses on an interaction of two factors to the exclusion of the rest of those in the field which influence the dynamics of that relationship. But despite the claims of some critics to be strictly objective and all-inclusive, no criticism is possible without bracketing the space. Life itself is a matter of bracketing.

Ironically, if a critical study succeeds greatly, it may alter the space, thus distancing it from itself. Or perhaps it will so capture readers' imagination that the space will be pressed temporarily into a static mold. The critic's presence itself may come to represent a force field within the space. Some participate in power by attaching themselves to whatever figure seems to excercise more gravitational pull at the time. Others have tried to appropriate the source of power to themselves, claiming the need to mediate experience, and even the right to be the primary contact between reader and society, offering their own presence as a more reliable bridge to other spaces. Although criticism can be seen to have a space of its own, it participates in the general one of cultural production; it is a matter of perspective, but a matter, nonetheless, that also has to be taken into account when charting the field, an action which itself also must be accounted for.

I have indulged this metaphor long enough, but then criticism often dons the cloak of metaphor, offering itself as something other than what it is, somewhat like Blanchot's cadaver, a once particular being which, while still clinging to individual appearances, already participates in Otherness where all is possible because materiality no longer exists to limit it (Blanchot, 257-60). In this characteristic, criticism also attempts to usurp literature's essence. Frankenstein's crime was that, like an author or critic or reader, he animated cadavers. I have pursued this metaphor to the point of death because it, too, is basic to my thought.

My Theory As Cultural Production

Although my approach has been associated by some with Formalism or even New Criticism, I believe that this is a misconception based on my wish that the text itself, and not the critic's interpretation, remain the central point of the reading encounter. I still believe that the critic's role is to lead readers back to the subject text better equipped to enjoy and understand the experience. This is founded in my faith that the texts contain and produce culture in a more direct, primary manner than criticism itself. Even texts with which we do not agree—and there have been a good number of them—reflect some aspect of our heterogeneous community. Thus, the creative work being analyzed is the beginning and end of the critical process, but that does not exclude the possibility and probability of going beyond it during the analysis, forming a sort of expansive parenthesis. Nor does it exclude the need for well-founded knowledge of broad contexts. But I reiterate: the text will lead one to these, explicitly or implicitly. To work outside it is another field of study, perhaps more appropriately designated the sociology of literature.

My critical orientation is best described as eclecticism—Annette Kolodny's term "playful pluralism" fits as well—or by other terminology popular in France: civilization and cultural production. This is the product of my interdisciplinary liberal arts training with Jesuits, who insisted on large blocks of courses dedicated to literature, history, philosophy and theology, and my own choice of history as an early focus of concentration. My rejection of a strictly historical—in the traditional sense of the term—basis for the eclectic synthesis can be attributed to my years of specialization in history, including teaching at the high school level, and a B.A. major.

My fascination with history began around age eight. Along with devouring all the books at the local libraries, I had the privilege of an intense and varied oral tradition experience. I overheard long conversations by Austrian Jewish refugees, Italian and French immigrants and, of course, Mexican nationals. Many entertaining hours were spent listening to a retired oil engineer recount the 1920s and '30s in Mexico. I witnessed intense arguments between the Mexican Consul and a Spaniard, or among university professors, or veterans from W.W.II—as well as reading antirepublican Franquista propaganda, which led me to seek republican responses. In Mexico I heard different views, from the poor indigenous to the upperclass. As a result, I came to realize, even while still in grade school, that history was susceptible to manipulation. One should know facts, such as dates and places, but "history" was how you used them in an argument to prove or disprove points, to sway your listener. The next step from this realization was a healthy cynicism with respect to any appeals to the priority of the historical text and context. Years later, when I first encountered Hayden White, I recognized a kindred spirit.

The interdisciplinary focus of my preparation lead me to develop a cultural view of all fields as part of a product of social orientation to basic questions of survival. My readings of the existentialists made me doubt transcendent essence, but Albert Camus' stand on the value of life in *The Rebel* brought me back to the basic question of survival. Phenomenology provided me with the rationale for, 1) suspending judgment on the basis of preestablished norms; 2) for attempting to allow specific objects to reveal their own interior structural dynamics; and, 3) to accept that the object will always be read—and therefore utilized—in different manners by different audiences according to their situational needs and perspectives. An early reading of Mircea Eliade was a revelation: the history of peoples could be seen as the repeated attempt to create a livable order in the midst of imminent chaos, to instill values in a world which denied them, and to provide meaningful patterns of behavior in the face of the one overriding fact of life—death. History was a series of attempts to provide people with the orientation of their own *axis mundi*. All human efforts seemed to be either consciously or unconsciously aimed at achieving what Eliade called cosmicization. History itself—the practice of textualizing and contextualizing events— was nothing more than this, as was the Bible, yet another fictional history designed to fabricate a cultural *axis mundi* for a displaced, migrant people in perpetual diaspora. Art serves the same function, whether at the social or the personal level.

When I entered graduate school, however, I found that my professors in Spanish and Latin American literature understood none of this. My first reaction was that I could not argue until I had mastered, as in history, the basic facts: dates, names, places. After I did, I found the problem to be more profound: my professors had no idea what literature was, not even an idea I could consider incorrect. Nor did they care. Their lack of orientation allowed me eventually to develop on my own along the lines begun years earlier. But I was in need of some guidance.

Fortunately, chance came to my rescue when in 1969, while starting to write a dissertation on Carlos Fuentes, I discovered the writings of Juan García Ponce, who became the teacher and mentor none of my professors had been. Not that I met him immediately—I was not that lucky—rather his essays provided the education and orientation I needed. In them once again I encountered phenomenology, this time heavily steeped in Merleau Ponty, but with the added dimensions of Maurice Blanchot and Georges Bataille. It was like rereading my old cultural studies through a dark, Nietzchean gaze. Even Octavio Paz paled in comparison.

García Ponce's brilliant essay "El arte y lo sagrado" reoriented my work after a chaotic graduate program, whose only virtue was an old-fashioned required reading list that excused no period nor genre. In that essay, García Ponce, while pretending to talk about painting, places into dialogue writers such as Hölderlin, Rilke, Pavese, Heidegger, Blanchot and Bataille, through which there develops an exposition on art as the sacrifice of material reality, a sacrifice in which spectators participate and from which they receive benefits of a sacred revelation:

> Which ever artist we refer to, be it the poet in relation to the word or the painter in regard to images, he strips both the world and its beings of their appearance, of their individuality, to turn them into words or images. In order to do so . . . it is indispensable that this individuality exist, that it be real; but after accepting this, which is equivalent of accepting the world and its apparent reality, what the artist does in truth is sacrifice the world. Through the artistic act, reality dies to transform itself, in the case of painting, into an image. However, this death is a new life. Reality is devoured by the work, by the image, so that the latter might show us the former as another life. But it is a dead life which precisely has been taken out of time, stripping it of its discontinuity, leaving it fixed forever outside of and within life simultaneously. In this fact is found the secret and power of the permanence of the work of art. In the work of art the sacrifice is repeated over and over again in front to the attentive spectator's gaze. And from the sacrifice is born the power to evoke the sacred. (95-96, translation mine)

Art, then, functions as a spiritual, moral force in the world, far beyond its prosaic, informational function. As explained by García Ponce, art fulfilled Eliade's definition of the cultural project of creating the *axis mundi*. Through the reading, literature seemed to assume a key topological characteristic that transcended the greatist topographical diversity.

About the time I was discovering the world through García Ponce, the Chicano Movement was discovering me. One was as inescapable as the other, but eventually I would have to bring them into harmony.

When I first started working in Chicano studies, much of our cultural space was being bracketed out by those ideologues who were defining Chicanismo in the most narrow terms and reducing literature to a mere adjunct of political rhetoric. Exclusionary practices of different groups competed for the position of sole authentic model of early Chicanismo. In Colorado, my home state, in the late '60s and early '70s, many students either turned, or were turned, away from new Chicano organizations because they could not fit into the characteristics of a Chicano as set down by the militants of different persuasions. I saw hundreds of Chicano students enroll in the university—recruited from all over the state, with divergent backgrounds—clash with organizers who would later declare that recruiting from certain geographic areas was a mistake because those young people were "not really Chicanos." I encouraged a young woman to publish her poetry, only to have her respond that another professor, a Chicana, had told her that her poetry was "not Chicano enough." Students were being expelled from the circle of our people by those few who arrogated to themselves the right to define Chicano authenticity. My immediate response was to tell my students that they were Chicanos, so whatever they did was Chicano culture. In my courses on Chicano literature, the students had to write stories and poetry. It wasn't all publishable, but it was Chicano. And I learned that their concerns exceeded what the ideologues were discussing. The most blatant exclusions from that early Movement rhetoric were women and the middle class Chicano.

At the same time, the relatively scarce literature available in those years already displayed a diversity that belied any narrow focus. Yet, especially when seen from one or another specific region of the Southwest, it seemed simple to dismiss divergent types as somehow not authentic. We functioned like tribes: those closest to the center were correct, authentic—but who was to fix the center? For us in Colorado, Chicanos from Texas and California could seem somewhat strange, each excentric in their own manner, although the Californians were always preferable. On the other hand, New Mexicans struck us as much more real, like country cousins, but at least first cousins. Of course, the farmworker transcended all regional categories—although one would have had to be blind not to notice that most of the urban students at the Denver

Center of the University of Colorado, where I served as director of our
program, had little direct knowledge of those people who most often
skirted the city in their movements along the farm roads.

There was much more to the culture than what was being discussed
in public, and in an attempt to speak for those not being represented,
I published my first essay: "Freedom of Expression and the Chicano
Movement." In brief, it asked for a more comprehensive view of our
culture and that of Mexico so as not to exclude any of our community
from the literature being produced. It was a call, not to U.S. mainstream
publishers, but to Chicano publishers to expand their conception of our
culture to reflect more accurately our diversity. I was already thinking
in terms of a phenomenological space with a much wider bracketing.
This would be necessary if I and many Chicanos I worked with were to
be included.

The need for some topological paradigm made itself apparent when
I tried, along with my students, to find relationships among the varied
surfaces of Chicano texts in the early '70s. Yet, teaching in Colorado
with mostly local students, I believe prevented me from seeing it clearly,
for the reasons mentioned above. It crystalized with surprising rapidity,
however, when I arrived at Yale University in 1974 and found myself
in an extremely heterogeneous congregation of students united under
the rubric of Chicanos. We were the metaphor of the literature and
an accurate microcosm of the general Chicano community: diversity in
search of a unifying principle, under the continual threat of extinction.
Distant as we were from any regionally defined community, authenticity
was not a matter of residence, but of essence. This situation made it
urgent that our specific cultural production—that is what we did, and
how we related as a group—not be divisive. It was in September of
1974 that the paradigm of Chicano literature was produced during my
first semester at Yale.

This interpretation stated that the major Chicano texts assumed the
rhetorical stance of responding to a threat to the existence of Chicano
culture in some representational form that, in so-called real life, oriented space into a meaningful cosmos; that those texts responded to
that threat by affirming the existence of the things or processes threatened, but transformed them into words, images, texts; that in the light of
the disappearance of the object in the so-called real world, or in some
cases the delayed appearance of a substitute, the text becomes a new
form of the object, actually an object and process and experience on its
own, that then functions as a new point of orientation; that the writ-
ing/reading of a Chicano text is a ritual of cultural orientation, perhaps
a reification of more concrete rituals, but none the less a ritual, a form
of sacred, orientating experience; that this new ritual is a reality in so-

ciety; it is not simply the reflection of culture—or of ideology if you will—but the producer and product of culture. The literature creates a space for culture to reflect itself in a written media formerly closed to self-produced Chicano images. It is also one of the spaces where one goes for symbolic action, which then, depending on the reader, can be transformed into other forms of praxis.

Chicano literature became a centering presence and practice. The reading of divergent texts as representatives of different aspects of a common space in and of itself authorized divergency in our immediate community, while serving as a communion ritual for those who wished to participate. Instead of dismissing texts because of distasteful ideological stands—which usually meant dismissing as non-Chicano those Chicano students who related to the images in those texts—I tried to open the students to the idea that the literature faithfully represented the variety of the community, whether we liked it or not. That is not to say that one simply accepts an ideology, but one must try to understand it on its terms before one can respond. More than this, without abandoning disagreement or conflict, one should try to embrace the community in its differences.

More importantly, we found that, despite differences in ideology, which could be explained by the specific context of the production of the text, the most significant writers concerned themselves with the same essential question of survival. Moreover, when the concept of art and the sacred was applied, the texts all were shown to function as ritual sacrifice which ordered the chaos of life. Literature was not a formalistic excercise, but a serious response to a death threat. It did not substitute for action in the real world, but rather often demanded just such action. Nevertheless, it was of itself another type of real action that could significantly alter one's experience by orienting and teaching.

Perhaps it is just an idealized memory, but something of that spirit seemed to spill over outside the classroom. The fact that what we were doing at Yale began to reverberate in other parts of the Chicano community helped us relate to Chicanos back home by giving us an identity within a national literary project. And what it told us about home, family and community were the basic facts of culture as real activity, as necessary signifying acts of cosmic orientation that provide a sense of place and identity from which all other actions could be attempted, and without which they were, at best, dubious. It revealed that we have lived, and continue to live, with the special sense of diaspora, despite a claim of rights to the land; that we are in constant need of reaffirming unity, because the threat of disintegration is ever present; that we see existence in the basic terms of struggle against the outsider, and that we do not tolerate well those of our own who do not remain faithful to the group, while at the same time we conserve a tradition of rebelliousness. Finally, and most importantly, through literature it became apparent that there was no one political ideology that united us, nor even one specific cultural code, because regionalism had never been transcended. The advantage of being at Yale, where the students came from all over the United States, was that they themselves incarnated the vast differences in the greater Chicano community. When they could not even agree on how to make an enchilada, then the ideal of a simple, superficial Chicanismo was obviously an illusion. Yet the literature became a binding factor when read for essence, despite surface difference.

After all these years, and the onslaught of the post-modern conceptualization of our historic moment, it may seem a romantic anachronism to still believe in the possibility of a transcendent function for art. Yet, even when critics and certain intellectuals dismiss the goal of transcendence, or deny the possibility of presence, it changes little. The necessity for the art of the sacred was the fact of absence at the heart of every apparent presence. What is now clearer than ever is that the word is not the thing, but the death of the thing, its absence, its cadaverous representation in our midst—but that's exactly the point. To flee from death into a series of ever altering mirror reflections of mere representation is not to exalt life, but just to delay and ironically multiply, the ephemeral quality of life. And in spite of it all, people still desire orientation rituals, and they find them in art, even when that art appears to be the monstrous, piecemeal work of a mad surgeon.

I am surprised that the paradigm I offered back in 1974 still functions for many texts today, perhaps because it is not unique to Chicano literature, but common to contemporary literature, in varying degrees, since the Romantic period, and the basis for religious experience, as we know it, from the start. That texts have appeared which do not stress this paradigm—I would say my own book of poetry would be included among them, although perhaps I am too close to it to read it correctly—can be seen in different ways. On the one hand, the existence of Chicano literature itself can make writers less concerned for their survival; they now have a space to work in. As Ramón Saldívar has said of the Chicano novel after *Pocho*, it is not a question of *if* the Chicano novel exists, but *how*. In addition, we must accept the fact that not all Chicano authors will share the most obvious and visible characteristics of the culture— and those who do in their life may not want to in their literature, which is a legitimate position. Also, the changing mood of the society can buffer writers from experiencing life as a struggle. We must remember that contemporary Chicano literature arose in the '60s when even the mainstream society questioned its own relevance. Things have changed, but one still finds the paradigm functioning in such works as Sheila Ortiz Taylor's *Faultline*, Cecile Pineda's *Face*, Lorna Dee Cervantes' *Emplumada*, Luis Valdez' *Zoot Suit*, Sandra Cisneros' *The House on Mango Street*, Jimmy Santiago Baca's *Martín and Meditations on the South Valley*, or *Reto al Paraíso* by Alexandro Morales, to name a few. But as I admitted back in 1974, the dynamic nature of cultural production can render incomplete or obsolete any interpretation, including this one. The critic should accept the role of just another force in the interplay of tensions. If what comes denies this paradigm, it matters little. Nothing is eternal, and very little is actually necesary. If my work has helped, or at least participated, in the expansion of our space to more of us, then it has served its purpose as cultural production. If it accurately portrayed the concerns of at least part of the community, then it has functioned as cultural criticism.

A Cursory Survey Of Chicano Literary Space

The space of Chicano criticism was not empty when I ventured into it, although it certainly was less congested. Some basic studies had been published. Looking back on that early period, contrary to the complaints that our criticism tends to ignore historical content or context, the dominant method of the first stage was historical and descriptive, with two main proponents: Philip Ortego and Luis Leal. They coincided in their view that Chicano literature should trace its existence back centuries through a historical presence of Spanish-speaking people in the northern colonies of New Spain, but they differed on the particulars of their explanation. In fact, Leal's "Mexican American Literature: A Historical Perspective" (1973) can be read as a dialogical appendix to, if not an emmendation of, Ortego's doctoral dissertation, *Backgrounds of Mexican American Literature* (1972).

Ortego, having graduated from an English Department, displayed some of the same limitations concerning the canon that he criticized in others. He was searching for written texts in the line of high culture literature. Leal, coming from a Spanish Department, sees the Southwest in terms of the Spanish Colonial period followed by a brief Mexican territorial one which was cut short by the U.S take over that brought into being what we now call the Southwest. This formulation of historical periods was a direct response to the question, raised by Ortego and others, as to where the silenced Chicano material would be found. Leal was gently suggesting that English trained critics had to learn Spanish and become familiar with Mexican literature.

During the same period of the late '60s and early '70s, however, Doris Meyer entered the dialogue to respond more directly. While Ortego called the Territorial Period a "Dark Age" of which little is known, Meyer published several articles on nineteenth-century New Mexican poetry, demonstrating that research could indeed prove a historical presence despite previous lagunae. Meyer's intertextual, implicit criticism of Ortego lies in her demonstration that serious research could prove the existence of materials to belie the "Dark Age" comment; even more to the point, she conducted her research in the very same geographic location, New Mexico, where Ortego had done his dissertation. The space of criticism contains dangers as well as opportunities.

Much lip service was paid to the need to continue this kind of historical investigation, but it would not be until the '80s that results would begin to materialize, as we will see later. Significantly, most of the work in this area attributes its source of orientation not to Ortego, who since has almost disappeared from the scene, but to Leal, thus creating one of those clusters of gravity within Chicano literary space, while, by preference of the users of the space, eclipsing another.

The majority of the very few essays that passed for criticism in the late '60s and early '70s, however, was based on political and ideological considerations. Chicano literature was judged on how it conformed to the goals of the Movement. There was much talk of committed literature, in the Sartrean sense, while at the same time people demanded that the literature accurately reflect the community. That there might be a difference between militant rhetoric and the community was not often discussed. This was the era of the ethnic slur; to question the Movement was to put in doubt your ethnicity.

When I read my paper at the conference in 1974, I intended, in a sense, to dialogue with the center of Chicano literary space from a position at the periphery. Mine was not an established voice, like Leal's, nor that of a highly visible print-media figure like Ortego's. Like many other beginning professors trained in the '60s, I wanted to incorporate the literature of my particular interest group into the canon of university letters. But I did not agree with much of what was said by other critics. As I have explained above, my experience with my students had taught me that not all of them felt themselves represented by the literature and that the majority cared little about the politcal standards applied by activists. Chicano students often asked basic questions, like what do different works have in common? Or, is this literature really any different from other ethnic writing? So in particular I wanted to go beyond the reductionist vision of our literature as political statement and find its human elements. Expressed in other terms that seem to have lost favor in political circles, I wanted to demonstrate its universality. In another way I wanted to voice the possibility of experiences silenced by the noise of politicians and ideologues. Where were the Chicano writers who could speak to and bespeak the lives of my students? My goal was to expand the space to allow discussion of concerns branded as non-Chicano, but which obviously were present in the works of writers who qualified as Chicano by birth and heritage.

Also, my experience with very contemporary Mexican literature differed, not only from Ortego's and Leal's, but from most of the critics active at that time. As mentioned above, my own graduate experience was so scandalously devoid of methodological orientation that I was forced to find my own. Luckily, I finally came across Juan García Ponce writings, which reaffirmed the phenomenological slant of my Jesuit undergraduate studies (see "Testimonio escrito con X"). But since I came from neither the East Coast new-formalists, nor from any English Department whatsoever, nor from the emerging socially oriented schools of the '60s, when I began to publish I found myself often dialoguing in silence. My students and a few interested readers responded. Yet someone else was listening as well who considered my concepts to be such a threat that a full scale attack was begun.

After the appearance of my first essay, the space of Chicano criticism heated up considerably. In 1977 Joseph Sommers published his only major article on Chicano literature: "From the Critical Premise to the Product." It called for a criticism rooted in history and conducted dialectically. No one really argues with Sommers' ideal methodology because it included almost everything anyone would do with a text. The critic was advised to synthesize the best from all existing approaches. What he insisted upon, however, was reduction of literature to reality. That is to say, the literary text was essentially the same in nature as any other phenomena, not to be privileged in any fashion. Sommers participated in that attack on art which attempts to bring it back to the realm of the everyday, the mundane. This had the effect of placing the value of literature in a scale of realism in which this key term was linked closely to ideological principles. If the work reflected class struggle and addressed directly the definition of oppressors and oppressed, then it was of value. If it did not, or seemed not to, or did not within what Sommers considered the correct manner, then it was declared a failure and harmful. He insisted on the critic's right and duty to judge a work and writer according to his—Sommers'—preconceived ideological standards. Even more, he believed in using criticism as a weapon against those with whom he did not agree, and it is here where I found fault with him then and still do. It is this use of criticism to impose an ideological criteria for good or bad literature that places Sommers back within the sociopolitical line of criticism of the earlier years. He differed in that his attack was aimed at those who had done the attacking before, the cultural nationalists. Yet his insistence on a Marxist or

pseudo-Marxist orientation was no less dogmatic than the one he attacked in others.

That behind his liberal façade Sommers attacked me by calling me a
formalist—the Marxist equivalent of *vendido*—should not be taken too
much to heart. I believe he was sincere—which does not erase defects—
for in my conversations with him I came to realize that he did not understand the difference between a formalist and a phenomenologist. Again
I would mention that my training in post-Octavio Paz Mexican thought
made my communication with Sommers difficult at a time when he was
moving back to a defense of *indigenismo*. However, that he would misrepresent my work through vulgar reductionism and false attribution of
principles should not be overlooked, because it is as an example that
Sommers is most fondly remembered and eulogized. I have no objection, since he was not a theoretician, so we can and should recall how
he went about his project of suggesting a proper Chicano canon.

For example, when he condemned Rudy Anaya's *Bless Me Ultima* as
a "harking back with sadness and nostalgia to a forgotten, idealized and
unobtainable past" (61), he did needless harm, while simultaneously revealing his own inability to read beyond the surface of a text. In this case,
as an example of a "dynamic" text and thus correct in his political view,
Sommers offered Raúl Salinas' poem "A Trip Through the Mind Jail,"
which he preferred for its capacity to provide the forms and encourage
the spirit of resistance. However, both texts are essentially retrospective voyages into childhood, a space which in the present of each writing
act has disappeared. So both look back nostalgically to an unobtainable
past. That one text idealizes this past more than the other is highly de-
batable, since both of them balance the positives and negatives of life
in the childhood neighborhood. And as for resistance, both texts find it
ultimately in the writing act itself, not in any political action outside of
the text. If anything, Salinas' poem can be seen as more attuned to indi-
vidualism and escapism than Anaya's. What Sommers liked in Salinas,
as is often the case with cultural outsiders, is the poem's urban ghetto
quality that seems more authentic and more accurate according to a certain preestablished picture of Chicano communities. Something similar
can be found in such works as *West Side Story* or *Tortilla Flat*. Anaya's
novel, when read carefully, is not a call for returning to a static past,
but for recuperating a traditional way of living the dynamic oppositions
of the present, yet updated to modern conditions. But because Sommers definition of good literature was that which espoused his view of
social evolution at the most superficial level, anything else, even when
it expressed an authentic experience of a member of the Chicano community, had to be, not only dismissed, but slurred. For Sommers, as for
some Chicano critics as well, his ideal of the community was more im-

portant than the community itself, which he knew very little. He had the
tendency to deny the reality of the values and the ideas of those authors
who did not blatantly encode the class struggle into their works.

Unfortunately, this strategy of the drawing of battle lines, along with
a general divisive tone, was and is still followed by a core group of disci-
ples. As I stated before, there is no real objection to using all the critical
approaches Sommers recommends in the utopian portion of his essay,
it is only when he practiced misrepresentation and censorship that he
fell from those lofty liberal heights.

Before the decade ended, a direct response to Sommers was eloquently formulated by Ramón Saldívar in "A Dialectic of Difference:
Toward a Theory of the Chicano Novel." Saldivar, much better prepared in literary theory than Sommers, picks up the challenge to practice dialectical criticism and offers a version derived from the post-
structuralist thought of Derrida, with a healthy dose of Adorno and
Bakhtin. His characterization of Chicano literature as the producer
and product of a culture of difference, one which constantly negates the
predominant cultural models, and simultaneously turns negation into
an affirmation of new existence as a culture different from the other,
but still related, is, in my opinion, a brilliant recasting and elaboration
of my own approach, with an added emphasis on ideological concerns.
He seems to differ in his negation of cultural synthesis, preferring to
emphasize Adorno's negative dialectics. However, within the continual
dynamism of literary space, my concept of synthesis also proves to be a
process always in progress, an ideal goal never achieved. The difference
between Saldívar and Sommers is essentially that the latter saw the text
as the product of an exterior reality which the author and work should
serve, and that praxis, to be real, had to come outside the realm of the
text or even literature; while the former studies it as a reality capable of
producing concrete effects in the world. Sommers saw and analyzed the
message; Saldivar accepts that symbolic action constitutes a real praxis
in itself.

When you add to Ramón's work that of his brother José David Saldívar, we have the most exciting theoretical thought in Chicano criticism. José Saldívar's application of negative dialectics and Jamesonian
theories of political unconsciousness promise to deliver what Sommers
called for: dialectical analysis that takes history into consideration as
another text. Yet the Saldívar brothers surpass Sommers in their aversion to tendentiousness, their healthy questioning of all ideologies, and
mostly for a self-consciousness that insists that true dialectical thought
is always self-critical. One's own assumption must come under the same
critical scrutiny as those of others.

In the '80s we have had the continuation of the approaches begun in

the '70s. Most exciting in the historical approach is Genaro Padilla's discovery of a wealth of autobiographies from the nineteenth century. Chicano literature has always been considered lacking in this genre. With
Padilla's work we now have fertile new material to research. Of special interest in Padilla's work is the fact that the lives he will soon make
available include figures from widely different backgrounds, once again
proving that earlier concepts of Chicanos as monolithic was not true
even in the nineteenth century. Also, the research of Juan Rodríguez,
Nicolás Kanellos, Juanita Lawhn and Luis Leal himself, along with others, into the Spanish language newspapers of the Southwest is continually forcing Chicano space to expand, while proving the need and validity of the historical approach in providing a background for the contemporary period. One thing that we have learned is that our community
was neither as singularly oral as we believed twenty years ago, nor was
it cut off from Latin American letters, especially Mexican literature.

My own work in the area of historical backgrounds has proved that
the Texan and Southern California Chicano communities of this century's first decades had weekly access to the best of Mexican writing,
sometime even before Mexicans themselves. This forces us to consider
other questions; for example, at what point can an immigrant Mexican writer be considered Chicano? What effect did the publication of
world-class authors have on the Chicano readership? What is the relationship between the Mexican exiles' rhetoric of self-justification between 1910-1936 and the Chicano Movement's rhetoric of separatist nationalism some three decades later? Why did these publishing outlets
attract so little direct participation by Chicano writers? Where are the
Chicano authors who read these papers? These new questions take us
back to reevaluate, for instance, Tomás Rivera and Rolando Hinojosa,
both of whom faithfully read *La Prensa*, or Tino Villanueva, who remembers how his grandfather received the newspaper and how one of
his own poetic images—the watchmaker's repair kit ("Escape," 44)—
can be traced back to an item advertised in the newspaper. Perhaps
Hinojosa's characteristic fragmentation of texts has some relationship
with the fragmented texts of the literary supplements of those newspapers. Thus, the historical research continually sparks reformulations.
Another example of research necessitating readjustments in assumptions we have taken for granted is Luis Leal's recent discovery that the
most commonly cited text of the Joaquín Murrieta Corrido was actually a superficially amended version of a corrido about a bandit from
northen Mexico. This information forces us to ponder the supposed
historical utility of the corridos, shifting them away from documentary,
factual status back into the province of oral tradition—docu-fiction at
best—where they belong.

In the Sommers line of criticism we have the book on Chicano novel in Spanish by Salvador Rodríguez del Pino who credits Sommers' article as the source of his methodology. Although claiming to follow Sommers' recommendations, del Pino strays into very traditional techniques of authenticating the factual content of texts by reference to interviews and biography. Ironically, del Pino's work is much closer to what Sommers attacked as formalist criticism than dialectics. A better attempt to follow the ideal can be found in Alurista's dissertation on Oscar Zeta Acosta. Most probably the best utilization of the Marxist dialectic has been Rosaura Sánchez' work, especially her linguistic studies. Presently she is writing essays of semiotic and political analysis that no longer fall in the field of literature, but more in sociology or perhaps communications.

Two significant new developments are 1) the rapidly growing body of feminist criticism, and 2) the emergence of a group of interested European critics. A fine example of a feminist critic is Diana Rebolledo. Her essays have focused on specific topics, like game playing or humor, instead of attempting to offer a comprehensive overview of the literature, thus providing solid building blocks for the new field. Norma Alarcón's as yet unpublished research will begin to provide the overview Rebolledo lacks. The most promising panoramic project, however, is being carried out by Rebolledo, Eliana Rivero, Carmen Salazar Parr and María Herrera-Sobek who have undertaken a lengthy and detailed analysis of Chicana rhetoric. The project is in completion stage and should change radically the dynamics of our critical space.

Another book attempts a more modest proposal, Marta Sánchez' *Contemporary Chicana Poetry*. Sánchez postulates that Chicana poets struggle with different identities modes: poet, woman, Chicana. Thus, the analysis of any Chicana poet can be formulated in terms of how she balances these forces, and what choices she makes concerning them. I find some of the analysis interesting, but I question the categories of identity. Must they be inherently in opposition? Also, I come away from the reading feeling that these writers have been subjected to, first, a categorization as schizophrenics, and secondly, a type of psychological analysis that may not always best explain the poetry. Also, as a methodology it requires much more research into the backgrounds of the writer than is normally possible. This is author-oriented analysis, not textual or even reader response. My discomfort with it has nothing to do with the feminism; I would feel equally uneasy with this method applied to men. But it does open an approach up to now little utilized by Chicano critics. Del Pino could be said to be similar, and the comparison makes one appreciate just how well Sánchez did her work, and how much effort was lacking in del Pino's.

The European criticism is stimulating and provocative. Dieter Herms' application of Lenin's theory of Second Culture is a good example. Our Marxists are so accustomed to formulating their arguments in the terms of U.S. academia's version of that philosophy that when one confronts a Marxist from another tradition it is like a breath of fresh air. Their ideas force us to reconsider what we have taken as given, as basic information universally understood, and explain it. They can place us in perspective in a manner that reveals our participation in U.S. literature, or our difference. For instance, why does Professor Ostendorf's theory of parody in U.S. Black literature —minstrellsy he calls it—not function in the case of Chicanos? This dialogue has already produced three major international conferences, with a fourth planned for Germany in 1990. They are the most significant and exciting happenings in Chicano criticism since the days of the Floricantos and the mid-seventies MLA conferences.

The interaction of all of these modes of criticism produces the space of Chicano criticism. It is absurd to complain that there is no agreement on what type of criticism is best or which theoretical approach more accurately represents a Chicano perspective. Just as our community is in reality a conglomeration of losely related but highly diverse communities, our criticism reflects multiple possibilities. This is healthy and promising. Ultimately it proves that criticism is just another element in cultural production, so as Chicano literature and arts expands to embrace ever more perspectives, criticism follows suit.

Conclusion

In closing this essay allow me to return again to the personal note. Too much attention has been given my "The Space of Chicano Literature" as the basic statement of my theories. I would simply remind readers that my first essay was titled "Freedom of Expression and the Chicano Movement." In it I called for artistic and ideological freedom for writers and the tolerance of differences by readers and critics. I made a plea for allowing our literature to develop as the expression of the entire community, not just those who speak the style or the message of one or another interest group. Chicano literature is to be made, not prescribed. Also I called for reading without fixed absolutes, eclectically. I have not changed. Back then I pondered the future of Chicano literature in the following fashion.

> Years from now, critics will come to study what were the characteristics of Chicano literature of our time. Hopefully, they will find such an enormous wealth of divergent material that simple classification will be

impossible. Not that they will be stopped, for literary historians make the impossible possible, usually through the process of falsification and amputation. (Or should that read mutilation?) Ni modo. But it will be tragic if they find their job already done, the censuring and excluding having been carried out by over zealous, narrow minded, misguided Chicanos themselves.

I did not foresee that I would come to be one of those beings called a critic—I never intended to be; in fact I never intended to do anything. For my amputations, I apologize; for my falsifications, I plead ignorance; for my classifications I plead necessity—or perhaps insanity. What we achieved sprang from specific, intense cultural needs. To create the space of Chicano literature was our response to the cultural chaos we found ourselves in. In this profoundly practical, pragmatic way, it is essentially cultural production. That it, like Frankenstein's invention, has become something more than what I intended at the start is both blessing and curse, but that, too, is a cultural commentary worthy of yet another venture into invention.

Previously unpublished

Notes

[1]"The ideologeme is an amphibious formation, whose essential structural characteristic may be described as its possibility to manifest itself either as a pseudoidea—a conceptual or belief system, an abstract value, an opinion or prejudice—or as a protonarrative, a kind of ultimate class fantasy about the 'collective characters' which are the classes in opposition." Fredric Jameson, *The Political Unconscious, Narrative as a Socially Symbolic Act*, 87.

[2]Pachucos came to national prominence during World War II, first with the Sleepy Lagoon incident. A young man was found dead near the Lagoon in Los Angeles, and the police arrested a gang of young Chicanos. The press sensationalized the case with accusations that Pachucos were un-American. The defendants were found guilty, but they were later released when a higher court overturned the decision. Another incident brought Pachucos to international attention. U.S. servicemen stationed in Southern California, their prejudice against Pachucos inflamed by yellow journalism, clashed with Pachucos on the streets of Los Angeles. Soon the military men were invading the city in larger numbers, attacking Pachucos and eventually any foreign looking person, beating and stripping them. These so-called *Zoot Suit Riots* drew criticism from U.S. allies and enemies alike.

Pachucos were distinguished by their extravagant clothes: fingertip-length, wide-lapel coat; narrow-brimmed hat; high, draped pants that ballooned at the knees and narrowed tightly at the ankles; and thick-soled shoes. They spoke a combination of Spanish, English and a slang mixture of the two. For a bibliography of basic studies on Pachucos, see Bruce-Novoa, *Chicano Poetry*, 218-219.

[3]I have used this term, coined by José Luis Cuevas in his essay of the same title, because, although Cuevas included Paz among those who supposedly were trying to open Mexico to the world, Paz' treatment of the Pachuco is a rhetorical drawing of a nationalistic curtain of sorts. The irony is deliberate.

[4]"Nortismo era, en realidad pochismo. Palabra que se usa en California para designar al descastado que reniega de lo mexicano aunque lo tiene en la sangre y procura ajustar todos sus actos al mimetismo de los amos actuales de la región [U.S.A.]" Vasconcelos, 789. *Nortismo*, or northernism, was attributed to the writings of Roberto Maytorena, whom Vasconcelos accused of inverse orientation: "Roberto era simple vehículo de ideas cuyo alcance le hubiera horrorizado si llegara a entenderlo. Producto de aristocracia pueblerina y de sangre pura española, sólo la ignorancia peculiar de los medios en que se criara explica que anduviese propagando la doctrina enemiga; la destrucción de la cultura latinoespañola de nuestros padres, para sustituirla con el primitivismo norteamericano que desde la niñez se infiltra en los pochos" (782). Here the inverse orientation is subconscious, but perhaps for this reason more sinister.

[5]First National Symposium on Chicano Literature and Critical Analysis, held at New Mexico Highlands University, Nov. 21-22, 1974.

[6]Freud employed a similar construction by opposing Reality Principle and Pleasure Principle, or, in lay terms, work versus play. Though Bataille does not treat Freud specifically, two authors who do, and who should be read in conjunction with Bataille, are Norman O. Brown—*Life Against Death, the Pyschoanalytical Meaning of History* and *Love's Body*—and Herbert Marcuse—*Eros And Civilization, A Philosophical Inquiry into Freud*—both of whom support Bataille's proposition that man should eroticize life.

[7]Bataille ends his introduction with a discussion of mysticism. He finally states that he could have spoken of poetry, but it would have plunged us into

177

an intellectual labyrinth. One feels poetry, but cannot talk about it. He goes on to quote Rimbaud, than adds: "Poetry leads to the same place as all forms of eroticism—to the blending and fusion of separate objects. It leads to eternity, it leads us to death, and through death to continuity" (25). In a very real manner, *Death and Sensuality* is a manual of literary aesthetics, metaphorically treated, a theory of poerotics.

[8]Mikel Dufrenne, in his monumental *The Phenomenology of Aesthetic Experience*, convincingly explains the temporal character of pictorial space. Though not in complete accord with my views on the simultaneity of the image, Dufrenne's treatment of the aesthetic object as quasi-subject and his stand on truth in regard to art are highly relevant to my work.

[9]This space is not a "gap" as someone has suggested, for gap implies that two elements should merge. I call it a space because I hope it will expand and prosper, not disappear.

[10]Marty Ulloa, unpublished essay written for a Chicano poetry course, Yale University, 1977.

[11]Bruce-Novoa, lectures at University of California, Santa Barbara and Los Angeles campuses, and the University of New Mexico, Albuquerque, March 1976.

[12]"A discourse moves 'to and from' between received encodations of experience and the clutter of phenomena which refuses incorporation into conventionalized notions of 'reality,' 'truth,' or 'possibility.' It also moves 'back and forth' (like a shuttle?) between alternative ways of encoding this reality, some of which may be provided by the traditions of discourse prevailing in a given domain of inquiry and others of which may be idiolects of the author, the authority of which he is seeking to establish. Discourse, in a word, is quintessentially a *mediative* enterprise. As such, it is both interpretative and pre-interpretive; it is always as much *about* the nature of interpretation itself as it is *about* the subject matter which is the manifest occasion of its own elaboration," Hayden White, *The Tropics of Discourse, Essays on Cultural Criticism*, 4.

[13]The context of White's statement may be of interest to readers more accustomed to utilizing the term dialectical criticism: "This twofold nature of discourse is sometimes referred to as dialectical. But apart from being fraught with ideological associations of a specific sort, the term *dialectical* too often suggests a transcendental subject or narrative ego which stands above the contending interpretations of reality and arbitrates between them. Let me offer another term to suggest how I conceive the dynamic movement of a discourse: *diatactical*. This notion has the merit of suggesting a somewhat different kind of relationship between the discourse, its putative subject matter, and contending interpretations of the latter. It does not suggest that discourses about reality can be classified as hypotactical (conceptually overdetermined), on the one side, and paratactical (conceptually underdetermined), on the other, with the discourse itself occupying the middle ground (of properly syntactical thought) that everyone is seeking. On the contrary, discourse, if it is genuine discourse—that is to say, as self-critical as it is critical of others—will radically challenge the notion of the syntactical middle ground itself. It throws all 'tactical' rules into doubt, including those originally governing its own formation. Precisely because it is aporetic, or ironic, with respect to its own adequacy, discourse cannot be governed by logic alone. Because it is always slipping the grasp of logic, constantly asking if logic is adequate to capture the essence of its subject matter, discourse always tends towards metadiscursive reflexiveness. This is why every discourse

is always as much about discourse itself as it is about the objects that make up its subject matter," 4.

Works Cited

Abelardo. See Delgado, Abelardo Lalo.

Acosta, Oscar Zeta. *The Autobiography of a Brown Buffalo*. San Francisco: Straight Arrow Books, 1972.

——. *The Revolt of the Cockroach People*. San Francisco: Straight Arrow Books, 1973.

Algarín, Miguel. *On Call*. Houston: Arte Publico Press, 1980.

Algarín, Miguel, ed. *Nuyorican Poetry*. New York: Morrow, 1978.

Alurista. *Floricanto en Aztlán*. Los Angeles: Chicano Studies Center of UCLA, 1971; no pagination, so references must be to poem number.

Alurista, et al., eds. *El Ombligo de Aztlán*. San Diego: Centro de Estudios Chicanos Publications, 1971.

Alvarez Acosta, Miguel. *La frontera plural, estancias de un amor indocumentado*. México D.F.: Editorial Joaquín Mortiz, 1979.

Anaya, Rudolfo A. *Bless Me, Ultima*. Berkeley: Quinto Sol, 1972.

Arana, Federico. *Enciclopedia de latinamericana omnisciencia*. México D.F.: Editorial Joaquín Mortiz, 1977.

Arias, Ron. *The Road to Tamazunchale*. Reno: West Coast Poetry Review, 1975.

Babín, Maria Teresa, and Stan Steiner, eds. *Borinquen, An Anthology of Puerto Rican Literature*. New York: Vintage Books, 1974.

Baca, Jimmy Santiago. *Martín and Meditations on the South Valley*. New York: New Directions, 1987.

Baker, Houston A., ed. *Three American Literatures*. New York: Modern Language Association of America, 1982.

Barrio, Raymond. *The Plum Plum Pickers*. Sunnydale: Ventura Press, 1969.

Bataille, Georges. *Death and Sensuality, a Study of Eroticism and Taboo*. New York: Walker & Co., 1962.

Blanchot, Maurice. *The Space of Literature*. Translated by Ann Smock. Lincoln: University of Nebraska Press, 1982.

Brawley, Ernest. *The Alamo Tree*. New York: Simon and Shuster, 1984.

——. *The Rap*. New York: Atheneum, 1974.

——. *Selena*. New York: Atheneum, 1979.

Brown, Norman O. *Life Against Death, The Psychoanalytical Meaning of History*. Middletown: Wesleyan University Press, 1959.

Bruce-Novoa. "Canonical and Non-canonical Texts." *The Americas Review* 14. 3-4 (Fall-Winter 1986): 119-135.

——. "A Case of Identity: What's in a Name? Chicanos and Riqueños," a translation of "Una cuestión de identidad: ¿Qué significa un nombre? Chicanos and Riqueños." *Imágenes e identidad: el puertorriqueño en la literatura*. Río Piedras: Ediciones Huracán, 1985: 283-288.

_____. "Charting the Space of Chicano Literature," Translation of "El deslinde del espacio literario chicano." *Aztlán* 11. 2 (Fall 1980): 323-338.

_____. *Chicano Authors, Inquiry By Interview*. Austin: University of Texas Press, 1980.

_____. "Chicano Literary Production, 1960-1980." *Les minorités en Amérique de Nord (1960-1980)*. Bordeaux: Presses Universitaires de Bordeaux, 1985: 115-132.

_____. "Chicano Poetry." *Chicano Literature, A Reference Guide*. Westport: Greenwood Press: 1985, 161-173.

_____. *Chicano Poetry, A Response to Chaos*. Austin: University of Texas Press, 1982.

_____. "Chicanos in Mexican Literature." *Missions in Conflict, Essay on U.S.-Mexican Relations and Chicano Culture*. Tübingen: Gunter Narr Verlag, 1986: 55-64.

_____. "*El Crepúsculo* & *Cuaderno*, Oldest Newspaper & Book in the Southwest." *La Luz* (Oct. 1973): 12-14.

_____. "Década literaria chicana." In *La Comunidad, Suplemento Dominical de LA OPINION* 128 (2 de enero, 1983): 12-13.

_____. "Freedom of Expression and the Chicano Movement." *La Luz*, Sept. 1973: 28-29.

_____. "Hispanic Literatures in the U.S." *American Writing Today* 2. Washington, D.C.: Forum Series, 1982: 250-61.

_____. "The Hollywood *Americano* in Mexico." *Mexico and United States: Intercultural Relations in the Humanities*, San Antonio: San Antonio College, 1984: 18-39.

_____. *Inocencia perversa/Perverse Innocence*. Phoenix: Baleen Press, 1977.

_____. "In Search of the Honest Outlaw, John Rechy." *Minority Voices* 3. 1 (Fall 1979): 37-45.

_____. "Literatura chicana: la respuesta al caos." *Revista de la Universidad de México* 29. 12 (agosto 1975): 20-24.

_____. "México en la literature chicana." *Revista de la Universidad de México* 29. 5 (enero 1975): 13-18.

_____. "Pluralism versus Nationalism: U.S. Literature." *Council of National Literatures Quarterly Report* 6. 1-2 (Jan.-April 1983): 13-18.

_____. "*Pocho* as Literature," *Aztlán* 7. 1 (Spring 1976): 65-77.

_____. "Portraits of Chicano Artists as Young Men: the Narrator in Three Chicano Novels." *Floricanto II*, Albuquerque: Pajarito Press: 1979, 150-161.

_____. "Report on El Quinto Festival de Teatros Chicanos." *De Colores* 2. 2 (1975): 66-72.

_____. "The Space of Chicano Literature." *The Chicano Literary World 1974*. Philip Ortego, ed. Las Vegas: New Mexico Highlands University, 1975: 22-51.

RetroSpace

——. "Testimonio escrito con equis." *Semanal de La Jornada*, 10 de enero, 1988: 7-9.

——. "The Topological Space of Chicano Literature." *Revue Francaise D'Etudes Americaines* 13. 36 (April 1988): 264-279.

Campbell, Joseph. *The Hero with a Thousand Faces*. New York: Bollingen Foundation, 1949.

Candelaria, Nash. *Inheritance of Strangers*. Binghamton: Bilingual Press, 1986.

——. *Memories of the Alhambra*. San Jose: Cibola Press, 1977.

——. *Not By the Sword*. Ypsilanti: Bilingual Press, 1982.

Cárdenas, Margarita Cota. *Noches despertando inconsciencias*. Tucson: Scorpion Press, 1975.

Castillo, Ana. *The Mixtahuala Letters*. Phoenix: Bilingual Press 1986.

Chacón, Eusebio. *El hijo de la tempestad; Tras la tormenta la calma*. Santa Fe: Tipografía de "El Boletín Popular, 1982

Chávez, Fray Angélico. *La Conquistadora, The Autobiography of an Ancient Statue*. Patterson, N.J.: St Anthony Guild Press, 1954.

Cervantes, Lorna Dee. *Emplumada*. Pittsburgh: Pittsburgh Press, 1980.

Cisneros, Sandra. *The House on Mango Street*. Houston: Arte Publico Press, 1983.

Cuevas, José Luis. *The Cactus Curtain. Evergreen Review* 7 (1959): 111-120.

Dante, Alighiere. *The Divine Comedy of Dante Alighieri*. Trans. Charles Eliot Norton. Chicaco: Encyclopaedia Britannica, 1952.

Delgado, Abelardo Lalo. *Letters to Louise*. Berkeley: Tonatiuh International, 1979.

Derrida, Jacques. *Of Grammatology*. Translated by Gayatari Chakravorty Spivak. Baltimore: John Hopkins Press, 1976.

Dufrenne, Mikel. *The Phenomenology of Aesthetic Experience*. Evanston: Northwestern University Press, 1973.

Edmonson, Munro E. *Lore : An Intorduction to the Science of Folklore and Literature*. New York: Holt, Rinehart And Winston, 1971.

Eliade, Mircea. *The Myth of the Eternal Return*. New York: Harper and Row Torchbooks, 1959.

——. *Patterns in Comparative Religion*. Cleveland: World Publishing Company, 1970.

——. *The Sacred and the Profane: The Nature of Religion*. Translated by Willard Trask. New York: Harcourt, Brace and World, 1959.

Elias, Leonardo. "Aztec Mother." In Harth, ed., *Voices*, op. cit, 177.

Elizondo, Sergio. *Libro para batos y chavalas chicanas*. Berkeley: Editorial Justa, 1977.

——. *Muerte en una estrella*. México D.F.: Tinta Negra Editores, 1984.

——. *Perros y antiperros: Una épica Chicana*. Berkeley: Quinto Sol, 1972.

Espinosa, Aurelio Macedonio. *Conchita Argüello, Historia y novela californi-ana*. New York: The Macmillan Co., 1938.

Falcon, Tep. "amerika, amerika . . . " In *Sirocco*, Denver: University of Col-orado, 1973: 18.

Fernández Méndez, Eugenio, ed. *Antología del pensamiento puertorriqueño, (1900-1970)* 2. Barcelona: Editorial Universitaria, 1975.

Flor i canto II. Albuquerque: Pajarito Press, 1979.

Fuentes, Carlos. *La región más transparente*. México D.F.: Fondo de Cultura Económica, 1957.

Galarza, Ernesto. *Barrio Boy*. Notre Dame, Ind.: University of Notre Dame Press, 1971.

García, Ricardo. *Selected Poetry*. Berkeley: Quinto Sol, 1973.

García Ponce, Juan. *Aparición de lo invisible*. México, D.F.: Siglo XXI Edi-tores, 1968.

———. *Entry Into Matter, Modern Literature and Reality*. Trans. David Parent and Bruce-Novoa. Ann Arbor: Applied Literature Press, 1976.

Gonzales, Laurence. *El Vago*. New York: Atheneum, 1983.

Gonzales, Rodolfo. *I Am Joaquín/ Yo soy Joaquín*. New York: Bantam Books, 1972.

Guzmán, Martín Luis. *El águila y la serpiente*. In *La novela de la revolución mexicana*, México D.F.: Aguilar, 1964: 207-424.

Harth E., Dorothy, and Lewis M. Baldwin, eds. *Voices of Aztlán: Chicano Literature Today*. New York: New American Library, 1974.

Herms, Dieter. "Chicano Literature: A European Perspective."*International Studies in Honor of Tomás Rivera*, Julián Olivares, ed. Houston: Arte Publico Press, 1985: 163-72.

Hernández Cruz, Victor. *Mainland*. New York: Random House, 1973.

———. *Tropicalization*. New York: Reed & Cannon, 1976.

Hinojosa S., Rolando. *Estampas del valle y otras obras*. Berkeley: Quinto Sol, 1973.

———. *Generaciones y semblanzas*. Berkeley: Justa Publications, 1977.

———. *Klail City y sus alrededores*. Havana: Casa de las Américas, 1976.

Islas, Artura. *The Rain God: A Desert Tale*. Palo Alto: Alexandrian Press, 1984.

James, Daniel. *Famous All Over Town*. New York: Simon and Shuster, 1983.

Jameson, Fredric. *Marxism and Form, Twentieth-Century Dialectical Theories of Literature*. Princeton: Princeton University Press, 1971.

———. *The Political Unconscious, Narrative as a Socially Symbolic Act*. Ithaca: Cornell University Press, 1981.

Kanellos, Nicolás. *Mexican American Theatre: Then and Now*. Houston: Arte Publico Press, 1983.

Katz, Friedrich. *The Secret War in Mexico*. Chicago: University of Chicago Press, 1983.

Klein, Marcus. *Foreigners, The Making of American Literature*. Chicago: University of Chicago Press, 1981.

Kolodny, Annette. "Some notes on Defining a 'Feminist Literary Criticism." *Critical Inquiry* 2 (1975): 75-92.

Lamb, Blaine P. "The Convenient Villain: The Early Cinema Views of the Mexican-American." *Journal of the West* 14 (Oct. 1975): 75-81.

Lahwn, Juanita. "Victorian Attitudes Affecting the Mexican Woman Writing in *La Prensa* During the Early 1900s and the Chicana of the 1980s." *Missions in Conflict. Essays on U.S.-Mexican Relations and Chicano Culture*, eds. Renate von Bardeleben, et al. Tübingen: Gunter Narr Verlag, 1986: 65-71.

Lauter, Paul. "Caste, Class, and Canon." In *A Gift of Tongues, Critical Challenges in Contemporary American Poetry*. Athens: University of Georgia Press: 1987, 57-82.

――――. "Race and Gender in the Shaping of the American Literary Canon," *Feminist Studies* 9 (Fall 1983): 435-563.

Laviera, Tato. *La Carreta Made a U. Turn*. Houston: Arte Publico Press, 1980.

Leal, Luis. "Mexican American Literature: A Historical Perspective." *Modern Chicano Authors*, Joseph Sommers and Tomás Ybarra-Frausto, eds. Englewood Cliffs: Prentice-Hall, 1979: 18-30.

Leal, Luis, et al., eds. *A Decade of Chicano Literature (1970-1980*. Santa Barbara: Editorial La Causa, 1982.

Leñero, Vicente. *El evangelio de Lucas Gavilán*. México D.F.: Seix Barral, 1980.

Lomelí, Francisco and Donaldo Urioste. *Chicano Perspectives in Literature: A Critical and Annotated Bibliography*. Albuquerque: Pajarito Publications, 1976.

López, Diane. *Victuum*. Ventura: Diana-Etna, 1976.

Lotman, Jurij M. "On the Metalanguage of a Typological Description of Culture." *Semiotica* 14. 2 (1975): 97-123.

MacConnell, Dean. "Ethnosemiotics." *Semiotics of Culture*. The Hague: Mouton Publishers, 1979.

Marcuse, Herbert. *Eros and Civilization, A Philosophical Inquiry into Freud*. Boston: Beacon Press, 1955.

Márquez, René. *La carreta*. Río Piedras: Editorial Cultural, 1963.

Méndez, Miguel. *Los criaderos humanos (épica de los desamparados) y Sahuaros*. Tuscon: Editorial Peregrinos, 1975.

――――. *Peregrinos de Aztlán*. Tucson: Editorial Peregrinos, 1974.

――――. "Tata Casehua." In Romano, Octavio, *El Espejo/ The Mirror*: 44-58.

Meyer, Doris. "Anonymous Poetry in Spanish-Language New Mexico Newspapers (1880-1900)." *Bilingual Review* 2. 3 (1975): 259-75.

———. "Early Mexican-American Responses to Negative Stereotyping." *New Mexico Historical Review* 53. 1 (January 1978): 75-91.

Moquin, Wayne, et al., eds. *A Documentary History of the Mexican Americans.* New York: Praeger, 1972.

Montoya, José. "El Louie." In Luis Valdez, *Aztlán*: 333-37.

———. *El sol y los de abajo.* San Francisco: Ediciones Pocho-Che, 1972.

Morales, Alejandro. *Caras viejas y vino nuevo.* México D.F.: Editorial Joaquín Mortiz, 1975.

———. *Reto en el paraíso.* Ypsilanti: Bilingual Press, 1983.

———. *La verdad sin voz.* México D.F.: Editorial Joaquín Mortiz, 1979.

Muckley, Robert F. *Introduction to Notes on Neorican Seminar.* San Germán: Interamerican University, 1972.

Navarro, J.L. "To a Dead Lowrider," in Valdez, 1972: 337-39.

Nelson, Eugene. *Bracero.* Berkeley: Thorp Springs Press, 1972.

Nichols, John. *The Milagro Beanfield War.* New York: Holt, Rinehart and Winston, 1978.

Niggli, Josephina. *Mexican Village.* Chapel Hill: University of North Carolina Press, 1945.

———. *Step Down, Elder Brother: A Novel.* New York: Rinehart and Company, 1947.

Ojeda, David. *Las condiciones de la guerra.* La Habana: Casa de las Américas, 1978.

Ong, Walter J. *Orality and Literacy, The Technologizing of the Word.* London and New York: Metheuen, 1982.

Ortego, Philip. *Backgrounds of Mexican-American Literature.* Dissertation, University of New Mexico, 1971.

———. "The Chicano Renaissance." *Social Casework* 52. 5 (May 1971): 294-307.

Paredes, Américo. *With a Pistol in His Hand: A Border Ballad and Its Hero.* Austin: University of Texas Press, 1958.

Paredes, Raymond. "The Evolution of Chicano Literature." In Baker: 33-79.

Paz, Octavio. *El arco y la lira, el poema, la revelación poética, poesía e historia.* México, D.F.: Fondo de Cultura Económica, 1967.

———. *El laberinto de la soledad.* México, D.F.: Fondo de Cultura Económica, 5th ed., 1967.

Pérez de Villagrá, Gaspar. *Historia de la Nueva México.* Alcalá: 1610.

Pettit, Arthur G. *Images of the Mexican American in Fiction and Film.* College Station: Texas A&M University Press, 1980.

Pietri, Pedro. *Puerto Rican Obituary.* New York: Monthly Review, 1974.

Pineda, Cecile. *Face.* New York: Viking Penquin, 1985.

———. *Frieze.* New York: Viking Penguin, 1986.

Pino, Salvador del. *La novela escrita en español: cinco autores comprometidos.* Ypsilanti: Bilingual Press, 1982.

Portillo, Estela. *Rain of Scorpions and Other Writings.* Berkeley: Tonatiuh International, 1975.

Quirarte, Jacinto. *Mexican American Artists.* Austin: University of Texas Press, 1973.

Ramírez, Orlando. *Speedway.* San José: Mango Press, 1979.

Rechy, John. *City of Night.* New York: Grove Press, 1963.

———. *The Fourth Angel.* New York: Viking Press, 1972.

———. *Numbers.* New York: Grove Press, 1967.

———. *This Day's Death.* New York: Grove Press, 1969.

Ríos, Isabella. see López, Diane.

Rivera, Tomás. "Pete Fonseca." In Harth: 52-58; and Tomás Rivera, *The Harvest, Short Stories / La cosecha, cuentos,* Julián Olivares, ed. Houston: Arte Público Press, 1989:29-39 / 91-101.

———. . . . *y no se lo tragó la tierra.* Berkeley: Quinto Sol, 1971.

Robinson, Cecil. *With the Ears of a Stranger, the Mexican in American Literature.* Tucson: University of Arizona Press, 1963.

Rodríguez, Juan, ed. *Crónicas diabólicas (1916-1926) de "Jorge Ulica*/Julio G. Arce. San Diego: Maize Press, 1982.

Rodríguez, Richard. *Hunger of Memory, The Education of Richard Rodriguez.* Boston: David R. Godine, 1982.

Romano-V., Octavio. "Goodbye Revolution—Hello Slum." In Romano 1969: 76-82.

———. . "A Rosary for Doña Marina." In Romano 1969: 104-22.

Romano-V., Octavio, and Herminio Ríos C., eds. *El Espejo/The Mirror: Selected Chicano Literature.* 2d ed., Berkeley: Quinto Sol, 1972.

———. . *El Espejo/The Mirror: Selected Mexican-American Literrture.* 1st ed., Berkeley: Quinto Sol, 1969.

Salas, Floyd. *Tattoo the Wicked Cross.* New York: Grove Press, 1967.

———. . *What Now My Love.* New York: Grove Press, 1969.

Saldívar, Ramón. "A Dialectic of Difference: Towards a Theory of Chicano Novel." *MELUS* 6. 3 (Fall 1979): 73-92.

Salinas, Omar. *Crazy Gypsy.* Fresno: Origenes Publications, 1970; also in *The Sadness of Days, Selected and New Poems.* Houston: Arte Publico Press, 1987.

Salinas, Raúl. *Un trip through the mind jail y otras excursiones.* San Francisco: Editorial Pocho-Che, 1980.

Sánchez, Marta Ester. *Contemporary Chicana Poetry, A Critical Approach to an Emerging Literature.* Berkeley: University of California, 1985.

Sánchez, Ricardo. *Canto y grito mi liberación (y lloro mis desmadrazgos).* Garden City: Doubleday, 1973.

_____. *Hechizospells*. Los Angeles: Chicano Studies Center Publications, University of California, 1976.

Sánchez, Rosaura. "Chicana Prose Writers: The Case of Gina Valdés and Sylvia Lizárraga." *Beyond Stereotypes, The Critical Analysis of Chicana Literature*, María Herrera-Sobek, ed. Binghamton: Bilingual Press, 1985: 61-70

Sánchez Cámara, Florencia. *El notata y las mujeres mágicas*. México D.F.: Editorial Joaquín Mortiz, 1980.

Santiago, Danny. See James, Daniel.

Segovia, Francisco. "Poemas." In *Triga*. México D.F.: Universidad Nacional Autónoma de México, 1983.

Shelley, Mary. *Frankenstein: or, the Modern Prometheus*. New York: Signet, 1965.

Shular, Antonia Castañeda, Tomás Ibarra-Frausto, and Joseph Sommers, eds. *Literatura chicana: Texto y contexto*. Englewood Cliffs: Prentice-Hall, 1972.

Sommers, Joseph. "From the Critical Premise to the Product: Critical Modes and Their Applications to a Chicano Literary Text." *New Scholar*, 6 (1977), 51-80.

Soto, Gary. *Living Up The Street*. San Francisco: Strawberry Hill Press, 1985.

Soto, Pedro Juan. *Hot Land, Cold Season*. New York: Dell Publishing Co., 1970.

_____. *Spiks*. Río Piedras: Editorial Cultural, 1973.

Spencer, Benjamin T. *The Quest for Nationality, An American Literacy Campaign*. Syracuse: Syracuse University Press, 1957.

Steiner, George. *After Babel, Aspects of Language and Translation*. London: Oxford University Press, 1975.

Taylor, Sheila Ortiz. *Faultline*. Tallahassee: Naiad Press, 1982.

The Americas Review 17. 3-4 (1989); on *La Prensa* and Hispanic journalism in the United States.

Thomas, Piri. *Down These Mean Streets*. New York: Knopf, 1967.

Tonn, Horst. *Zeitgenössische Chicano-Erzählliteratur in englischer Sprache: Autobiographie und Roman*. Frankfurt: Peter Lang, 1988.

Trujillo, Roberto G. and Andres Rodríguez. *Literatura Chicana: Creative and Critical Writings Through 1984*. Oakland: Floricanto Press, 1985.

Ulica, Jorge. *Crónicas Diabólicas*. San Diego: Maize Press, 1982.

Vaca, Nick C. "The Week in the Life of Manuel Hernández." In *El espejo*: 135-43.

Valdez, Luis. *Actos: The Teatro Campesino*. San Juan Bautista: Cucaracha Press, 1971.

Valdez, Luis and Stan Steiner, eds. *Aztlán, An Anthology of Mexican American Literature*. New York: Vintage Books, 1972.

Vasconcelos, José. *Obras completas* 1. México D.F.: Libreros Mexicanos Unidos, 1957.

Vásquez, Richard. *Chicano*. Garden City: Doubleday, 1970.

Velasco, Luis Casas. *Death Show*. México D.F.: Editorial Joaquín Mortiz, 1981.

Villanueva, Alma. *Blood Root*. Austin: Place of the Heron Press, 1977.

Villanueva, Tino. *Hay otra voz poems*. Staten Island: Editorial Mensaje, 1972.

Villarreal, Jose Antonio. *The Fifth Horseman*, Garden City: Doubleday, 1974.

——. *Pocho*. New York: Doubleday, 1959.

White, Hayden. *Tropics of Discourse, Essays in Cultural Criticism*. Baltimore: John Hopkins University Press, 1978.

Yañez, Agustín. *Al filo del agua*. México D.F.: Editorial Porrúa, 1963.

Yarbro-Bejarano, Yvonne. "From *acto* to *mito*: A Critical Appraisal of the Teatro Campesino." In *Modern Chicano Writers, A Collection of Critical Essays*. Englewood Cliffs: Prentice-Hall, 1979.

Ybarra-Frausto, Tomás. "The Chicano Movement and the Emergence of a Chicano Poetic Consciousness." New Scholar 7 (1977): 81-109.

Zamora, Bernice. *Restless Serpents*. Menlo Park: Diseños Literarios, 1976.